MODERN LEGAL STUDIES

THE COURT OF JUSTICE
OF THE
EUROPEAN COMMUNITIES

MODERN LEGAL STUDIES

L. NEVILLE BROWN and FRANCIS G. JACOBS

THE COURT OF JUSTICE
OF THE
EUROPEAN COMMUNITIES

Third edition by L. Neville Brown, OBE
Solicitor; Professor of Comparative Law
at the University of Birmingham

LONDON
SWEET & MAXWELL
1989

First Edition 1977
Second Impression 1979
Second Edition 1983
Third Edition 1989
Second Impression 1991

Published by
Sweet & Maxwell Limited of
South Quay Plaza, 183 Marsh Wall, London E14 9FT
Laserset by P.B. Computer Typesetting,
Pickering, N. Yorks.
Printed in Scotland

British Library Cataloguing in Publication Data

Brown, L. Neville (Lionel Neville), *1923–*
    The Court of Justice of the European Communities.—
    3rd ed. — (Modern legal studies)
    1. Court of Justice of the European Communities
    I. Title   II. Jacobs, Francis G. (Francis Geoffrey),
    1939–   III. Series
    341.24′22

    ISBN 0–421–41460–x

PREFACE

A third edition of this book has been necessitated by the many developments since 1983 in the law and practice of the Court of Justice, by the institutional changes consequent upon the accession in 1986 of Spain and Portugal, and by the setting up in 1989 of the Court of First Instance. This edition also looks forward to the completion of the single market scheduled for 1992. How much the judicial arm of the Communities has grown, and will continue to grow, may be seen from the massive extensions, built or planned, to the original Courthouse (compare the two drawings preceding the title page).

In preparing this edition, I worked with the co-author of the previous editions until his appointment in September 1988 as an advocate general at the Court of Justice. The completion of the text has been my responsibility alone, and we agreed that this edition should therefore appear under my name only.

I must express my gratitude to Mr Tom Kennedy of the Court's Information Service for his ready help and advice.

Much of the joint planning of this edition was done over tea and teacakes off Pall Mall where this preface is signed.

The Library,
United Oxford and   L. NEVILLE BROWN
   Cambridge University Club,
S.W.1.
July 4, 1989

The publishers thank the artist, Mr. Edmond Goergen of Luxembourg, for his kind permission in allowing us to reproduce his drawing of the original Court building. The other drawing shows the enlarged judicial complex as it will appear in 1991 with the completion of an additional court-house (left foreground) for the Court of First Instance.

PREFACE TO THE FIRST EDITION

In teaching the elements of Community law to English undergraduates, each of us felt the need for a fuller account of the Court of Justice than is normally included in the standard textbooks on Community law. Yet, for the readership we had in mind, the large practice books on the Court were not appropriate.

When we found that our ideas for a short monograph were running along parallel lines, we decided to collaborate in the present work. Our primary aim has been to provide a study of the composition, jurisdiction and practice of the Court, a subject which we believe to be essential for the student or practitioner seeking to understand the Community legal system and its substantive law. But we also believe that the Court deserves study in its own right as a remarkable judicial institution of modern times. On either count, our book was able, much to our satisfaction, to be included in *Modern Legal Studies.*

Although each of us undertook the first draft of particular chapters, our many meetings in London and Birmingham led to so much rewriting that the final text may truly be described as an amalgam of our several labours. As such, its imperfections must be our joint responsibility.

Platform 6	L. Neville Brown
Euston	Francis G. Jacobs
June 1977	

CONTENTS

	Page
Preface	vii
Preface to the first edition	ix
Table of Cases before the Court of Justice	xv
(in alphabetical order)	
Table of Cases before the Court of Justice	xxv
(in numerical order)	
Table of Cases before Other Courts	xxxiii
Table of Community Treaties	xxxv
Table of Community Legislation	xxxviii
1. General Introduction	1
PART ONE: ORGANISATION AND	
COMPOSITION	13
2. Court Organisation	14
Appendix	32
Organigramme of the Court of Justice	
3. Judges	33
4. Advocates General	53
5. The Court of First Instance	64
Appendix	69
First Judges of the Court of First Instance	
PART TWO: FUNCTIONS AND JURISDICTION	71
6. Actions against Member States	76
Appendix	94
Enforcement Actions against Member States	
7. Judicial Review of Community Acts	95
8. Plenary Jurisdiction	131
Appendix	158
Methods to challenge the Validity of a Regulation	

9. Staff Cases   159
Appendix   168
Recognised Unions and Professional Organisations
    of Community Employees
10. Preliminary Rulings   169
11. Opinions: External Relations   203
Appendix   209
Judicial Statistics

PART THREE: PROCEDURE AND PRACTICE   219
12. Procedure and Practice   222
Appendix   247
Notes for the Guidance of Counsel at Oral Hearings
13. Lawyers in the Court   252

PART FOUR: THE COURT AS LAW-MAKER   265
14. Methods of Interpretation   268
15. General Principles of Law   293
16. Precedent and the Court   311
17. Future of the Court: Conclusions   323

Select Bibliography   337
Index   339

OTHER BOOKS IN THE SERIES

Anatomy of International Law (Second Edition) by J. G. Merrills

Breach of Statutory Duty in Tort by K. M. Stanton

Children, Parents and the State by A. Bainham

Confessions by Peter Mirfield

Constructive Trusts (Second Edition) by A. J. Oakley

Development Control by J. Alder

The Governance of Police by Laurence Lustgarten

Grievances, Remedies and the State by Patrick Birkinshaw

Human Rights and Europe (Second Edition) by Ralph Beddard

Immigration Law (Second Edition) by John Evans

Law and the Electoral Process by H. F. Rawlings

Law, Legitimacy and the Constitution by McAuslan and McEldowney

Law of the Common Agricultural Policy by Francis G. Snyder

Local Government in the Modern State by Martin Loughlin

Misrepresentation by David K. Allen

Product Liability by Alistair Clark

Quasi-Legislation by G. Ganz

Rape and the Legal Process by Jennifer Temkin

Registered Land (Third Edition) by David J. Hayton

Remedies for Breach of Contract by Hugh Beale

Security of Tenure under the Rent Act by Jill E. Martin

Sex Discrimination in Employment by R. Townshend-Smith

TABLE OF CASES
BEFORE THE COURT OF JUSTICE

(in alphabetical order)

ALBAKO v. B.A.L.M. (249/85) 2 [1987] ECR 2354 298
AM & S Europe Limited v. Commission (155/79) [1982] 2 CMLR
    264 .... 232, 240, 285, 332
ASSIDER (3/54) [1954–1956] ECR 63 .... 275, 284
—— (5/55) [1954–1956] ECR 135 241
Adams v. Commission (145/83) [1986] (1985) ECR 3539 .... 140, 144
Adlerblum v. Caisse Nationale d'Assurance Vieillesse des Travail-
    leurs Salariés (93/75) [1975] ECR 2147 183
Adoui and Cornuaille (115 & 116/81) [1982] ECR 1665 315
Alcan v. Commission (69/69) [1970] ECR 385 113
Algera and Others v. Assembly (7/56 & 3–7/57) [1957 and 1958]
    ECR 39 .... 146, 162, 166, 285
Allied Corporation v. Commission (239 and 275/82) [1984] ECR
    1005 107
Alvis v. Council (32/62) [1963] ECR 49 .... 164, 285
Amylum and Tunnel Refineries v. Council and Commission (116 &
    124/77) [1979] ECR 3497 143
Apples Cases. See International Fruit Company and Others v.
    Commission (41–44/70) [1971] ECR 411 109
Associazione Industrie Siderurgiche Italiane (ASSIDER) v. High
    Authority (3/54) [1954–1956] ECR 63 .... 275, 284

B.R.T. v. S.A.B.A.M. (127/73) [1974] ECR 51 245
Bakels v. Oberfinanzdirektion München (14/70) [1970] ECR
    1001 313
Bayerische HNL v. Council and Commission (83 & 94/76, 4, 15, &
    40/77) [1978] ECR 1209 .... 141, 142, 143
Becher v. Hauptzollamt München (13/67) [1968] ECR 187 244
Becker v. Finanzamt Münster (8/81) [1982] ECR 53 .... 47, 244, 314
Belgische Radio en Televisie v. SABAM and Fonior (127/73)
    [1974] ECR 51 245
Bellintani v. Commission (116/78) [1980] ECR 23 241
Bergmann v. Grows-Farm GmbH (114/76) [1977] ECR 1211 142
Blaizot v. University of Liège (24/86), The Times, April 4,
    1988 .... 197, 289
Bock v. Commission (62/70) [1971] ECR 897 .... 108, 113, 301

xv

Bollmann Paul G. *v.* Hauptzollamt Hamburg-Waltershof (62/72)
    [1973] ECR 269 245
Bonsignore *v.* Oberstadtdirektor der Stadt Köln (67/74) [1975]
    ECR 297 170
Borker (138/80) [1980] ECR 1975 187
Bosch (13/61) [1962] ECR 45 .... 59, 178, 183
Bouchereau, R. *v.* (30/77) [1977] ECR 1999 275
Brack *v.* Insurance Officer (17/76) [1976] ECR 1429 .... 10, 187, 284
Breedband N.V. *v.* Société des Aciéries du Temple (42 & 49/59)
    [1962] ECR 145 242
Bresciani *v.* Amministrazione Italiana delle Finanze (87/75) [1976]
    ECR 129 185
British Beef Co. *v.* Intervention Board for Agricultural Produce
    (146/77) [1978] ECR 1347 10
Broekmeulen *v.* Huisarts Registratie Commissie (246/80) [1981]
    ECR 2311 .... 188, 189
Brunner *v.* Hauptzollamt Hof (9/72) [1972] ECR 961 279
Budget (1986), *Re* the Council *v.* European Parliament (34/86)
    [1986] 3 CMLR 94 .... 101, 105

COFAZ (Compagnie Française de L'Azote) S.A. *v.* Commission
    (169/84) [1986] ECR 391 112
C.A.M., SA *v.* Commission (100/74) [1975] ECR 1393 110
C.I.L.F.I.T. (283/81) [1982] ECR 3415 195
CNTA *v.* Commission (74/74) [1975] ECR 533 .... 146, 301
Calpak S.p.A. and Società Emiliana Lavorazione S.p.A. *v.*
    Commission (789/79) [1980] ECR 1949 106
Camera Care Ltd. *v.* Commission (792R/79) [1980] ECR 119 238
Cement-Convention (8–11/66) [1967] ECR 75 98
Centrafarm BV and de Peijper *v.* Sterling Drug Inc. and Winthrop
    BV (15 & 16/74) [1975] ECR 1147 and 1183 170
Chasse (15/57) [1957 and 1958] ECR 211 263
Cimenteries CBR and Others *v.* Commission (8–11/66) [1967]
    ECR 75 117
Coenen and Others *v.* Sociaal-Economische Raad (39/75) [1975]
    ECR 1547 256
Colditz *v.* Caisse d'Assurance Vieillesse des Travailleurs Salariés
    de Paris (9/67) [1967] ECR 229 290
Commission *v.* Belgium (157/77) [1978] ECR 1881 130
—— *v.* —— (283/86) 76
—— *v.* Council (22/70) [1971] ECR 263 .... 60, 98, 100, 101, 103
—— *v.* —— (81/72) [1973] ECR 575 .... 4, 103, 122, 300
—— *v.* —— (70/74) [1975] ECR 795 .... 103, 104
—— *v.* —— (59/81) [1982] ECR 3329 104
—— *v.* —— (45/86) [1987] ECR 1493 .... 4, 104, 118
—— *v.* French Republic (6 & 11/69) [1969] ECR 523 114

Commission *v.* French Republic (26/69) [1970] ECR 565   82
—— *v.* —— (167/73) [1974] ECR 359 .... 84, 90, 317
—— *v.* —— (Mutton and Lamb) (232/78) [1979] ECR 2729 .... 79, 90
—— *v.* —— (24/80) [1980] ECR 1319 .... 79, 80
—— *v.* —— (97/80) [1980] ECR 1319   80
—— *v.* —— (42/82R) [1982] ECR 841   238
—— *v.* Germany (70/72) [1973] ECR 813   89
—— *v.* —— (116/82) [1986] ECR 2519   46
—— *v.* —— (205/84) [1987] 2 CMLR 69   255
—— *v.* Ireland (61/77) [1978] ECR 417   93
—— *v.* —— (414/85)   76
—— *v.* Italian Republic (7/61) [1961] ECR 317 .... 80, 98
—— *v.* —— (7/68) [1968] ECR 423   79
—— *v.* —— (24/68) [1969] ECR 193   282
—— *v.* —— (48/71) [1972] ECR 527   79
—— *v.* —— (257/86)   76
—— *v.* Luxembourg and Belgium (2 & 3/62) [1962] ECR 425   82
—— *v.* —— (90 & 91/63) [1964] ECR 625   83
—— *v.* Luxembourg (58/81) [1982] 3 CMLR 482   84
—— *v.* United Kingdom (31/77R & 53/77R) [1977] ECR 921 .... 87, 91
—— *v.* —— (231/78) [1979] ECR 1447 .... 80, 93
—— *v.* —— (353/85), *The Times*, February 24, 1988   76
—— *v.* —— (416/85), *The Independent*, June 28, 1987 .... 22, 76
—— *v.* Zoubek (426/85) (1986) ECR 4057   133
Compagnie Continentale France *v.* Council (169/73) [1975] ECR
    117   148
Compagnie d'Approvisionnement *v.* Commission (9 & 11/71)
    [1972] ECR 391 .... 141, 147, 148
Compagnie des Hauts Fourneaux de Chasse *v.* High Authority (15/
    57) [1957 and 1958] ECR 211   296
Compagnie Française Commerciale et Financière *v.* Commission
    (64/69) [1970] ECR 221 .... 109, 283
Conegate *v.* H.M. Customs and Excise (121/85) [1986] 2 All E.R.
    688 .... 170, 315
Consten and Grundig *v.* Commission (56 & 58/64) [1966] ECR
    299 .... 106, 122
Continental Can (6/72) [1973] ECR 215 .... 60, 106, 273, 274, 287, 291
Costa *v.* ENEL (6/64) [1964] ECR 585 .... 47, 179, 190, 199, 200, 201,
                                                              244, 280
Council *v.* Parliament (72/82) (discontinued) 6, 100

DGV Deutsche Getreideverwertung und Rheinische Kraftfutter-
    werke GmbH and Others *v.* Council and Commission (241,
    242 & 245–250/78) [1979] ECR 3017 .... 143, 146
Da Costa en Schaake NV and Others *v.* Nederlandse Belastingad-
    ministratie (28–30/62) [1963] ECR 31 .... 196, 319

Dairy Products Case: Commission v. Luxembourg and Belgium
(90 & 91/63) [1964] ECR 625 .... 83, 280
D'Amario: Benito D'Amario v. Landesversicherungsanstalt
Schwaben (320/82) [1983] ECR 3811 263
Dautzenberg v. Court of Justice (2/80) [1980] ECR 3107 161
De Franceschi S.p.a. Monfalcone v. Council and Commission (51/
81) [1982] ECR 117 144
Defrenne v. Sabena (43/75) [1976] ECR 455 ..... 170, 197, 199, 257, 289,
314
De Geus v. Bosch (13/61) [1962] ECR 45 .... 59, 178, 183
Demirel (M.) (12/86) Judgment of September 30, 1987 185
De Peijper (104/75) [1976] ECR 613 .... 170, 298
Donington, Lord Bruce of (208/80) [1981] ECR 2205 187
Du Pont (234/81) [1982] ECR 3515 258
Deutsche Bakels GmbH v. Oberfinanz-direktion München (14/70)
[1970] ECR 1001 313
Dietz v. Commission (126/76) [1977] ECR 2431 156
—— v. —— (126/76–Costs) [1979] ECR 2131 237
Drake v. Chief Adjudication Officer (150/85) [1986] 3 All E.R.
65 170
Dumortier and Others v. Council (64 & 113/76, 167 & 239/78, 27,
28 & 45/79) [1979] ECR 3091 .... 143, 146
Dundalk Water Scheme (45/87R) [1987] 2 CMLR 197 and 536 91
Dunstan Curtis v. Commission and Parliament (167/80) [1981]
ECR 1499 167
Dyestuffs Cases (48 etc./69) [1972] ECR 619 316

EMI v. CBS (51, 86 & 96/75) [1976] ECR 811 171
ERTA Case. See Commission v. Council (22/70) [1971] ECR
263 .... 60, 98, 100, 101, 103, 272, 280, 287
Elz v. Commission (56/75–rev.) [1977] ECR 1617 241
Einfuhr- und Vorratsstelle für Getreide- und Futtermittel v. Mack-
prang (2/75) [1975] ECR 607 301
Eunomia di Porro v. Italian Ministry of Education (18/71) [1971]
ECR 811 79
European Parliament v. Council (13/83) [1985] ECR 1513 123
—— v. —— (302/87) *The Times*, October 11, 1988 105
Europemballage Corporation and Continental Can Co. Inc. v.
Commission (6/72) [1973] ECR 215 287
Export Credits Case: Opinion 1/75 [1975] ECR 1355 207

Fédéchar v. High Authority (8/55) [1954–1956] ECR 245 .... 59, 119,
121, 274, 290, 296
FEDIOL v. Commission (191/82) [1983] ECR 2913 112
Foglia v. Novello (104/79) [1980] ECR 745 .... 180, 181, 245
—— v. —— (244/80) [1981] ECR 3045 .... 181, 245, 315

Foto-Frost (314/85) (1989) 13 E.L.Rev. 125 .... 173, 174
Fournier *v*. Commission (39/69) [1970] ECR 267 166
France *v*. European Parliament (358/85) (1988) 13 E.L.Rev. 293 ... 12
French Republic *v*. High Authority (1/54) [1954–1956] ECR 1 121
—— *v*. United Kingdom (141/78) [1979] ECR 2923 85–86
Frilli *v*. Belgian State (1/72) [1972] ECR 457 299

GEMA *v*. Commission (125/78) [1979] ECR 3173 124
Geitling and Others *v*. High Authority (36–38 & 40/59) [1960] ECR
    423 304
Germany *v*. Commission (24/62) [1963] ECR 63 117
—— *v*. —— (34/62) [1963] ECR 131 290
Geweise *v*. Mackenzie (24/83) [1984] ECR 817 260
Gingerbread Case. *See* Commission *v*. Luxembourg and Belgium
    (2 & 3/62) [1962] ECR 425 .... 273, 280, 281
Granaria *v*. Hoofdproduktschap voor Akkerbouwprodukten
    (Skimmed milk powder) (116/76) [1977] ECR 1247 142
Groupement des Industries Sidérurgiques Luxembourgeoises *v*.
    High Authority (7 & 9/54) [1954–1956] ECR 175 .... 59, 114
Gullung: Claude Gullung *v*. Conseil de L'Ordre des Avocats du
    Barreau de Colmar (292/86) [1988] 2 CMLR 57 255

Haegeman *v*. Belgian State (181/73) [1974] ECR 449 185
—— *v*. Commission (96/71) [1972] ECR 1005 .... 154, 155, 314
Hauer *v*. Land Rheinland-Pfalz (44/79) [1979] ECR 3727 .... 308, 309
Hoogovens *v*. High Authority (14/61) [1962] ECR 253 294
Humblet *v*. Belgian State (6/60) [1960] ECR 559 .... 274, 278

IBM *v*. Commission (60/81) [1981] ECR 2639 98
I.C.I. and Others *v*. Commission (48, 49, 51–57/69) [1972] ECR
    619 316
Importazione Bestiame Carni *v*. Commission (46/75) [1976] ECR
    65 154
Import Gadgets, S.a.r.l., Paris *v*. L.A.M.P. S.p.A., Pavia (22/76)
    [1976] ECR 1371 .... 43–45, 56, 181, 229, 243, 273, 279, 313
International Fruit Company and Others *v*. Commission (41–44/
    70) [1971] ECR 411 109
Internationale Handelsgesellschaft *v*. Einfuhr- und Vorratsstelle
    für Getreide und Futtermittel (11/70) [1970] ECR
    1125 .... 120, 194, 305, 309
Interquell Stärke-Chemie and Diamalt *v*. Council and Commission
    (261 & 262/78) [1979] ECR 3045 .... 143, 147
Ireks-Arkady *v*. Council and Commission (238/78) [1979] ECR
    2955 .... 143, 146
Italian Republic *v*. Commission (41/83) [1985] 2 CMLR 368 103
Italy *v*. Council and Commission (32/65) [1966] ECR 389 129

Italy v. High Authority (20/59) (1960) ECR 325 290

Japanese Ball-Bearings Cases: Toyo Bearing Co. and Others v. Council and Commission (113 & 118–121/77) [1979] ECR 1185 .... 107, 113

KSH v. Council and Commission (143/77) [1979] ECR 3583 143
Kampffmeyer and Others v. Commission (5, 7 & 13–24/66) [1967] ECR 245 .... 138, 141, 146, 153
—— v. Commission and Council (56–60/74) [1976] ECR 711 146
Kenny v. Insurance Officer (1/78) [1978] ECR 1489 170
Kergall v. Common Assembly (1/55) [1954–1956] ECR 151 134
Klopp (107/83) [1984] ECR 2971 .... 170, 255
Kolpinghuis Nijmegen (80/86) [1988] P.L. 317 320
Koninklijke Scholten-Honig v. Council and Commission (143/77) [1979] ECR 3583 143
Koschniske v. Raad van Arbeid (9/79) [1979] ECR 2717 275
Kramer and Others (3, 4 & 6/76) [1976] ECR 1279 206
Krohn & Co. Import-Export v. Commission (175/84) [1987] ECR 97 156

LTU v. Eurocontrol (29/76) [1976] ECR 1541 284
Lamb War Cases: Commission v. France (24/80R & 97/80R) [1980] ECR 1319 .... 90, 91
Lee v. Minister for Agriculture (152/79) [1981] ECR 1495 263
Leonesio v. Italian Ministry for Agriculture and Forestry (93/71) [1972] ECR 287 170
Lesieur Cotelle S.A. and Others v. Commission (67–85/75) [1976] ECR 391 154
Lord Bruce of Donington (208/80) [1981] ECR 2205 187
Ludwigshafener Walzmühle Erling (197–200, 243, 245, 247/80) [1981] ECR 3211 154
Lütticke v. Commission (48/65) [1966] ECR 19 124
—— v. —— (4/96) [1971] ECR 325 .... 139, 146, 314
Luxembourg v. European Parliament (230/81) [1983] ECR 255 ...... 12, 99

Mackprang v. Commission (15/71) [1971] ECR 797 124
—— (2/75) [1975] ECR 607 301
Maizena v. Council (139/79) [1980] ECR 3393 119
Manghera (59/75) [1976] ECR 91 .... 281, 289
Manzoni v. Fonds National de Retraite des Ouvriers Mineurs (112/76) [1977] ECR 1647 313
Markus & Walsh v. Hauptzollamt Hamburg-Jonas (14/69) [1969] ECR 349 279
Marshall v. Southampton etc. A.H.A. (152/84) [1986] ECR 737 47

Matisa-Maschinen GmbH *v.* Hauptzollamt Berlin-Packhof (35/75)
[1975] ECR 1205 313
Meijer *v.* Department of Trade (118/78) [1979] ECR 1387 .... 80, 93
Merkur *v.* Commission (43/72) [1973] ECR 1055 .... 145, 314
Meroni *v.* High Authority (9/56) [1957 and 1958] ECR 133 ... 117, 128,
141, 274
Metro *v.* Commission (26/76) [1977] ECR 1875) 111, 113
Meyer-Burckhardt *v.* Commission (9/75)ECR 1171 .... 134, 194
Milchkontor *v.* Hauptzollamt Saarbrücken (29/68) [1969] ECR
165 195
Mills *v.* European Investment Bank (110/75) [1976] ECR 955 166
Minister for Fisheries *v.* Schoenenberg (88/77) [1978] ECR 473 93
Muller-Collignon *v.* Commission (4/67) [1967] ECR 365 145
Münchener Import-Weinkellerei GmbH *v.* Commission (147/83)
[1985] ECR 257 45

Nederlandse Spoorwegen *v.* Minister van Verkeer en Waterstaat
(36/73) [1973] ECR 1299 186
Netherlands *v.* High Authority (6/54) [1954–1956] ECR 103 . 103, 122,
278
—— *v.* —— (25/59) [1960] ECR 355 290
—— *v.* Rüffer (814/79) [1980] ECR 3807 284
Niemann *v.* Bundesversicherungsanstalt für Angestellte (191/73)
[1974] ECR 571 174
Nold *v.* Commission (4/73) [1974] ECR 491 .... 120, 307, 309
—— *v.* High Authority (18/57) [1957 and 1958] ECR 121 317
Nordsee *v.* Nordstern (102/81) [1982] ECR 1095 188

Officier van Justitie *v.* van Haaster (190/73) [1974] ECR 1123 280
Opinion 1/75 Export Credits Case 205
—— 1/76 Draft agreement establishing laying-up fund for inland
waterway vessels [1977] ECR 741 206
—— 1/78 concerning the International Agreement on National
Rubber [1979] ECR 2811 206
Oryzomyli Kavallas *v.* Commission (160/84) [1985] ECR 675;
[1986] ECR 633 228

Partie Ecologiste 'Les Verts' *v.* European Parliament (294/83)
[1982] 2 CMLR 343 .... 101, 105, 110
Pellegrini *v.* Commission (23/76) [1976] ECR 1807 133
Petroni *v.* ONPTS (24/75) [1975] ECR 1149 174
Pigmeat Case: Commission *v.* Italy (7/61) [1961] ECR 317 .... 80, 98
Pig Producers Case: Commission *v.* United Kingdom (31/77R &
53/77R) [1977] ECR 921 87
Pigs Marketing Board *v.* Redmond (83/78) [1978] ECR 2347 260

Pinna: Pietro Pinna *v.* Caisse d'Allocations Familiales de la Savoie
(41/84) [1988] 1 CMLR 350 .... 198, 199, 289
Pioneer Electronic and Pioneer High Fidelity *v.* Commission (102
& 103/80) [1983] ECR 1825 332
Plaumann *v.* Commission (25/62) [1963] ECR 95 .... 47, 108, 109, 111,
144, 314
Polydor Ltd. *v.* Harlequin Record Shops Ltd. (270/80) [1982] ECR
329 185
Portelange *v.* Smith Corona Marchant International and Others
(10/69) [1969] ECR 309 180
Prais *v.* Council (130/75) [1976] ECR 1589 .... 161, 261, 330
Pretore di Salo *v.* X. (14/86) [1987] ECR 2565 187
Procureur de la République *v.* Waterkeyn (314/81) [1982] ECR
4337 89
Procurator Fiscal *v.* Marshall (370/88) 260
Providence Agricole de la Champagne and Others *v.* ONIC (4, 109
& 145/79) [1980] ECR 2823 198
Pubblico Ministero *v.* Manghera and Others (59/75) [1976] ECR
91 .... 281, 289
—— *v.* Ratti (148/78) [1979] ECR 1629 47

R. *v.* Bouchereau (30/77) [1977] ECR 1999 275
—— *v.* Henn and Darby (34/79) [1979] ECR 3795 .... 170, 315
—— *v.* Intervention Board for Agricultural Produce, *ex p.* Man
(Sugar) (181/84) [1986] 2 All E.R. 115 296
—— *v.* Kirk (63/83) [1984] ECR 2689 83
—— *v.* Secretary of State for Home Affairs, *ex p.* Santillo (131/79)
[1980] ECR 1585 .... 234, 276, 292
Racke *v.* Hauptzollamt Mainz (98/78) [1979] ECR 69 301
Ratti (148/78) [1979] ECR 1629 47
Rau *v.* De Smedt (261/81) [1982] ECR 3961 181
Razanatsimba (65/77) [1977] ECR 2229 187
Razzouk and Beydoun *v.* Commission (75 & 117/82) [1984] ECR
1509 163
Rewe Handelsgesellschaft Nord and Rewe Markt Steffen *v.*
Hauptzollamt Kiel (158/80) [1981] ECR 1805 241
Reyners *v.* Belgian State (2/74) [1974] ECR 631 255
Rey Soda *v.* Cassa Conguaglio Zucchero (23/75) [1975] ECR
1279 280
Rheinmühlen *v.* Einfuhr- und Vorratsstelle für Getreide und
Futtermittel (6/71) [1971] ECR 719 321
—— *v.* —— (146 & 166/73) [1974] ECR 33 and 139 .... 174, 178, 180,
193, 321, 322
Richez-Parise *v.* Commission (19, 20, 25 & 30/69) [1970] ECR
325 139
Roquette *v.* Council (138/79) [1980] ECR 3333 119

Royal Scholten-Honig (Holdings) and Tunnel Refineries *v*. Intervention Board for Agricultural Produce (103 & 145/77) [1978] ECR 2037 299
Rüffer (814/79) [1980] ECR 3807 275
Rutili *v*. Minister for the Interior (36/75) [1975] ECR 1219 ... 307, 308, 309

SNUPAT *v*. High Authority (42 & 49/59) [1961] ECR 53 .... 120, 127
Saar Tubes *v*. High Authority (1 & 14/57) [1957 and 1958] ECR 105 97
Sabbatini *v*. European Parliament (20/71) [1972] ECR 345 .... 127, 163, 300
Santillo (131/79) [1980] ECR 1585 .... 234, 276, 292
Sayag (5/68) [1968] ECR 395 .... 150, 151, 152
—— *v*. Leduc (9/69) [1969] ECR 329 .... 150, 151
Schertzer *v*. European Parliament (25/68) [1977] ECR 1729 262
Schots-Kortner and Others *v*. Council and Commission (15–33 etc./73) [1974] ECR 177 .... 145, 163, 300
Schwarze: Firma C. Schwarze *v*. Einfuhr- und Vorratsstelle für Getreide und Futtermittel (16/65) [1966] CMLR 172 183
Sermes *v*. Commission (279/86R) [1987] ECR 3110 107
Sgarlata *v*. Commission (40/64) [1965] ECR 215 .... 295, 304
Simmenthal (106/77) [1978] ECR 629 201
—— *v*. Commission (92/78) [1979] ECR 777 126
Simon *v*. Court of Justice (15/60) [1961] ECR 115 161
Société de Fonderies de Pont-à-Mousson (14/59) [1959] ECR 215 .. 229
Société des Grands Moulins des Antilles *v*. Commission (99/74) [1975] ECR 1531 154
Sotgiu *v*. Deutsche Bundespost (152/73) [1974] ECR 153 280
Staff Salaries Cases (81/72 and 70/74) 4, 103
Stauder *v*. Ulm (26/69) [1969] ECR 419 .... 120, 275, 305
Stork *v*. High Authority (1/58) [1959] ECR 17 304
Suiker Unie and Others *v*. Commission (40–48 etc./73) [1975] ECR 1663 .... 240, 331

Thieffry: Jean Thieffry *v*. Conseil de L'Ordre des Avocats à la Cour de Paris (7/76) [1977] ECR 765 255
Timex *v*. Council and Commission (264/82) [1985] ECR 849 112
Tither *v*. Commission (175/80) [1981] ECR 2345 .... 261, 262
Toepfer *v*. Commission (106 & 107/63) [1965] ECR 405 .... 108, 111, 113, 138
Torrekens (28/68) [1969] ECR 125 283
Toyo Bearing Co. and Others *v*. Council and Commission (113 & 118–121/77) [1979] ECR 1185 .... 107, 113
Transocean Marine Paint Association *v*. Commission (17/74) [1974] ECR 1063 .... 106, 120, 302, 313

United Brands v. Commission (27/76R [1976] ECR 425 .... 238, 241
United Kingdom v. European Parliament (23/86R) [1986] CMLR
    82 101
Union Syndicale v. Council (72/74) [1975] ECR 401 167

Vaassen-Göbbels v. Beambtenfonds voor het Mijnbedrijf (61/65)
    [1966] ECR 261 185
van Binsbergen v. Bestuur van de Bedrijsfsvereniging voor de
    Metaalnijverheid (33/74) [1974] ECR 1299 255
van Duyn v. Home Office (41/74) [1974] ECR 1337 ... 10, 273, 314, 315
van Gend en Loos v. Nederlandse Administratie Belastingen (26/
    62) [1963] ECR 1 .... 10, 47, 60, 92, 183, 196, 197, 199, 274, 313
van Haaster (190/73) [1974] ECR 1123 280
Vinal v. Orbat (46/80) [1981] 3 CMLR 524 181
Vloeberghs v. High Authority (9 & 12/60) [1961] ECR 197 .... 141, 149
von Colson v. Land Nordrhein-Westfalen (14/83) [1984] ECR
    1891 320
von Lachmüller v. Commission (43, 45 & 48/59) [1960] ECR 463 134

Walter Rau v. B.A.L.M. (133–136/85) (1987) 12 E.L.Rev. 451 298
—— v. EEC (279, 280, 285 & 286/84) *The Times*, March 23,
    1987 .... 22, 299
Watson and Belmann (188/75) [1976] ECR 1185 .... 257, 308
Wöhrmann and Lutticke v. Commission (31 & 33/62) [1962] ECR
    501 127
Wollast v. EEC (18/63) [1964] ECR 85 228
Woodpulp Cases (89/85); Opinion of May 25, 1988 317
Wünsche Handelsgesellschaft, (197/83) *Re* [1987] 3 CMLR
    225 .... 194, 307, 309

Zuckerfabrik Schöppenstedt v. Council (5/71) [1971] ECR
    975 .... 47, 141, 143, 145

TABLE OF CASES
BEFORE THE COURT OF JUSTICE

(in numerical order)

1/54 French Republic *v.* High Authority 121
3/54 ASSIDER *v.* High Authority 275, 284
6/54 Netherlands *v.* High Authority 103, 122, 278
7 & 9/54 Groupement des Industries Sidérurgiques Luxembourgeoises *v.* High Authority 59, 114
1/55 Kergall *v.* Common Assembly 134
5/55 ASSIDER 241
8/55 Fédéchar *v.* High Authority 59, 119, 121, 274, 290, 296
7/56 & 3–7/57 Algera and Others *v.* Assembly 146, 162, 166, 285
9/56 Meroni *v.* High Authority 117, 128, 141, 274
1 & 14/57 Saar Tubes *v.* High Authority 97
15/57 Compagnie des Hauts Fourneaux de Chasse *v.* High Authority 296
18/57 Nold *v.* High Authority 317
1/58 Stork *v.* High Authority 304
14/59 Société de Fonderies de Pont-à-Mousson 229
20/59 Italy *v.* High Authority 290
25/59 Netherlands *v.* High Authority 290
36–38 & 40/59 Geitling and Others *v.* High Authority 304
42 & 49/59 SNUPAT *v.* High Authority 120, 127
42 & 49/59 Breedband N.V. *v.* Société des Aciéries du Temple 242
43, 45 & 48/59 von Lachmüller *v.* Commission 134
6/60 Humblet *v.* Belgian State 274, 278
9 & 12/60 Vloeberghs *v.* High Authority 141, 149
15/60 Simon *v.* Court of Justice 161
7/61 Commission *v.* Italian Republic 80, 98
13/61 De Geus *v.* Bosch 59, 178, 183
14/61 Hoogovens *v.* High Authority 293
2 & 3/62 Commission *v.* Luxembourg and Belgium 82, 273, 280, 281
24/62 Germany *v.* Commission 117
25/62 Plaumann *v.* Commission 47, 108, 109, 111, 144, 314
26/62 van Gend en Loos *v.* Nederlandse Administratie Belastingen 10, 47, 60, 92, 183, 196, 197, 199, 274, 313
28–30/62 Da Costa en Schaake NV and Others *v.* Nederlandse Belastingadministratie 196, 319
31 & 33/62 Wöhrmann and Lütticke *v.* Commission 127

XXV

32/62 Alvis v. Council 164, 285
34/62 Germany v. Commission 290
18/63 Wollast v. EEC 228
90 & 91/63 Commission v. Luxembourg and Belgium 83, 280
106 & 107/63 Toepfer v. Commission 108, 111, 113, 138
6/64 Costa v. ENEL 47, 179, 190, 199, 200, 201, 244, 280
40/64 Sgarlata v. Commission 295, 304
56 & 58/64 Consten and Grundig v. Commission 106, 122
16/65 Schwarze: Firma C. Schwarze v. Einfuhr- und Vorratsstelle
    für Getreide und Futtermittel 183
32/65 Italy v. Council and Commission 129
48/65 Lütticke v. Commission 124
61/65 Vaassen-Göbbels v. Beamtenfonds voor het Mijnbedrijf 185
5, 7 & 13–24/66 Kampffmeyer and Others v. Commission 138, 141,
                                                                                      146, 153
8–11/66 Cimenteries CBR and Others v. Commission 98, 117
4/67 Muller-Collignon v. Commission 145
9/67 Colditz v. Caisse d'Assurance Vieillesse des Travailleurs
    Salariés de Paris 290
13/67 Becher v. Hauptzollamt München 244
5/68 Sayag 150, 151, 152
7/68 Commission v. Italy 79
24/68 Commission v. Italian Republic 282
25/68 Schertzer v. European Parliament 262
28/68 Caisse régionale de sécurité sociale du nord de la France v.
    Torrekens 283
29/68 Milchkontor v. Hauptzollamt Saarbrücken 195
4/69 Lütticke v. Commission 139, 146, 314
6 & 11/69 Commission v. French Republic 114
9/69 Sayag v. Leduc 150, 151
10/69 Portelange v. Smith Corona Marchant International and
    Others 180
14/69 Markus & Walsh v. Hauptzollamt Hamburg-Jonas 279
19, 20, 25 & 30/69 Richez-Parise v. Commission 139
26/69 Commission v. French Republic 82
29/69 Stauder v. Ulm 120, 275, 305
39/69 Fournier v. Commission 166
48, 49, 51–57/69 I.C.I. and Others v. Commission 316
64/69 Compagnie Française Commerciale et Financière v. Com-
    ission 109, 283
69/69 Alcan v. Commission 113
11/70 Internationale Handelsgesellschaft v. Einfuhr- und Vorrats-
    stelle für Getreide und Futtermittel 120, 194, 305, 309
14/70 Deutsche Bakels GmbH v. Oberfinanzdirektion München ... 313
22/70 Commission v. Council (ERTA Case) 60, 98, 100, 101, 103,
                                                                                272, 280, 287

41–44/70 International Fruit Company and Others *v.* Commission 109

62/70 Bock *v.* Commission 108, 113, 301

5/71 Zuckerfabrik Schöppenstedt *v.* Council 47, 141, 143, 145

6/71 Rheinmühlen *v.* Einfuhr- und Vorratsstelle für Getreide und Futtermittel 321

9 & 11/71 Compagnie d'Approvisionnement *v.* Commission .. 141, 147, 148

15/71 Mackprang *v.* Commission 124

18/71 Eunomia di Porro *v.* Italian Ministry of Education 79

20/71 Sabbatini *v.* European Parliament 127, 163, 300

48/71 Commission *v.* Italy 79

93/71 Leonesio *v.* Italian Ministry for Agriculture and Forestry 170

96/71 Haegeman *v.* Commission 154, 155, 314

1/72 Frilli *v.* Belgian State 299

6/72 Europemballage Corporation and Continental Can Co. Inc. *v.* Commission 60, 106, 273, 274, 287, 291

9/72 Brunner *v.* Hauptzollamt Hof 279

43/72 Merkur *v.* Commission 145, 314

62/72 Bollmann *v.* Hauptzollamt Hamburg-Waltershof 245

70/72 Commission *v.* Germany 89

81/72 Commission *v.* Council 4, 103, 122, 300

4/73 Nold *v.* Commission 120, 307, 309

15–33 etc./73 Schots-Kortner and Others *v.* Council and Commission 145, 163, 300

36/73 Nederlandse Spoorwegen *v.* Minister van Verkeer en Waterstaat 186

40–48 etc./73 Suiker Unie and Others *v.* Commission 240, 331

127/73 B.R.T. *v.* SABAM 245

146 & 166/73 Rheinmühlen *v.* Einfuhr, etc. 174, 178, 180, 193, 321, 322

152/73 Sotgiu *v.* Deutsche Bundespost 280

167/73 Commission *v.* French Republic 84, 90, 317

169/73 Compagnie Continentale France *v.* Council 148

181/73 Haegeman *v.* Belgian State 185

190/73 Officier van Justitie *v.* van Haaster 280

191/73 Niemann *v.* Bundesversicherungsanstalt für Angestellte 174

2/74 Reyners *v.* Belgian State 255

15 & 16/74 Centrafarm BV and de Peijper *v.* Sterling Drug Inc. and Winthrop BV 170

17/74 Transocean Marine Paint Association *v.* Commission ... 106, 120, 302, 313

33/74 van Binsbergen *v.* Bestuur van de Bedrijsfsvereniging voor de Metaalnijverheid 255

41/74 van Duyn *v.* Home Office 10, 273, 314, 315

56–60/74 Kampffmeyer and Others *v.* Commission and Council 146

67/74 Bonsignore v. Oberstadt-direktor der Stadt Köln 170
70/74 Commission v. Council 103, 104
72/74 Union Syndicale v. Council 167
74/74 CNTA v. Commission 146, 301
99/74 Société des Grands Moulins des Antilles v. Commission 154
100/74 C.A.M., SA v. Commission 110
Opinion 1/75 concerning Export Credits Case 205
2/75 Einfuhr- und Vorratsstelle für Getreide- und Futtermittel
    v. Mackprang 301
9/75 Meyer-Burckhardt v. Commission 134, 194
23/75 Rey Soda v. Cassa Conguaglio Zucchero 280
24/75 Petroni v. ONPTS 174
35/75 Matisa-Maschinen GmbH v. Hauptzollamt Berlin-Packhof .. 313
36/75 Rutili v. Minister for the Interior 307, 308, 309
39/75 Coenen and Others v. Sociaal-Economische Raad 256
43/75 Defrenne v. Sabena 170, 197, 199, 257, 289, 314
46/75 Importazione Bestiame Carni v. Commission 154
51, 86 & 96/75 EMI v. CBS 171
56/75–rev. Elz v. Commission 241
59/75 Pubblico Ministero v. Flavia Manghera and Others 281, 289
67–85/75 Lesieur Cotelle SA and Others v. Commission 154
87/75 Bresciani v. Amministrazione Italiana delle Finanze 185
93/75 Adlerblum v. Caisse Nationale d'Assurance Vieillesse des
    Travailleurs Salariés 183
104/75 De Peijper 170, 298
110/75 Mills v. European Investment Bank 166
118/75 Watson and Belmann 257, 308
130/75 Prais v. Council 161, 261, 330
Opinion 1/76 Draft Agreement establishing laying-up fund for
    inland waterway vessels 206
3, 4 & 6/76 Kramer and Others 206
7/76 Thieffry: Jean Thieffry v. Conseil de L'Ordre des Avocats à
    la Cour de Paris 255
17/76 Brack v. Insurance Officer 10, 187, 284
22/76 Import Gadgets v. L.A.M.P. ... 43–45, 56, 181, 229, 243, 273, 279,
    313
23/76 Pellegrini v. Commission 133
26/76 Metro v. Commission 111, 113
27/76R United Brands v. Commission 238, 241
29/76 LTU v. Eurocontrol 284
64 & 113/76, 167 & 239/78, 27, 28 & 45/79 Dumortier and Others v.
    Council 143, 146
83 & 94/76, 4, 15 & 40/77 Bayerische HNL v. Council and
    Commission 141, 142, 143
112/76 Manzoni v. Fonds National de Retraite des Ouvriers
    Mineurs 313

114/76 Bergmann v. Grows-Farm GmbH 142
116/76 Granaria v. Hoofproduktschap voor Akkerbouwproduk-
    ten 142
126/76 Dietz v. Commission 156
126/76–Costs: Dietz v. Commission 237
30/77 Bouchereau 275
31/77R & 53/77R Commission v. United Kingdom 87, 91
61/77 Commission v. Ireland 93
65/77 Razanatsimba 187
88/77 Minister for Fisheries v. Schoenenberg 93
103 & 145/77 Royal Scholten-Honig (Holdings) and Tunnel
    Refineries v. Intervention Board for Agricultural Pro-
    duce 299
106/77 Simmenthal 201
113/77 NTN Toyo 107, 113
116 & 124/77 Amylum and Tunnel Refineries v. Council and
    Commission 143
143/77 Koninklijke Scholten-Honig v. Council and Commission 143
146/77 British Beef Co. v. Intervention Board for Agricultural
    Produce 10
156/77 Commission v. Belgium 130
Opinion 1/78 concerning the International Agreement on National
    Rubber 206
1/78 Kenny v. Insurance Officer 170
83/78 Pigs Marketing Board v. Redmond 260
92/78 Simmenthal v. Commission 126
98/78 Racke v. Hauptzollamt Mainz 301
116/78 Bellintani v. Commission 241
118/78 Meijer v. Department of Trade 80, 93
125/78 GEMA v. Commission 124
141/78 French Republic v. United Kingdom 85–86
148–78 Pubblico Ministero v. Ratti 47
21/78 Commission v. United Kingdom 80, 93
232/78 Commission v. French Republic 79, 90
238/78 Ireks-Arkady v. Council and Commission 143, 146
241, 242 & 245–250/78 DGV and Others v. Council and Commis-
    sion 143, 146
261 & 262/78 Interquell Stärke-Chemie and Diamalt v. Council and
    Commission 143, 147
4, 109 & 145/79 Providence Agricole de la Champagne and Others
    v. ONIC 198
9/79 Koschniske v. Raad van Arbeid 275
34/79 R. v. Henn and Darby 170, 315
44/79 Hauer v. Land Rheinland-Pfalz 308, 309
104/79 Foglia v. Novello 180, 181, 245, 315

131/79 R. *v.* Secretary of State for Home Affairs, *ex p.* Santillo 234, 276, 292
138/79 Roquette *v.* Council 119
139/79 Maizena *v.* Council 119
152/79 Lee *v.* Minister for Agriculture 263
155/79 A.M. & S. Europe Limited *v.* Commission ... 232, 240, 285, 332
789/79 Calpak S.p.A. and Società Emiliana Lavorazione Frutta S.p.A. *v.* Commission 106
792R/79 Camera Care Ltd. *v.* Commission 238
814/79 Netherlands *v.* Rüffer 275, 284
2/80 Dautzenberg *v.* Court of Justice 161
24/80 Commission *v.* France 79
24/80R & 97/80R Commission *v.* France 90, 91
46/80 Vinal *v.* Orbat 181
97/80 Commission *v.* France 80
102 & 103/80 Pioneer Electronic and Pioneer High Fidelity *v.* Commission 332
130/80 Borker 187
158/80 Rewe Handelsgesellschaft Nord and Rewe Markt Steffen *v.* Hauptzollamt Kiel 241
167/80 Dunstan Curtis *v.* Commission and Parliament 167
175/80 Tither *v.* Commission 261, 262
197–200, 243, 245, 247/80 Ludwigshafener Walzmühle Erling 154
208/80 Lord Bruce of Donington 187
244/80 Foglia *v.* Novello 181, 245, 315
246/80 Broekmeulen *v.* Huisarts Registratie Commissie 188, 189
270/80 Polydor Ltd. *v.* Harlequin Record Shops Ltd. 185
8/81 Becker *v.* Finanzamt Münster 47, 314
51/81 De Franceschi S.p.A. Monfalcone *v.* Council and Commission 144
58/81 Commission *v.* Luxembourg 84
59/81 Commission *v.* Council 104
60/81 IBM *v.* Commission 98
102/81 Nordsee *v.* Nordstern 188
115 & 116/81 Adouai and Cornuaille 315
230/81 Luxembourg *v.* European Parliament 12, 99
234/81 Du Pont 258
261/81 Rau *v.* De Smedt 181
283/81 C.I.L.F.I.T. 195
314/81 Procureur de la République *v.* Waterkeyn 89
42/82R Commission *v.* French Republic 238
72/82 Council *v.* Parliament 6, 100
75 & 117/82 Razzouk and Beydouin *v.* Commission 163
116/82 Commission *v.* Germany 46
191/82 FEDIOL *v.* Commission 112
239 & 275/82 Allied Corporation *v.* Commission 107

264/82 Timex v. Council and Commission 112
320/82 D'Amario: Benito D'Amario v. Landesversicherungsanstalt Schwaben 263
13/83 European Parliament v. Council 123
14/83 von Colson 320
24/83 Geweise v. MacKenzie 260
41/83 Italian Republic v. Commission 103
63/83 R. v. Kirk 83
107/83 Klopp 170, 255
145/83 Adams v. Commission 140, 144
147/83 Munchenen Import-Weinkellerei GmbH v. Commission 45
197/83 Wünsche Handelsgesellschaft 194
294/83 Partie Ecologiste 'Les Verts' v. European Parliament 101, 105, 110
41/84 Pinna: Pietro Pinna v. Caisse d'Allocations Familiales de la Savoie 198, 199, 289
152/84 Marshall v. Southampton etc. A.H.A. 47
160/84 Oruzomyli Kavallas v. Commission 228
169/84 COFAZ v. Commission 112
175/84 Krohn & Co. Import-Export v. Commission 156
181/84 R. v. Intervention Board for Agricultural Produce, ex p. Man (Sugar) 296
205/84 Commission v. Germany 255
279, 280, 285 and 286/84 Walter Rau v. EEC 22, 299
89/85 Woodpulp 317
105/85 Drake v. Chief Adjudication Officer 170
121/85 Conegate v. H.M. Customs and Excise 170, 315
133–136/85 Walter Rau v. B.A.L.M. 298
249/85 ALBAKO v. B.A.L.M. 298
314/85 Foto-Frost 173, 174
353/85 Commission v. United Kingdom 76
358/85 France v. European Parliament 12
414/85 Commission v. Ireland 76
416/85 Commission v. United Kingdom 22, 76
426/85 Commission v. Zoubek 133
12/86 Demirel (M.) 185
14/86 Pretore di Salo v. X. 187
23/86R United Kingdom v. European Parliament 101
24/86 Blaizot v. University of Liège 197, 289
34/86 Budget (1986), Re the Council v. European Parliament 101, 105
45/86 Commission v. Council 4, 104, 118
80/86 Kolpinghuis Nijmegen 320
257/86 Commission v. Italy 76
279/86R Sermes v. Commission 107
283/86 Commission v. Belgium 76

292/86 Claude Gullung *v*. Conseil de L'Ordre des Avocats du
   Barreau de Colmar 255
45/87 Dundalk Water Scheme 91
302/87 European Parliament *v*. Council 105
370/88 Procurator Fiscal *v*. Marshall 260

TABLE OF CASES
BEFORE OTHER COURTS

Avilar (Conseil d'Etat, March 23, 1984) 78

Bourgoin v. Ministry of Agriculture, Fisheries and Food [1985] 3
    All E.R. 585 78
Buchanan (James) & Co. v. Babco Forwarding and Shipping
    (U.K.) [1978] A.C. 141 (H.L.) 335
Bulmer v. Bollinger [1974] Ch. 401 .... 189, 193, 268

Cohn-Bendit [1980] 1 CMLR 543 .... 193, 194
Concorde Express Transport v. Traffic Examiner, Metropolitan
    Area [1980] 2 CMLR 221 193
Cunningham v. Milk Marketing Board for Northern Ireland [1988]
    3 CMLR 815 276
Customs and Excise v. Samex [1983] 1 All E.R. 1042 175

Duke v. GEC Reliance [1988] 1 All E.R. 626 320

Garden Cottage Foods v. Milk Marketing Board [1985] 2 All E.R.
    770 78
Garland v. British Rail Engineering [1982] 2 CMLR 174 193

Hagen v. Moretti [1980] 3 CMLR 253 191
Heydon's Case (1584) 3 Co.Rep. 7a 276
Hoffman-La Roche & Co. v. Secretary of State for Trade and
    Industry [1975] A.C. 295 (H.L.) 141
Holiday in Italy, Re a [1975] 1 CMLR 184 192

Kloppenburg [1988] 3 CMLR 1 265

Lee v. Minister for Agriculture 262

Macarthys v. Smith [1979] 1 W.L.R. 1189; [1979] 3 All E.R. 325 335
Minister for Economic Affairs v. Fromagerie Franco-Suisse "Le
    Ski" [1972] CMLR 330 83
Minister for the Interior v. Cohn-Bendit [1980] 1 CMLR 543 4
Moorcock, The, (1889) 14 P.D. 64 290

Noncyp [1988] 3 CMLR 84 315

Portsmouth City Council *v.* Richards [1988] , *The Times*, November 21, 1988 171

R. *v.* Barnsley Metropolitan Borough Council, *ex p.* Hook [1976] 1
  W.L.R. 1052 296
—— *v.* Henn and Darby [1982] A.C. 850 292
—— *v.* Marlborough Street Stipendary Magistrate, *ex p.* Bouchereau [1977] 1 W.L.R. 414 263
—— *v.* Secchi [1975] 1 CMLR 383 292
Roussel Laboratories (Hague District Court, July 18, 1984) 78
Russell *v.* Duke of Norfolk [1949] 1 All E.R. 109 188

SA Magnavision *v.* General Optical Council (No. 2) [1987] 2
  CMLR 262 .... 171, 191
Schorsch Meier *v.* Hennin [1975] Q.B. 416 292
Steinhauser *v.* City of Biarritz (Tribunal Administratif de Pau,
  November 12, 1985) 78
Steinike and Weinlig *v.* Bundesamt für Ernährung und Forstwirtschaft [1980] 2 CMLR 531 307

Terrapin (Overseas) Ltd. *v.* Terranova Industrie [1978] 3 CMLR
  102 196

TABLE OF COMMUNITY TREATIES

ECSC Treaty
Art. 4 79
Art. 31 297
Art. 32 37
  (1) 26
Art. 33 .... 96, 98, 113, 114, 115,
  117, 121, 124, 127, 128, 129,
  171, 275, 296
Art. 34 .... 122, 149
Art. 35 ... 96, 123, 124, 127, 149
Art. 36 .... 114, 126, 128
  (2) 132
  (3) 127, 128, 129
Art. 38 .... 99, 100
Art. 40 . 132, 135, 138, 149, 150
Art. 41 ... 27, 169, 171, 173, 184
Art. 60 121
Art. 61 121
Art. 65 121
Art. 80 .... 113, 149
Art. 88 .... 78, 87, 88, 149
Art. 89 85
Art. 92 128
Art. 95 74
EEC Treaty
Art. 2 .... 286, 288, 294
Art. 3 288
Art. 4 160
  (1) 2
Art. 7 299
Art. 9 .... 273, 281, 283
Art. 12 .. 79, 183, 184, 197, 199,
  273, 274, 281, 283, 294
Art. 13 .... 273, 283
Art. 16 .... 79, 273, 279, 283
Art. 30 ..... 78, 79, 170, 282, 297
Art. 31 .... 80, 81, 170, 297
Arts. 32–35 .... 170, 297
Art. 36 .... 170, 282, 284, 297

EEC Treaty—*cont.*
Art. 37 288
  (1) 280
Art. 38(1) 293
Art. 40(3) 142, 299
Art. 48 .... 84, 273, 290
  (3) 274
Arts. 49, 50 290
Art. 51 ... 66, 173, 174, 283, 290
Arts. 52–58 254
Arts. 59–66 255
Art. 74 123
Art. 84(2) 84
Art. 85 .... 10, 111, 122, 182
  (1) 273
  (2) 182
Art. 86 .... 111, 140, 273, 274,
  287, 288, 291
Art. 92 .... 87, 89, 112
Art. 93 .... 76, 86, 87, 88, 89, 90,
  91, 112, 130
  (2) 88
  (3) 87
Art. 94 112
Art. 113 ...... 106, 118, 203, 204,
  205
  (3) 204
Art. 117 289
Art. 119 .... 289, 299, 300
Art. 144 3
Art. 148 7
Art. 149 8
Art. 164 ... 3, 297, 303, 305, 323
Art. 165(2) 26
Art. 166 .... 53, 54, 66
Art. 167 .... 3, 15
Art. 168 .... 19, 35, 53
Art. 168A 64, 68
  (1) 66

EEC Treaty—*cont.*
  Art. 168A—*cont.*
      (3) 65
      (4) 66
  Art. 169 .. 28, 76, 77, 79, 80, 81,
      82, 83, 85, 86, 87, 88, 89,
      90, 91, 93, 98, 183, 184,
      194, 198, 238, 256
  Art. 170 .. 76, 85, 88, 89, 90, 91,
      93, 183, 184
      (3) 86
  Art. 171 .... 77, 79, 89, 90, 91
  Art. 172 .... 131, 132
  Art. 173 .... 65, 67, 87, 96,
      97–123, 124, 125, 126,
      127, 129, 130, 141, 143,
      144, 145, 158, 162, 165,
      167, 198, 204, 240, 272,
      275, 295, 296
      (1) 97, 98, 99, 102, 105
      (2) 105, 106, 109, 111,
      157, 239
      (3) 115
  Art. 174(2) 122, 198
  Art. 175 .. 65, 96, 104, 123–125,
      144
      (1) 123
      (2) 124
      (3) 123
  Art. 176 122
  Art. 177 .... 27, 56, 59, 84, 93,
      107, 120, 142, 145, 158,
      169, 172, 173, 174, 176,
      179, 180, 181, 182, 184,
      185, 186, 187, 188, 189,
      190, 193, 194, 195, 197,
      198, 199, 200, 201, 206,
      244, 296, 319, 321, 322,
      327, 331
      (2) 191
      (3) 190, 191
  Art. 178 .... 132, 133, 134, 136
  Art. 179 .... 26, 132, 134, 150,
      160, 161
  Art. 180 74
  Art. 181 .... 74, 133

EEC Treaty—*cont.*
  Art. 182 .... 74, 75
  Art. 183 134
  Art. 184 ...... 115, 125–130, 145,
      158, 163, 197, 300
  Art. 186 .... 80, 88, 91, 92
  Art. 188 220
  Art. 189 .... 5, 97, 99, 272
  Art. 190 .... 117, 118
  Art. 192 235
  Art. 193 9
  Art. 215 ...... 119, 132, 134, 137,
      141, 143, 144, 145
      (1) 132
      (2) .. 47, 135–139, 141–143,
      145, 150, 155–158,
      273, 285, 286
  Art. 216 11
  Art. 219 75
  Art. 220 176
  Art. 223 86
  Art. 224 86
  Art. 225 86
  Art. 226 .... 81, 82
  Art. 228 .... 74, 185, 203,
      204, 207
      (1) 205
  Art. 229 204
  Art. 235 118
  Art. 236 203
  Art. 238 .... 185, 204, 205
  Annex. II 242
Euratom Treaty
  Art. 103 .... 203, 207
  Art. 150 .... 27, 169, 184
  Art. 153 .... 74–75, 133
  Art. 188 286
      (2) 135
Merger Treaty
  Art. 2 7
  Art. 4 8
  Art. 10(2) 8
  Art. 11 3
  Art. 13 .... 3, 74
Act of Accession
  Art. 102 206

Protocol on the Statute of
the Court of Justice
Art. 4 41
Art. 18 257
Art. 43 143
Rules of Procedure of the
Court of Justice 67, 219
Art. 9(1) 26
Art. 37 251
Art. 38(3) 258
Art. 70 166
Art. 80 80
Art. 95 .... 27, 28
(2) 28
(3) 28, 165
(4) 315

Rules of Procedure of the
Court of Justice—*cont.*
Art. 104 .... 246, 259
1972 European Communi-
ties Act 201
s. 3 318
(1) 196, 269, 320
1972 Treaty of Accession 34,
148, 149
1984 Draft Treaty 5
Art. 4 310
Art. 43 104
Art. 44 92
1986 Single European
Act 3, 6, 7, 9, 11, 12,
64, 65, 71, 336
Art. 2 7

TABLE OF COMMUNITY LEGISLATION

Regulations
Reg. 3, J.O. 1958, 561 283
Reg. 17, J.O. 1962,
204 .... 98, 111
Art. 15 98
Art. 17 131
Reg. 99/63, J.O. 1963,
2268 .... 302, 303
Reg. 1408/71, J.O. 1971,
L.149/2 284
Reg. 1111/77, J.O. 1977,
L.134/4 299

Decisions and Directives
Dec. 22/54, J.O. 1954,
346 128
Dec. 14/55 .... 115, 128
Dir. 64/221, J.O. 1964,
850 .... 234, 273
Dec. 88/591 under Art.
168A, EEC
Art. 3(1) 65
Art. 3(2) 65
Art. 3(3) 65
Art. 7 66
Art. 11 66
Art. 15 98
Art. 17 131

Chapter 1

GENERAL INTRODUCTION

When on May 9, 1950, the French Foreign Minister, Robert Schuman, announced his proposal to place the whole of French and German coal and steel production under a common High Authority, in an organisation open to the participation of other European countries, he took care to include in the proposal the establishment of a court of justice which would subject the new Authority to judicial control.

Less than one year later, on April 18, 1951, the Treaty establishing the European Coal and Steel Community (the ECSC) was signed in Paris, creating, among other institutions, the Court of Justice. The elaborate institutional apparatus, including, as well as the High Authority and the Court, a Special Council of Ministers and a Common Assembly, was no doubt intended to ensure that the new Community should be based on democratic principles and the rule of law. The judicial structure was strongly influenced by ideas derived from continental, especially French, administrative law. But there was also a hint, in the Preamble to the Treaty, of a wider function for the institutions; the Preamble recalled that the six founding Member States—Belgium, France, Germany, Italy, Luxembourg and the Netherlands—were resolved "to lay the foundations for institutions which will give direction to a destiny henceforward shared."

When the same States signed the two Treaties of Rome, on March 25, 1957, establishing the European Economic Community (the EEC) and the European Atomic Energy Community (Euratom) respectively, the institutions were indeed given a wider task. Each of the

1

new Communities was endowed with a Court of Justice,
as well as a Commission (rather than a High Authority),
a Council of Ministers, and an Assembly. At the same
time it was provided that there should be a single Court
(and a single Assembly) to serve all three Communities;
this was effected by the Convention on Certain
Institutions Common to the European Communities.
Thus the Court of the ECSC became the Court of
Justice of the European Communities.

Later, the "Merger Treaty" of 1965 provided that
there should be a single Council and a single Commission for all three Communities. But the functions and
powers of all four institutions—Council, Commission,
Court and Assembly—are separately assigned in the
three founding Treaties. In practice the EEC Treaty is
by far the most important, and it is with the working of
the Court under the EEC Treaty that this book is
primarily concerned. The provisions governing the
Court are substantially identical in the EEC and
Euratom Treaties; they differ in more or less important
respects from those in the earlier ECSC Treaty.
Frequently, where provisions of the EEC Treaty are
cited in this book, there are corresponding provisions in
the other founding Treaties. The composition of the
institutions is the same under all three Treaties. When,
on January 1, 1973, the three Communities were
enlarged to include Denmark, Ireland and the United
Kingdom, the institutions were correspondingly enlarged
under the Treaty of Accession, but their jurisdiction was
not affected except in its territorial extent. The same
can be said of the further enlargements by the accession
of Greece on January 1, 1981, and of Spain and
Portugal on January 1, 1986.

In addition to their specific functions, the four
institutions are required, under Article 4(1) of the EEC
Treaty, to carry out the tasks entrusted to the
Community; each institution is to act within the limits of
the powers conferred upon it by the Treaty, as amended

now by the Single European Act of 1986. Both the Council, composed of government ministers from the Member States, and the Commission, an entirely independent body, are given legislative and decision-making powers. The Single European Act recognised that the Assembly should officially be known as the European Parliament, a style which the Assembly had assumed for itself in 1962; in this respect the Act reflects the enhanced role of the Parliament in the legislative process through the so-called "co-operation procedure" introduced by the Act and discussed below. The role of the Court, in the pregnant formula of Article 164 EEC, is to ensure that, in the interpretation and application of the Treaty, the law is observed. It is thus required to ensure that the other bodies act within the limits of their respective powers. Subsequent Articles of the Treaty spell out the Court's wide-ranging and multifarious jurisdiction, the main aspects of which will be discussed in Part Two of this book.

All four institutions are in principle equal under the Treaties; but, inevitably in the real world of politics as in the world of George Orwell, some are more equal than others. The formal equality of the institutions is symbolised by the fact that the members of the Court and of the Commission are appointed not by the Council—for that might be taken to imply the superior-ity of the Council—but "by common accord of the Governments of the Member States" (Article 167 EEC; Article 11 of the Merger Treaty). On the other hand, the Commission may be collectively dismissed by the Parliament (Article 144 EEC); and an individual member of the Commission may be compulsorily retired by the Court (Article 13 of the Merger Treaty).

We shall see that the relationship between the Council and the Commission is by no means that between political superior and inferior, even though the Council is undoubtedly the supreme expression, subject only to summit meetings of heads of government (below, p. 7), of the political will (or absence of will) in the Community. The relationship between the Council and the Court is also very different from that between government (or legislature) and judiciary, at least as it is known in the United Kingdom. While a decision of even the highest court in the United Kingdom can be reversed by Act of Parliament, even with retroactive effect, the decisions of the Court of Justice cannot be reversed by an act of the Council; on the contrary, any measure of the Council having legal effect can be annulled by the Court if contrary to the Treaties or other provisions of Community law. This has not infrequently happened; we shall see examples in Case 81/72, the first *Staff Salaries* case (below, p. 103) and the *GSP case* (Case 45/86, below, p. 118). In fact a ruling of the Court could be reversed only by the Court itself in a subsequent case, or by an amendment of the Treaties which, since it requires the unanimous approval of the Member States, each acting through its own constitutional processes, is not normally a practical possibility. Conversely, the political obstacles to amending the Treaties lend added significance to the Court's rulings on their interpretation, especially as the Court (as we shall see in Chapter 14) has been ready to interpret boldly in the face of political deadlock between the Council and the Commission. This boldness has at times led to a hostile reaction from national supreme courts; thus, the French *Conseil d'Etat* rebelled against the well-settled case-law of the Court of Justice on the direct effect of directives, partly on the ground that law-making by the Court was less to be tolerated once there was a directly elected European Parliament to take political initiatives (*Cohn-Bendit* C.E. December 12, 1979, *conclusions* Genevois [1980] 1 CMLR 543). In Germany, both the Federal Constitutional Court and the Federal Finance Court expressed reservations about the case-law of the Court of Justice, although those reservations have now been overcome: see

T.C. Hartley, *Foundations of European Community Law* (2nd ed., 1988), p. 227.

We shall have occasion to revert to the novel character of Community law which it is the Court's business to interpret and apply; here we must say a word about the sources of that law. In addition to, and derived from, the founding Treaties which make up the constitution of the Communities, it includes the regulations, directives and decisions of the Council and of the Commission, made under Article 189 EEC. These instruments are officially styled "acts" of the institutions. The acts of general application—regulations and directives—are sometimes referred to as "secondary legislation," the implication presumably being that the Treaties are in some sense "primary legislation." This classification is misleading since, although the implementing regulations of the Commission are often akin to subordinate or delegated legislation, there is nothing secondary, in character or in scope, about the basic regulations of the Council in such fields as agriculture, the free movement of workers, social security, and competition. This legislation is both as fundamental in character and as broad in scope as any national legislation, and its relationship to the founding Treaties is comparable to that which national legislation has to a national constitution, with the Court of Justice fulfilling the role of a constitutional court. Consequently we shall refer to regulations and directives of the Council as Community legislation, and for convenience we shall include in that term all enactments of both the Council and the Commission.

The European Parliament has no autonomous legislative powers. Under numerous provisions of the founding Treaties, its opinion must be sought by the Council before legislation can be enacted, but this need not be followed. The Parliament's own Draft Treaty (1984) for establishing the European Union suggested a two-chamber system for legislation. But these proposals

were not fully adopted in the Single European Act
(1986), which introduces instead a new "cooperation
procedure" involving Council, Commission and Parliament. The procedure is complex but involves the
proposed legislation receiving both a first and a second
reading in the Council and also in the Parliament: for
details, see Hartley, *Foundations of European Community Law*, (2nd ed., 1988), pp. 32–35. Although the
scope of the new procedure is limited, it does give the
Parliament somewhat more influence in the legislative
process.

Parliament also has the power, in certain circumstances, to take part in proceedings before the Court: we
revert to this in Chapter 7 (see pp. 99 and 104 below).
In other respects the European Parliament is more like
a national parliament. It has been given gradually
increasing control over the Community budget; historically, budgetary powers have been of much importance
to national parliaments in their struggles with the
executive. The European Parliament also exercises
supervisory functions over the Community executive: its
members can put questions to the Commission (and to
the Council), and it can even dismiss the Commission.
Until 1979, its effectiveness had been limited by many
factors, not least by the fact that its members had to
combine their duties with serving the national parliaments, from which they had been appointed. With
direct elections, although such a "dual mandate"
remains possible, most M.E.P.s are able to give more
time to their duties, and their increased authority as a
result of direct election led them to reject the
Community budget in 1979 and subsequently to exercise
their budgetary powers up to (and even beyond) the
limit (see, *e.g.* Case 72/82 *Council* v. *European
Parliament*, below, p. 100). Clearly, the European
Parliament is destined in future to play a greater role,
and perhaps to arrogate to itself a more active part in
the legislative process. Nevertheless, for the present, the

supreme Community legislature remains the Council, representing the Governments of the Member States.

The founding Treaties conceived of the Council as a Community institution rather than as an intergovernmental body. Thus, although the Council consists of representatives of the Member States (Article 2 of the Merger Treaty), each State being represented either by the foreign minister or by the minister responsible for the subject in question (agriculture, education, finance, transport, etc.), nevertheless the Treaties provide for majority voting on most matters, in contrast with the unanimity rule often found in intergovernmental organisations. Again, in contrast with the normal rule of one State, one vote, the Treaties provide for weighted voting (Article 148 EEC) in certain important areas of Community activity. But in practice, under the so-called "Luxembourg Accords" of 1966, unanimity became the rule in cases where vital national interests were claimed to be at stake. Now, under the Single European Act, the increased use of majority voting in the Council has raised the question whether the new political will to achieve a single market by 1992 means the Accords are becoming a dead letter. In the past, the obstacles to legislative progress caused by disagreements at the political level have been partially overcome, as we shall see, by the creative use of its powers by the Court of Justice and by the development there of judicial law-making.

Apart from the four institutions set up under the Treaties, mention must be made of the "summit" meetings of heads of government, formerly arranged ad hoc when the occasion arose—a famous occasion being the Hague summit of November 1969 which opened the way to the first enlargement of the Communities—but regularised at the Paris summit of 1974 under the name of "European Council," to which the Single European Act has given Treaty recognition in Article 2. This European Council however is not an institution of the

European Communities, a term restricted to the four
original Treaty bodies, which include the Council of the
European Communities, a permanent institution based,
like the Commission, in Brussels.

The Council and the Commission are sometimes
contrasted as the legislature and executive respectively
of the Community. This contrast accords well with the
traditional doctrine of the separation of powers,
distinguishing legislature, executive and judiciary. The
Commission, however, should not be regarded as a
mere administration, for it has important political
responsibilities which it exercises in its own right.

Of most importance in this respect is the crucial role
of the Commission in the legislative process. In almost
every area of major policy under the EEC Treaty, the
Council can legislate only on a proposal of the
Commission. This exclusive "right of initiative" is
vested in the Commission to ensure that legislation
respects the Community interest; for "The members of
the Commission shall, in the general interest of the
Communities, be completely independent in the performance of their duties... they shall neither seek nor
take instructions from any Government or from any
other body" (Article 10(2) of the Merger Treaty).
Moreover, under Article 149 EEC, a proposal of the
Commission can be amended only by a unanimous vote
of the Council; so that if there is disagreement among
the ministers, no decision at all can be taken until the
Commission puts forward a different proposal. This has
important consequences: not only is the Council unable
to legislate unilaterally; the Commission is also actively
involved in the law-making process within the Council.
In practice, the Commission will have discussed its
proposals with the Committee of Permanent Representatives of the Member States, which prepares the work
of the Council (Article 4 of the Merger Treaty); the
proposals will have been considered, in collaboration
with the Commission, by the European Parliament, and

by the Economic and Social Committee (Article 193 EEC) if the Treaty so requires; the Commissioner most closely concerned with the proposal will attend the meetings of the Council at which the proposal is discussed, and will take part in the discussion. The Commission thus has, in a sense, its own seat at the Council table, although the Commission has no vote in the Council. To describe the Commission, therefore, as the Community executive is misleading unless the notion of executive is understood as including responsibility for policy and for implementing the aims and general programme of the Community.

The Court of Justice has normally no direct part to play in this formal legislative process. No doubt it will be consulted if the proposals affect its jurisdiction (indeed, the Court of First Instance was instituted on the basis of a proposal from the Court, as provided by the Single European Act); generally its concern is only with the end-product, the law. Here, as has been mentioned, the Court may have to adjudicate on the limits of the powers of the other institutions. In this way it has a constitutional role in determining the balance of power between the Community on the one hand and the Member States on the other, as well as the institutional balance between the Council, the Commission and the European Parliament. In exploring the jurisdiction of the Court in Part Two we shall have frequent occasion to illustrate this constitutional role of the Court.

The description of the Commission as the Community executive is also misleading about the nature of the Communities themselves, for it conceals the fact that, except to some extent under the ECSC Treaty, and in the field of competition under the EEC Treaty, the Community executive is not a Community body at all. Generally, Community policies are carried out, and Community legislation applied, by the national authorities of the Member States. It is the national customs administrations which are responsible for applying the common customs tariff, *e.g.* Case 26/62 *Van Gend en Loos* v. *Nederlandse Administratie der Belastingen* (below, p. 183); it is the national intervention agencies which implement the common agricultural policy, *e.g.* Case 146/77 *British Beef Co.* v. *Intervention Board for Agricultural Produce* [1978] ECR 1347; it is the national social security offices which apply the regulations on the social security of migrant workers, *e.g.* Case 17/76 *Brack* v. *Insurance Officer* (below, p. 284).

The Community is not, therefore, a State writ large; or at least not a centralised State, like France or the United Kingdom. Community policies are made in Brussels and the legislation enacted there, but the regulations, directives and decisions of the Council and Commission are implemented by the Member States themselves. In this sense the Community's administration is decentralised.

So too with the judicial organisation of the Community: litigation involving questions of Community law is normally for the national courts. A dispute between individuals, or between an individual and the national authorities, falls within the jurisdiction of the appropriate national court or tribunal. It may come before the Court of Justice on a reference from the national court, as will be seen in Chapter 10, but it cannot be brought directly before that Court.

Thus a person claiming the right to enter a Member State, under the Treaty provisions on the free movement of workers and the implementing Community legislation, must seek his remedy before the courts of that State against the immigration authorities who have refused the right he claims, as in the *Van Duyn* case (below, p. 273). Or if the defendant, in an action for breach of contract, alleges that the contract was void under Article 85 of the Treaty, that defence must be decided upon by the national court, subject again to the possibility of a reference to the Court of Justice on the interpretation, or validity, of Community law.

Only if the individual litigant seeks to challenge directly some Community measure affecting his interests may he go directly to the Court of Justice or to the new Community Court of First Instance authorised by the Single European Act; and even then, his right to do so, as will be seen in Chapters 5 and 7, is limited. In most cases, his forum is the national court.

It follows that, although the Court in Luxembourg is often described as the Community Court (in company now with the Court of First Instance), an essential role in the application of Community law is played by the whole range of national courts and tribunals. In civil and commercial matters, in administrative and industrial disputes, and even in criminal cases, all these courts may have to apply Community law, and they too are therefore, in a very real sense, Community courts. In this capacity they are to be guided and assisted by the Court of Justice, and to adopt the principles of interpretation developed by the Court—principles which, as we shall see, have had a far-reaching effect on the evolution of Community law.

This introduction would be incomplete without mention of a matter of geography. Article 216 EEC provides that the seat of the institutions of the Community shall be determined by common accord of the Governments of the Member States. No such accord has yet been reached upon permanent seats for the institutions, and even their provisional places of work have, for political reasons, not been gathered together in one place but are spread between the cities of Brussels, Luxembourg and Strasbourg, to the inconvenience of those who work in, or have business with, the institutions: see the Decision (of April 8, 1965) of the Representatives of the Governments of the Member States on the provisional location of certain Institutions and Departments of the Communities. Thus, the Council and Commission are based in Brussels, while the European Parliament sits at present in Strasbourg.

Before 1981 the Parliament also sat occasionally in
Luxembourg, where its officials had (and still have)
their headquarters. There have been cases before the
Court concerning the venue of the Parliament (see Case
230/81 *Luxembourg* v. *European Parliament* [1983] ECR
255, below; p. 99, Case 358/85 *France* v. *European
Parliament* (1988) 13 E.L.Rev. 293).

The Court of Justice has its seat in Luxembourg,
where it is in permanent session. Luxembourg is also
the seat of the Court of First Instance: this is not only
an obvious convenience but also a legal requirement.
For by the Single European Act the new jurisdiction is
"attached" to the Court; and it has no separate
administration or organisation. Moreover, the 1965
Decision stipulated that any future judicial (and quasi-
judicial) organ of the Communities should be based in
Luxembourg.

That Luxembourg, the mini-State among the Twelve,
should have become the judicial centre of the Communities, has consequences that may escape the notice
of anyone unfamiliar with the Grand Duchy and its
capital. The City of Luxembourg, where the Court has
sat since its inception, numbers some 80,000 inhabitants
and has very much the atmosphere of a pleasant
provincial town. There is neither the bustle of Brussels
nor the sophistication of Strasbourg. Letzebuergers (as
the natives of Luxembourg call themselves) are sober
and hardworking people. There are no frivolities and
few distractions, apart from the quiet charm of the
surrounding countryside. Expatriates who work at the
Court tend to entertain each other in their homes and
to restrict their social life to a small circle of colleagues.
This helps produce a sense of camaraderie and of
loyalty to the Court that transcends national differences.
On the other hand, narrowness of outlook is avoided
because of the great diversity of backgrounds from
which the personnel of the Court are drawn: this aspect
is returned to in Chapter 3.

PART ONE: ORGANISATION AND COMPOSITION

Introductory

This part will be devoted to what may be termed the judicial administration of the Court. Chapter 2 will examine the administrative organisation of the Court and of its non-judicial staff, of which the head is the Registrar. Chapters 3 and 4 concern the two categories of members of the Court, the judges and advocates general. Considerable descriptive and biographical information is included in this part, the better to convey to those who have not visited it the atmosphere of the Court and the character of the men and women who operate there the central machinery of Community justice. Chapter 5 gives the background leading to the setting up of the Court of First Instance and outlines its organisation, composition and jurisdiction: the complex division of jurisdiction between this new court and the Court of Justice will be examined in Part Two.

Chapter 2

COURT ORGANISATION

Introduction

The Court shares certain organisational features generally found in most courts. But it has also certain
peculiar features of its own.

Among features generally present in any court, one
may mention the Registry under its administrative head,
the Registrar, which carries out the normal administrative functions associated with a court Registry. There is
also at Luxembourg the dichotomy made in several
continental legal systems between, on the one hand,
those who sit in judgment—the Bench, as we would say
in England, or *la magistrature assise* as the French
jargon puts it, and, on the other, "the standing
magistracy" (*la magistrature debout*), by which are
meant the six advocates general. The latter do not
themselves sit in judgment but rather stand to proffer
advice to the Bench on how it should decide the cases
before the Court: their distinctive function will be
examined further in Chapter 4.

At Luxembourg both judges and advocates general
together constitute the judicial personnel of the Court
and as such are to be contrasted with the members of
the Bar who represent the parties and plead before the
Court. But "the Bar" entitled to practise in the Court
of Justice is very different from any single national Bar:
its potential membership includes every member of the
national Bars of the twelve Member States, and in the
case of the United Kingdom this may include solicitors
as well as members of the Bar in certain circumstances
(see Chapter 13, below).

Again, like any court, the Court of Justice has a certain defined jurisdiction. This jurisdiction however is not open-ended in character, in the way, for example, that the English High Court has a certain *inherent* jurisdiction. Rather, as the French would say, the Court has only a *compétence d'attribution,* that is, only such jurisdiction as is expressly conferred upon it by the Treaties or by a convention. In Part Two we shall see how extensive that attribution is; nevertheless its limits are precise.

Finally, the Court is sub-divided into Chambers. This common device to enable a greater work-load to be handled or a greater specialisation achieved is being extensively resorted to at Luxembourg, there now being six Chambers which, under the latest revision of the rules, deal severally with the greater part of the cases before the Court. The most important cases, however, are still reserved to the full Court.

Features peculiar to the Court of Justice arise from its multi-national and multi-lingual character.

Thus, its judges are of 12 different nationalities—one from each of the Member States, together with an additional judge drawn in rotation from one of the "big four," France, Germany, Italy and the United Kingdom. In 1988 Spain joined the big four in this rotation of the additional judge, although it is not (as they are) entitled always to have its own advocate general: instead, for this purpose Spain shares with the other seven smaller States in the rotation of the fifth and sixth posts of advocate general (see p. 61, below). This arrangement is nowhere prescribed by rule but is a necessary consequence of the principle under Article 167 EEC that membership of the Court requires a unanimous decision of the 12 governments (see p. 35, below). The judges (like the advocates general) do not of course in any sense represent their governments or their countries but must, and do, reach their decisions (or deliver their opinions) with complete independence and impartiality. Nevertheless, the fact that each nationality of the Twelve has its place on the bench of the Court does bring to its decisions a special authority transcending national viewpoints. The authority of the Court is also enhanced by the invariable practice of framing its decision as a single collegiate judgment: the oracles of Community law thus speak with one voice.

The Court functions in no fewer than 10 languages, Irish being accepted there in addition to the nine official Community languages. Thus, a case may be conducted in Danish, Dutch, English, French, German, Greek, Irish, Italian, Portuguese or Spanish. But, as we shall see below (p. 23), Irish has not yet been used in any case. Rules have been framed to determine the language of the particular case: these will be discussed later (below, p. 224). For practical convenience, however, as we shall see, French has been adopted as the working language of the Court—at least up to the present time. But the variety of languages available and the inevitable need for assistance from translators and interpreters have determined, to some extent, the procedures which the Court follows in handling its case-load. This will become apparent in the discussion of these procedures; but one general influence of the problem of language diversity has been to emphasise written procedure at the expense of orality and to diminish the impact of counsel when pleading in the less familiar languages.

Cabinets

Each judge or advocate general has a *cabinet,* translated into English as "chambers," although the French word refers ambiguously both to the suite of rooms and to the staff housed there. For the judge or advocate general has a small team of personal assistants and secretaries working exclusively for him. *Cabinet* in this sense is also used for "the private office" of each Commissioner in

Brussels and of the President, Lord Plumb, of the European Parliament in Strasbourg. At Luxembourg the *cabinet* also houses the archives and personal library of the judge or advocate general. The entrance door to the *cabinet* bears his name and designation in his national language. These *cabinets* are mostly grouped on the third floor of the Court building.

The *cabinets* (or chambers) should not, of course, be confused with the use of the word "Chamber" for a subdivision of the Court (see p. 26, below).

Legal Secretaries

Key figures in the work of the Court are the "legal secretaries," three (usually) are attached to each judge and advocate general as personal assistants. Commonly, they undertake the preliminary research on a case and help draft essential documents required by the procedure. They work in the closest association with the judge or advocate general to whom they are attached. This personal relationship is reinforced by physical proximity: the legal secretary will occupy an office as close as possible to the judge's or advocate-general's "chambers."

Legal secretary is the term in English which has come to be preferred since British members joined the Court. The previous term employed was either, in French, *Attaché* or the more imposing title *Référendaire.* *Conseiller-référendaire* is used in the French *Cour de Cassation* to describe a class of career judges who are attached to that Court to assist its senior members. In Germany, *Referendar* is used to denote a legal apprentice, and to avoid this confusion the word *Referent* has been adopted to designate the German legal secretaries. The closest analogy in the common law world is the law clerk of the American judicial system. In the United States, an outstanding law graduate may be invited upon graduation to serve for a year or two as

personal assistant to a senior judge. Such law clerks
often rise to high distinction in their subsequent careers,
as may also legal secretaries. The American analogy
breaks down in that at Luxembourg a legal secretary
usually has had other legal experience after qualifying,
commonly serves a longer term, and some used to serve
in that rank for a considerable period of years.
Nevertheless, "law clerk" is the term officially used for
legal secretary in the Staff Regulations. Usually but not
invariably the legal secretary is of the same nationality
as the judge or advocate general to whom he (or she) is
attached.

In the earliest days of the Court, a single legal
secretary sufficed for each member. Now that a team is
needed, inevitably the closeness of the relationship of
each to his or her judge or advocate general has
suffered. On the other hand, increase in the sheer
pressure of work means that each bears a heavier
professional responsibility: more must be delegated to
the legal secretary. The danger which some critics have
associated with American law clerks is that the clerk's
draft of a judgment may be merely rubber-stamped by
the judge. This situation could not arise at Luxembourg
because (as we shall see) a single collegiate judgment
has to emerge from the secret deliberations of the Court
(from which legal secretaries are excluded). And, while
it is true that the advocate-general's opinion might be
much influenced by the ideas of a legal secretary
(indeed, it should be so influenced if the ideas are
sound), each advocate general develops his own style
which indelibly stamps his opinion as his own.

Assistant Rapporteurs

The Statute provides for the appointment of assistant
rapporteurs to co-operate with the judge-rapporteur
(whose function is described in Chapter 12): no such
appointments have yet been made.

The Registry

The duties of the Registrar are set out in the Protocol on the Statute of the Court and the Rules of Procedure. The Treaties merely require that "the Court shall appoint its Registrar and lay down the rules governing his service" (Article 168 EEC). Like the Registrar of the International Court of Justice in The Hague or that of the European Court of Human Rights in Strasbourg, the Registrar in Luxembourg is dignified with an importance and status quite unlike that normally associated with the officer of the same name in the English court system or the French *greffier*. This difference is evident from his being seated at the bench of the Court, to one side of but at the same level as the judges; he wears the same formal robes, though of humbler fabric in place of silk, and will accompany the members of the Court upon ceremonial visits; his photograph and *curriculum vitae* are given equal prominence with those of the judges and advocates general in the official handbook of the Court; and like them he is mentioned in the founding Treaties.

According to the Protocol the Registrar must reside in Luxembourg as the seat of the Court. The Rules of Procedure require that he be appointed by secret ballot by the judges and advocates general for a term of six years. He is eligible for re-appointment, and the first holder of the office, Mr. Albert Van Houtte, had the remarkable distinction of having served as Registrar for 29 years from 1953 when the Court began its existence as the Court of the Coal and Steel Community. Previously, Mr. Van Houtte, a doctor of laws and *avocat*, had held academic and governmental posts in his native Belgium; from 1945 to 1952 he was attached to the Food and Agriculture Organisation of the United Nations. Mr. Paul Heim, who succeeded Mr. Van Houtte in February 1982, was British and a member of the English Bar; he had previously served as a senior official in the Council of Europe and the European Parliament. He was succeeded in February 1988 by a Frenchman, M. Jean-Guy Giraud, an official for many years in the European Parliament—latterly, in the *cabinet* of its President, Lord Plumb. His previous career, after law studies in Paris and Washington, included a period as legal and economic adviser at the French Embassy in Canberra.

Upon appointment (or re-appointment) the Registrar swears an oath to perform his duties impartially and conscientiously and to preserve the secrecy of the Court's deliberations, although, in contrast to the Registrar of the European Court of Human Rights, he does not accompany the Court when it withdraws to deliberate nor take part in the drawing up of the judgment. He performs all his duties under the authority of the President. These duties are two-fold.

In the first place, he is responsible, under the President of the Court, for the conduct, at all stages, of proceedings before the Court. The Registry serves all documents upon the parties, verifies that the documents comply with the Rules of Procedure, and gives the parties the notices and communications required under the Rules. It also distributes copies of the documents in all cases to each member of the Court. The emphasis on the written procedure, which will be considered in Part Three, results in a considerable volume of documents being distributed in the Court; in the corridors of the Court the visitor is most likely to be met by the sight of trolleys laden with piles of documents, being circulated by a small army of porters (or *huissiers*), sometimes with the help of miniature lift-cum-railways specially installed for the transport of documents and books within the building. The Registry is responsible also for publishing the Court's decisions.

Secondly, the Registrar is the head of the administration of the Court. When the Court is convened for an administrative meeting (as distinct from its judicial sittings) the Registrar is always present, although, unlike the judges and advocates general (all of whom attend) he has no vote. In general, he has a heavier responsibility than the Registrar of a national court whose administration and finances would be the ultimate responsibility of a Minister of Justice.

Reports of Cases before the Court

The official series of reports of cases before the Court is known (in English) as the European Court Reports, which are cited as "ECR" with the year of publication preceding in square brackets. As this series is published in all nine official languages (*i.e.* Danish, Dutch, English, French, German, Greek, Italian, Portuguese and Spanish—but not Irish), the different versions are distinguished by the colour of their binding: the English series is bound in purple (like this book).

An alternative, but unofficial, series in English is the Common Market Law Reports (cited as "CMLR"). This series has the advantage not only of more speedy publication of cases before the Court, but it also includes reports of cases before national courts involving important points of Community law. By reporting foreign cases in English, the series provides a particularly valuable service.

Both the ECR and the CMLR include not only the judgment of the Court but also the opinion of the advocate general delivered in the case. In advance of publication of the printed reports in the ECR the Registry makes available photostat copies of both judgments and opinions as soon as they are delivered: a limited number of copies of these are made available free of charge at the door of the courtroom. Further copies may be obtained from the Internal Services Department of the Court, for 200 Luxembourg or Belgian Francs each or, provided the subscriber already takes the ECR, by subscription.

The official ECR series published by the Registry
provides the only authentic source for citation of
judgments of the Court. Authenticity, moreover,
attaches only to the judgment in the original procedural
language of the case (for the choice of this language,
see p. 224, below), even though the judgment may have
been drafted in some other language.

Law reports prepared by a barrister should be
distinguished from reports by journalists of court
decisions. The regular European Law Reports in *The
Times* of London fall into the former category as do
those occasionally published in the *Financial Times* and
The Independent: see, *e.g.* Cases 279, 280, 285 and 286/
84 *Walter Rau* v. *EEC* [1987] ECR 1069; Case 416/85
Commission v. *United Kingdom, The Independent*, June
28, 1987 ("VAT zero rating on building work breaks
Community law").

Journalists' reports are assisted by press summaries of
judgments issued by the Court's Information Office.

Library and Documentation Service

In addition to the Registry, of which the day-to-day
running is in the hands of the Assistant Registrar, there
are five other departments which make up the administration of the Court.

The first of these is "the Library and Documentation
Directorate." The library has a very extensive collection
of legal materials, especially those published in the 12
Member States. As well as a complete collection in the
field of Community law, it maintains comprehensive
collections of the laws of all the Member States. It is
open to any lawyer of a Member State. It is in the
charge of the Librarian, whose staff includes lawyers
trained in each of the principal legal systems (and
languages) of the Twelve. The Librarian also organises
a "Documentation Service": his staff provides the

judges and advocates general (and their legal secretaries) with background papers on problems currently before the Court. These papers will set out relevant Community law, in particular, case-law of the Court, and may survey relevant provisions of the laws of the Member States.

Translation Service

A vital branch of the Court's administration is the Translation Directorate. A team of some 180 legally qualified linguists have to cope with the heavy demand for translations which the multi-lingual character of the Court promotes. Pleadings may need to be translated into French as the working language as well as into whatever language is prescribed for the particular case; for publication the opinions of the advocates general and the Court's judgments have to be translated into all nine languages. The three enlargements of the Community produced a need for the pre-1973, pre-1981 or pre-1986 decisions of the Court to be translated into English, Danish, Greek, Portuguese and Spanish. All the Court's decisions between 1953 and 1972 are now available in English. Only the principal decisions prior to 1973 have been translated into Danish: they extend to six volumes as compared with the 20 volumes of the complete reports. A similar abridgement is in preparation in Greek of the principal decisions prior to 1981. With regard to Portuguese and Spanish, decisions have still to be taken whether to translate the whole corpus prior to 1986 or only a selection.

The Directorate is divided into nine language divisions, to correspond with the official languages, and a terminology branch.

Irish is a special case. Although it is accepted as a procedural language (below, p. 224), in practice, all cases emanating from Ireland have been conducted so far in English. There are no official versions in Irish of the Court's decisions. Indeed, the Translation Directorate has no translators for the Irish language, nor does the Interpretation Division (below) have interpreters competent in that language. If it should be necessary for a case to be conducted in Irish, linguists would need to be specially hired for the purpose. Hitherto, however, the Irish Government has adopted English when faced with the choice of the language of the case. If it should happen, as one day it may, that a reference is made for a preliminary ruling (see Chapter 10) from an Irish court or tribunal where the proceedings have been conducted in Irish, or a disgruntled Community official exercised his or her option to use Irish in a staff case, Irish would become the procedural language of the case, the judgment would be authentic only in that language, and presumably the Court would publish an official report in Irish of the opinion and judgment. By way of analogy, there have been occasional publications of the Official Journal in Irish in order to provide official texts in Irish of certain Community acts or conventions: see, *e.g.* Final Act of Single European Act, OJ 1987 L 169 p. 28.

However, a court in Wales could not rely upon the Welsh Courts Act in order to submit a preliminary reference in Welsh: unlike Irish, Welsh is not accepted under the rules as a procedural language.

Interpretation Service

Besides its team of translators, the Court has need of interpreters to provide simultaneous translations during the oral proceedings or at other meetings organised by the Court (such as judicial conferences). Before 1980 the Court did not have these scarce specialists in its exclusive employ but used to hire a number of free-lance interpreters who also served the European Parliament (which frequently met in Luxembourg where it has its administrative headquarters, although it now generally meets in Strasbourg). In recent years, the Court has recruited its own specialists in legal interpretation. This Interpretation Division, as it is termed, falls under the direct control of the Registrar. By 1988 it included 18 interpreters but is being expanded so as to provide, eventually, interpretation from and into all the official languages. The possible combinations amount, in theory, to an horrendous total of 72; in practice, the burden may be lessened by using an interpreter in one of the principal languages (usually English or French) to act as a link in a relay, so that, for example, in proceedings conducted in Danish, an English interpreter will translate from Danish into English while a Spanish interpreter will listen to the English interpretation and interpret this into Spanish.

Information Office

The Court maintains an information service which is also, in effect, a press office and public relations department. Like other Community institutions, the Court is inundated by requests from interested individuals and groups to visit the Court. National judges, professors and law students flock to Luxembourg to study its working.

This service also issues press statements on new judgments. It publishes weekly summaries of proceedings, which are very widely distributed.

Administration and Personnel

The staff of the Court numbered 636 permanent and 46 temporary posts in January 1989, and because the Court has to be administered as a self-contained institution, it requires the services of a personnel department. This department, together with a Finance Department and a Department of "Internal Services," constitutes the Directorate of Administration. Internal Services is the "house-keeping" branch, responsible for the Court building, furnishings, equipment, security and such like.

Organigramme

Reference may be made to the organigramme of the Court included as an Appendix to this chapter.

Chambers

To facilitate its work the Court has been divided into six Chambers, two consisting of six judges and four of three judges. One judge in each Chamber is designated as President of that Chamber. The advocates general, by contrast, are no longer attached to particular Chambers.

Power to set up Chambers was included in the Treaties (see, *e.g.* Article 32(1) ECSC, Article 165(2) EEC), and the Rules of the Court now provide that "The Court shall set up Chambers" in accordance with the Treaty provisions "and shall decide which judges shall be attached to them" (Article 9, r. 1). The Rules further provide that "The Court shall lay down general principles governing the assignment of cases to Chambers."

On a point of nomenclature, the term "Chamber" is used in the texts to translate the French "Chambre" as indicating a division or section of the court. It does not, of course, carry the connotation of the English term "Chambers" as suggesting a hearing *in camera* or in the private room of the judge or judges.

The use of Chambers has evolved considerably. Originally, a Chamber of three was used in lieu of the full Court only for the hearing of "staff cases," that is, cases where the Community civil servants or officials are in dispute with the Community institution which employs them: here the Court, under jurisdiction conferred by Article 179 EEC, sat in effect as an industrial tribunal of first and last resort. Staff cases are more fully considered in Chapter 9; they have formed in the past a significant part of the business of the Court but have now been transferred to the Court of First Instance and will only reach the Court upon appeal.

A modest extension of the use of Chambers took place in 1974 by an amendment of the Rules so as to provide that a reference for a preliminary ruling under Article 177 EEC (or Article 41 ECSC, Article 150 Euratom) could be assigned to a Chamber if it was "of an essentially technical nature" or concerned "matters for which there was already an established body of case-law." The first such assignment took place in 1976.

Following a substantial increase in the Court's workload, a more drastic amendment of the rules was made in 1979. The new text of Article 95 of the Rules extends not only to references for preliminary rulings but also to direct actions other than those instituted by a Member State or a Community institution. Under the new provisions, the Court may assign to a Chamber any reference for a preliminary ruling or any direct action instituted by a natural or legal person, in so far (in either case) "as the difficulty or importance of the case or particular circumstances are not such as to require that the Court decide it in plenary session."

Consequent upon the further enlargement of the Court by the accession of Greece in 1981, the three existing Chambers of three judges were supplemented by the establishment of two further Chambers of five judges. And upon the accession of Spain and Portugal in 1986, the two larger Chambers were expanded to include six judges each, although continuing to sit usually as Chambers of five (six may sit, but then only five sign the judgment). These larger Chambers, representing as they do a broader cross-section of legal systems than the Chambers of three, have been entrusted with cases which it was formerly thought necessary to reserve for the full Court.

The decision whether to assign to a Chamber and, if so, whether to a three-judge or five-judge Chamber, is taken by the Court at the end of the written procedure upon consideration of the preliminary report of the judge-rapporteur and after the advocate general has been heard (Article 95(2)). A case may not, however, be assigned to a Chamber if trial by the full Court is requested by a Member State or a Community institution taking part in the proceedings whether as a party, or as intervenor in a direct action, or by submitting written observations on a reference for a preliminary ruling (Article 95(3)). These detailed matters of procedure are more fully explained in Chapter 12, as is the function of a Chamber in undertaking the *instruction*, or preparatory inquiry, which may be an important phase of the procedure in very rare instances. (below, p. 226).

The formulation of the new rule in Article 95 and the use made of it by the Court in practice has meant that since October 1979 cases have been commonly heard by a Chamber rather than by the full Court; and this has become more markedly so since the establishment of the larger Chambers. But cases brought by a Member State or by a Community institution must still be heard by the full Court; of these the most significant group numerically are actions brought by the Commission against a Member State under Article 169 EEC (below, p. 77).

The device of subdividing a court to enable it to handle a heavier case-load is a familiar one in the Member States. Thus the French *Conseil d'Etat* has 10 *sous-sections* of its *Section du Contentieux*. Subdivision of a court may also be a means for ensuring specialisation, as with the Divisions of the English High Court, but there has not yet developed any such specialisation at Luxembourg, although it has long been mooted as a development for the new Court of First Instance (see Chapter 5, below).

The Court Building

Pericles expressed the view that it was not walls that made a city great but the men within them. Physical environment however does have important influences, both practical and psychological, upon human activity. Some description therefore is appropriate here of the actual premises and location in which the Court operates.

In January 1973 the enlargement of the Community was the occasion of the addition to the Court of three new judges and an advocate general. On the same day as they swore their judicial oaths, the Luxembourg Government handed over to the President of the Court the new Courthouse (if we may so translate *Palais de Justice*). Previously the Court had enjoyed no permanent home. From 1953, as the Court of the Coal and Steel Community, it had occupied the Villa Vauban, a large mansion in a suburb of Luxembourg, now used as an art gallery; in 1959 it became the Court of Justice of the European Communities and moved to a more modern building in the city centre.

The new building is situated on the Kirchberg Plateau, a magnificent, elevated site on the further bank of one of the deep ravines which encircle the ancient fortified City of Luxembourg. The Plateau was mostly woodland and fields until acquired in 1961 by the Luxembourg Government to provide a special precinct for the various European institutions based in the Grand Duchy. As well as the Court, the Plateau contains the Parliament Building (the administrative headquarters of the European Parliament), a "Hemicycle" where the Parliament occasionally sat before 1981 (see p. 12, above), the Council Building and the Commission Building (where some staff of the Council and the Commission work on detachment from Brussels), the Computer Centre for the Communities, the Court of Auditors and the European Investment Bank.

The complex of buildings also includes the large European School to provide schooling in English and other languages for the children of the international community, and, inevitably (until 1987), that commercial enterprise found at every international crossroads— a Holiday Inn.

The Courthouse is a remarkable building on many counts. Despite its five storeys it appears squat because of its large dimensions. Its exterior structure is predominantly of glass and rustproof steel, left unpainted and now acquiring a natural brown hue. The interior is functional but elegant with much use of granite, marble and plain carpeting. The library has extensive stack-space and staff offices but a relatively small reading-room.

Already the Courthouse has proved too small for the needs of the enlarged Community. The large Translation Directorate has had to move out into the Commission Building, and the third floor is no longer adequate to provide separate "chambers" for the increased number of judges and advocates general. To help relieve the congestion, an extensive annexe adjoining the Courthouse was opened in 1988. The main feature of the present Courthouse, indeed its *raison d'être*, is the set of three courtrooms, a main courtroom for plenary sittings of the Court and two for use by the Chambers. Each courtroom has striking and distinctive colour schemes and they are decorated with modern tapestries or mural paintings; the public accommodation is spacious and consists of luxurious tip-up seats, each fitted with ear-phones for simultaneous translation.

Across the head of each courtroom is the raised bench for the judges and at each end of the bench a separate seat for the advocate general (from the public seats, on the left) and the Registrar (on the right).

The judges, advocates general and Registrar wear dignified robes of deep crimson; their French-style caps of the same colour have been discarded (alas) even for ceremonial occasions. Lawyers appearing before them wear the gowns of their own national profession: the wig made its appearance with British entry.

The judicial sittings are held on Tuesdays, Wednesdays and Thursdays. The overall impression upon most visitors is one of a dignified and orderly procedure. No time is wasted but there is no feeling of haste: the mills of Community justice grind smoothly. There is none of the drama, the cut and thrust and impromptu repartee of an English trial. The advocates deliver their set speeches: the rhetoric is subdued and often misunderstood, and humour intervenes rarely, and then lightly.

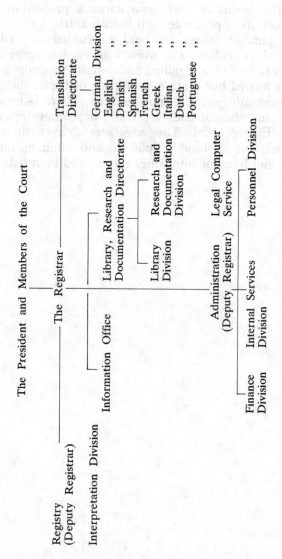

ORGANIGRAMME OF THE COURT OF JUSTICE

The President and Members of the Court

The Registrar

Registry (Deputy Registrar)

Interpretation Division

Information Office

Library, Research and Documentation Directorate
- Research and Documentation Division
- Library Division

Translation Directorate
- German
- English ,,
- Danish ,,
- Spanish ,,
- French ,,
- Greek ,,
- Italian ,,
- Dutch ,,
- Portuguese ,,

Administration (Deputy Registrar)
- Legal Computer Service
- Personnel Division
- Internal Services Division
- Finance Division
- Financial Controller
- Staff Committee

Chapter 3

JUDGES

Introduction

The reputation of a court depends upon the quality of its judges. Judicial quality is itself dependent upon the ability of an institution to attract outstanding lawyers into its service. Long-established institutions like the English High Court or the French *Conseil d'Etat* exert this attraction by the prestige accumulated over generations or even centuries. A new institution such as the Court of Justice lacks this power in its formative years: those called to serve it have been attracted rather by a sense of mission or vocation. But within the 36 years of its existence the Court has built up, by bold and imaginative judgments, its own tradition that should ensure the highest level of recruits to its ranks.

In this chapter, we will examine the Treaty provisions governing the appointment of members of the Court and their conditions of service. Much of what is said will apply both to the judges and the advocates general, although the distinctive function of the latter warrants their being made the subject of a separate chapter. Some account will be given of the backgrounds from which the past and present judges of the Court have been drawn. In order to show the end-product of their labours, the judgments of the Court will be considered, especially from the point of view of their form and style. Judgments are further considered in later parts, but it is thought desirable to provide this early introduction to their form and to the way in which they should be read.

Appointment

Number

The Court now consists of 13 judges, assisted by six advocates general. This makes it possible for the Court to sit (without the President) in two Chambers of five or four Chambers of three: this use of Chambers has already been discussed in the previous chapter (above, p. 26).

The number of judges is mainly a reflection of the number of the Member States. The principle, however, of collegiality, whereby the Court, when sitting *in pleno*, must reach a single judgment, if necessary by a majority, means that an uneven number of judges is required. Thus, in the original Community of the Six the Court was composed of seven judges; at one time, two of these were Dutch, and at the moment of the Six becoming the Nine, two were Italian. For the same reason, the Accession Treaty of 1972, in anticipation of Norway's entry, raised the required number of judges to 11 and so had to be amended later to nine when the Norwegian people decided, by referendum, against entry. Since the accession of Greece in 1981, and the consequent raising of the Member States to an even number, there has been an additional judge who serves a single term and is drawn in turn from the five larger Member States, France, Germany, Italy, Spain and the United Kingdom. The accession of Spain and Portugal in 1986 maintained the need for this additional (now thirteenth) judge.

Entitlement to this additional judge is determined, in the absence of agreement, by drawing lots. Thus, on the accession of Greece, it was agreed that France should have the additional judge, and Grévisse was appointed (see p. 51 below), whilst in the ballot Germany was successful in drawing the lot to nominate the next additional judge—in the event, Bahlmann (see p. 48 below). His successor, as additional judge, is from Spain

Diez de Velasco Valleja (see p. 52 below). There was protracted wrangling in the Council on the question whether this appointment should belong to Italy or to Spain (España), as prior to Italy in alphabetical order. Rotation, once the first in sequence has been determined, is normally in alphabetical order: Italy would therefore have followed Germany as entitled to the additional judge, had the accession of Spain not intervened. The consequence now for the United Kingdom is that its turn to nominate a British additional judges has been postponed by six years, *i.e.* to the year 2000.

In contrast with the membership of the Commission, it is nowhere stipulated that each Member State shall provide a judge for the Court. In an interview with *The Times* (August 18, 1988), the then President of the Court, Lord Mackenzie Stuart, remarked that the Court could be made up "entirely of Russians." Inevitably, in practice, the members are all drawn from the Member States. For every appointment of a judge (or advocate general) requires the common accord of the Governments of the Member States (Article 167 EEC): no State is likely to forego its representation on the Court, nor has this happened. Again, whereas the Treaties expressly restrict membership of the Commission to citizens of the Member States, there is no such restriction in regard to the Court. But political considerations make it almost inconceivable that someone who is not a national of a Member State would be appointed. The general acceptability of each State's candidate is a matter of prior informal consultations between the 12 Governments.

Appointment of the members of the Court by common accord of the Member States has not escaped criticism. In a resolution of July 6, 1982, the European Parliament expressed the view that it should be involved in the appointment of the members of the Court. Various possibilities might be considered: nominations

might be subject to ratification by the Parliament, a
solution similar to that in the United States where the
appointment by the President of Supreme Court judges
is subject to ratification by the Senate. In the European
Court of Human Rights, the judges are elected by the
Council of Europe's Parliamentary Assembly from lists
drawn up by the Governments. The European Parliament proposed in its Draft Treaty establishing the
European Union (above, p. 328), that half the members
of the Court of Justice should be appointed by the
Parliament and half by the Council. There would be no
requirement that the Court should include at least one
citizen from each Member State.

Qualifications

The Treaties require that judges and advocates
general "shall be chosen from persons whose independence is beyond doubt and who possess the qualifications
required for appointment to the highest judicial offices
in their respective countries or who are jurisconsults of
recognised competence." This formulation follows closely that for appointment to the International Court of
Justice at The Hague which also provided the model for
judicial appointment to the European Court of Human
Rights. It has been retained in a modified form for
judicial appointments to the new Court of First
Instance.

It is significant that the independence of candidates is
made a first and paramount consideration. This moral
requirement counters any notion that a judge is
representing his Member State or the Government
which has nominated him. Nevertheless, the criticism
has been made that political considerations have entered
into the selection of judges from some Member States
where party affiliation is an important consideration in
domestic judicial appointments. Once so appointed, a
judge who failed "to please" his Government might
then be in danger of not being re-appointed; but the

principle of collegiality and the secrecy of the Court's deliberations would appear adequate safeguards against this risk.

The professional qualifications for appointment are expressed in the alternative. In some countries of the common law tradition, such as England or Ireland, the alternative is a real one, inasmuch as legal scholarship as such is not in itself a qualification for appointment to the highest judicial office. In most civil law countries, on the other hand, the second alternative is subsumed in the first. Thus, in all the original six Member States the holder of a University chair of law may be translated to the bench, sometimes at the highest levels.

So far as the United Kingdom is concerned, up to 1988, only the first alternative was used, although there were not lacking precedents for academic appointments by the British Government to international courts and tribunals. The first two British appointments to the Court in 1972 involved, respectively, a judge of the Scottish Court of Session and a leading English barrister who held the post of Junior Counsel to the Treasury, the third most senior government lawyer. The eligibility of a Treasury Junior to be appointed to the English High Court was properly regarded as fulfilling the first alternative. The third British appointment, in 1981, was that of an English High Court judge, at the time of his translation President of the Employment Appeal Tribunal. The fourth appointment, in 1988, was that of a professor of law, although, as a Q.C., he also qualified for appointment under the first alternative.

Under the ECSC Treaty a prior legal qualification was not necessary: Article 32 ECSC, as originally drafted, merely stipulated that candidates should be "persons of recognised independence and competence." Two of the original judges of the Coal and Steel Court were not possessed of formal professional qualifications in law. The Dutchman Joseph Serrarens was a parliamentarian and a leading figure in the international

labour movement, and the Frenchman Jacques Rueff
was an expert in finance and banking who had
distinguished himself in administrative and ministerial
posts in France. The former was replaced in 1958 when
the Court became the Court of the three Communities
but the latter continued as a judge until 1962 when he
was succeeded by Robert Lecourt.

Oath

On taking up their appointment, the judges take an
oath in the following terms: "I swear that I will perform
my duties impartially and conscientiously; I swear that I
will preserve the secrecy of the deliberations of the
Court."

Term of appointment

Appointment is for a term of six years, but a judge
(or advocate general) is eligible for re-appointment for a
further term or terms. Appointments are "staggered" in
such a way that six or seven of the 13 judges (and three
of the six advocates general) come up for renewal at
triennial intervals. This guarantees a measure of
continuity of membership even if new appointments
were always made. In practice, most of the members of
the Court (the additional judge apart) have had their
terms of office renewed at least once, and some twice or
thrice. There is no prescribed age for retirement.
Indeed, at least one judge was a septuagenarian when
appointed.

Nevertheless, despite the practice of renewal, the
term of six years can be objected to as too short and in
conflict with that security of tenure which is the
hallmark of judicial independence in all the legal
systems of the Member States. Such relatively short
terms of appointments are commonly adopted for
international courts or tribunals (for example, nine
years in the case of a judge of the International Court
of Justice), but they seem undesirable in what is held

out to be, and is, a distinct legal order of a novel kind, neither international nor national but more akin to an embryonic federation. Even with a quasi-federal judiciary the impression should not be created that those appointed may be looking over their shoulders every six years towards their political masters, the Governments of the Member States. In practice such decisions are no doubt rarely taken on political grounds, but appearances are also of importance on so sensitive a matter. Moreover, too rapid a turnover—in 1988, on the triennial renewal of half the judges and advocates general, six members were replaced—may be unduly disruptive.

Dismissal

As we have seen, the opportunity to discard a judge occurs every six years. During the term of appointment dismissal can only take place by the unanimous decision of the other judges and advocates general that their colleague no longer fulfils the requisite conditions or no longer meets the obligations arising from his office. This procedure of trial by one's peers (copied from the International Court of Justice) provides a very effective safeguard against dismissal. The procedure has never yet been invoked. A judge may, however, submit his resignation at any time, and this has happened on several occasions. Thus, Judge O'Dalaigh resigned in 1975 in order to become the President of the Republic of Ireland.

President of the Court and Presidents of Chambers

The judges (but not the advocates general) choose one of their number to serve as President of the Court for a term of three years. This appointment is renewable. Thus, President Robert Lecourt, who retired in October 1976, served three terms as President (1967–1976); his immediate predecessor was Charles Hammes of Luxembourg. The President from 1958 to 1964 was a

Dutchman, Professor A. M. Donner, who remained a judge of the Court until his retirement in 1979. The German judge, Hans Kutscher, succeeded Robert Lecourt as President in October 1976, and upon his resignation in October 1980 was in turn succeeded as President by the Belgian judge, J. Mertens de Wilmars. From 1984 to 1988 the British judge Lord Mackenzie Stuart, was President. His successor is the Danish judge, Ole Due.

The President's functions, in the words of the Rules of the Court, are to direct the judicial business and the administration of the Court and to preside at hearings and deliberations.

The choice of President is made by secret ballot, being determined by a simple majority. The same process is used to elect annually a President for each of the Chambers of the Court, the composition of which is also determined annually. In practice the composition of each Chamber remains constant, but its presidency rotates annually.

After the President, the Presidents of the Chambers and the First Advocate General, the members of the Court (both judges and advocates general) rank equally in precedence according to their seniority in office. Where there is equal seniority in office, by reason of appointments having been made on the same date, precedence is determined by age. When the Court sits *in pleno* the President will be flanked to right and left by his fellow judges seated in order of seniority, a right-hand seat being superior to the equivalent position on the left, although this practice is not slavishly observed.

Immunities, privileges and salary

The judges (and advocates general) enjoy, as might be expected, immunity from suit or legal process. This immunity is retained after they vacate office in respect of acts performed by them in their official capacity. This is provided by the respective Protocols of the Statute of the Court of Justice annexed to the three founding Treaties.

Under the Protocol on the privileges and immunities of the Communities annexed to the Merger Treaty, the judges have the benefit of certain privileges, *e.g.* as to tax and customs duties. In particular, they are exempt from national taxes on their Community salaries; but they are liable to Community income tax, the rates for which rise to 45 per cent. In addition to their other privileges, each judge (and advocate general) is supplied with a car and chauffeur.

Judicial salaries (and those of the advocates general, which are identical) are fixed according to scales determined by the Council. A judge's salary is the same as that of a member of the Commission and is very substantial. It would however be very misleading to compare it to the salary of an English High Court judge, for, with the exception of the Luxembourg judge, the members of the Court of Justice naturally have to maintain two homes; they also find themselves called upon to fulfil a semi-diplomatic function and to foster links with judges and lawyers in their own countries.

Incompatibilities

It is incompatible with his appointment for a judge to hold any political or "administrative" (that is, governmental) office (Article 4 of the Statute of the Court). Nor may he be engaged in any occupation, whether gainful or not, unless exemption is exceptionally granted by the Council (*ibid.*). In practice, several members of the Court have been permitted to undertake teaching engagements in University faculties and institutes.

In addition, when taking up their duties, the judges undertake that they will behave with integrity and discretion as regards the acceptance, after they have ceased to hold office, of certain appointments or benefits. Not to canvas more extravagant possibilities, this would, it was thought, prevent a former judge from appearing as counsel at the bar of the Court: this has, however, occurred.

Composition of the Court

When the Court sits as a full court, a quorum of seven judges is required. A relatively low quorum is felt desirable to allow for illness or other unavoidable absences. But normally all 13 judges attend when the Court sits *in pleno*: such a Court of all 13 is, by usage, referred to as a 'Grand Plenum' as opposed to a 'Petit Plenum' (see further Chapter 12, p. 227, below).

As the President has no casting vote, an uneven number must sit for decisions to be valid. If a judge is prevented from attending the hearing (*e.g.* through illness), the most junior judge drops out to maintain an uneven number.

The Statute of the Court provides specifically that a party may not apply for a change in the composition of the Court (or of a Chamber) on the grounds of either the nationality of a judge or the absence from the Court (or Chamber) of a judge of the nationality of that party. This is in contrast with the Statute of the International Court of Justice which allows an ad hoc judge in certain circumstances; similar provision exists for the European Court of Human Rights at Strasbourg.

Form of Judgment

The Court follows the general continental practice in delivering judgment as a collegiate body. In contrast to the International Court of Justice and the European Court of Human Rights, no separate or dissenting judgments are permitted. The strict secrecy which surrounds the Court's deliberations means that only the judges themselves know whether their decision was reached unanimously or by a majority. The natural desire to achieve unanimity will lead to compromises which are then reflected in the somewhat equivocal language of the judgments, criticised by one English practitioner as "simply oracular and almost apocryphal" (L. Melville in (1978) 75 L.S. Gaz. 567).

Help in understanding a judgment can be derived from the opinion of the advocate general in the case. Usually, it is better to start by reading this opinion and then to turn to the judgment. Often, the Court follows the path urged upon it by the advocate general, but as mentioned in the next chapter (below, p. 59), there have been notable instances where the Court has gone its own way.

The form of the judgment is very different from that of an English or Scottish judgment. In the formative years of the Court's history, after essaying other styles, it decided to adopt the practice of the higher French courts in framing the whole judgment as, grammatically, a single Ciceronian sentence, with the facts of the case, the steps in the procedure and the legal reasons all recited in a long series of subordinate clauses leading eventually to the main sentence: "the Court hereby rules." Thus, in Case 22/76 *Import Gadgets* [1976] ECR 1371, the preliminary recitals extend over some nine pages, culminating in 15 numbered paragraphs of reasoning, before we arrive at the very short ruling: "Laughing devices suitable for use principally in dolls that are representations of human beings come within heading 97.02 B of the Common Customs Tariff."

As is apparent, the English version of the judgment has departed from the French model by the conversion of the subordinate clauses from ablative absolutes into separate sentences. Nevertheless, as judgments are normally drafted first in French, even the English version retains the succinct, even sybilline, quality of the original; notionally, it remains if not a single sentence, at least a single coherent whole. The influence which this style of drafting judgments has upon the law which they contain is not to be underestimated, even though it be intangible.

In 1979 the Court decided, even for its judgments in French, to move away from the original model and no longer to confine its reasoning within the grammatical strait-jacket of a single sentence. The increased linguistic diversity of the Court has also led, on rare occasions (but these may now increase) to a judgment being drafted first in English and then translated into French, especially where English has been the language of the case.

As a typical example, in Case 22/76 *Import Gadgets* [1976] ECR 1371 (set out in full in previous editions of this book), the judgment starts "In Case 22/76" (each case being referred to by the docket number and the year) and after mentioning the parties, the subject-matter of the case, and the composition of the Court, the main body of the judgment is in two parts, facts and law, ending with the ruling of the Court.

The first part is entitled "Facts" in *Import Gadgets* (but, since 1977, the title "Facts and Issues" has been adopted). Originally, in the French text (before the relaxation introduced in 1979) this part was introduced by the conjunction "attendu que" which might be rendered in English "whereas," although the conjunction was omitted in the English text. The part summarises, first, the facts of the case and the procedure before the Court, secondly the submissions made to the Court. As the case was a reference from a national court for a preliminary ruling, observations in writing were invited from the parties, the Member States and the Commission. In the actual case the defendant in the main action (*i.e.* the action before the national court) and the Commission put in observations which are summarised. This part of the judgment is based on the "report for the hearing" which is described in Chapter 12. Then the oral hearing and the delivery of the advocate-general's opinion are mentioned.

The second part of the judgment contains the law and is so entitled in *Import Gadgets*; but since 1978 the title "Decision" is preferred. After an introduction explaining how the question or questions for decision have arisen, this part sets out the *motifs* or reasons for the Court's ruling, followed by the ruling itself. This part is set out in a series of propositions, again linked in the French version by the conjunction "*Attendu que*," omitted in the English text. The paragraphs are numbered for ease of reference. The ruling, introduced by the phrase "On those grounds" (*pour ces motifs*), is usually quite short, as in the example chosen, which reads:

> "The Court, in answer to the question referred to it by the Tribunale di Pavia by order of January 22, 1976, hereby rules:
>> Laughing devices suitable for use principally in dolls that are representations of human beings come within heading 97.02 B of the Common Customs Tariff."

The original copy of the judgment bears the signatures of all the participating judges and is authenticated by the President and the Registrar.

For about 18 months from the end of 1984 the Court decided to omit the part entitled "Facts and Issues" from the version of the judgment published in the reports. This was to reduce the burden on the translation directorate. The first judgment to follow the new style was the judgment of the Fifth Chamber of the Court of January 25, 1985 in Case 147/83 *Munchenen Import-Weinkellerei Gmbh* v. *Commission* [1985] ECR 257. The change met with considerable dissatisfaction amongst practitioners and law teachers, in response to which the Court decided to restore in the published report the statement of "facts and issues" by simply reproducing the report for the hearing (for the *rapport d'audience*, see p. 230, below). The current sequence

therefore of the report (beginning with Case 116/82
Commission v. *Germany* [1986] ECR 2519) follows the
order: title of the case, the summary of the subject-
matter, the report for the hearing (giving the facts and
issues), the advocate-general's opinion and finally the
judgment itself. The new arrangement has the merit of
reflecting the actual sequence of events.

Judicial Style

The collegiate nature of the Court's judgments lends
them a certain flatness such as we associate with the
language of a government report. The tone is measured;
there is neither excitement nor humour. One must not
expect the often elegant, sometimes idiosyncratic, prose
of an English judgment, upon which the individual
judge will have imprinted his own personality and
particular style. At Luxembourg the individual voices
are muted; they blend in unison; there is a single
refrain. The only solo will have been that of the
advocate general.

On the other hand, collegiality has in no way
inhibited the development of Community law through
judicial decisions. The Court's judgments have become
an important, if secondary source of that law, as this
book will demonstrate. Here mention may be made
of one particular technique which law-making in committee, Luxembourg-style, appears to encourage.

Study of the case-law of the Court reveals certain
leitmotifs that recur through whole sequences of its
decisions. Phrases or passages will be repeated in case
after case, sometimes in identical terms, sometimes with
subtle variations. By constant rehearsal the Court, like a
Welsh choir, finds the exact note it wants to sound.
Examples abound of this technique whereby phrase-
building becomes law-making: elsewhere in these pages
we refer to the Court's classic definition of the nature of
the Community legal order (below, p. 200, Case 6/64

Costa v. *ENEL* [1964] ECR 585 at 593, which refined the
definition in Case 26/62 *Van Gend en Loos* [1963] ECR 1
at 12); to the *Zuckerfabrik Schöppenstedt* formula as a
yardstick for certain actions for damage under Article
215(2) EEC (p. 141, below, Case 5/71 [1971] ECR 975 at
984); and to the *Plaumann* test for locus standi of "non-
privileged" applicants under Article 173 EEC (p. 108,
below, Case 25/62 [1963] ECR 95 at 107). The same
technique has defined, and is still refining, the key concept of the direct effect of Community law, in a sequence
of cases extending from Case 26/62 *Van Gend en Loos* to
Case 148/78 *Ratti* [1979] ECR 1629, Case 8/81 *Becker* v.
Finanzamt Münster [1982] ECR 53 and Case 152/84 *Marshall* v. *Southampton etc. Area Health Authority* [1986]
ECR 737.

Biographical Background of the Judges

During the 36 years of its existence the Court has had
over 50 members, if we include for this purpose both
judges and advocates general. Some account is given in
the next chapter of the background of the past and
present advocates general. Here it is proposed to give
brief biographical details of those (all men) who have
served, or are serving, as judges of the Court: a woman
has still to be appointed to this office, although (as we
shall see) the French, with true republican *"égalité"*,
chose a woman for appointment as advocate general in
1981. Our attention will be directed mainly to the
present membership, but some knowledge of the
previous careers of the past as well as present judges
will be helpful to a proper understanding of the Court's
philosophy and approach to its daily tasks.

Of the past judges of the Court (29 in number),
mention has already been made of Serrarens and Rueff
as exemplifying appointees to the Coal and Steel Court
without formal legal qualifications. The other 27 had a
variety of legal backgrounds. Only ten, Bahlmann,

Hammes, Galmot, Grévisse, Kutscher, Mackenzie
Stuart, O'Keeffe, Riese, Rossi and Touffait had extensive judicial experience in their own countries; Pilotti,
van Kleffens and Strauss also began their careers as
judges, but Pilotti turned to international law (he was
Assistant Secretary General of the League of Nations
from 1932 until 1937), van Kleffens moved into legal
practice and then held important posts in the Dutch
Ministry of Economics, and Strauss served in high
administrative and governmental posts in post-war
Germany as well as being politically active in the
Christian Democratic Party.

Several judges had held ministerial posts in their own
countries. Delvaux was Belgian Minister of Agriculture
in 1945–46. Lecourt had been French Minister of Justice
for several periods between 1948 and 1958 and was
Minister for Overseas Departments shortly before his
appointment to the Court in 1962. Strauss was Secretary
of State in the Federal Ministry of Justice from 1949 up
to his appointment to the Court in 1963; Bahlmann had
held important posts in the same Ministry after serving
as a judge in Cologne. Rueff had been French Minister
of Finance in Poincaré's Government as long ago as
1926. Catalano held senior governmental posts in Italy.
O'Dalaigh was the Irish Attorney-General before being
appointed to the Supreme Court: he resigned from the
Court in Luxembourg in order to become President of
the Irish Republic. Pescatore, who served the Court as
Luxembourg judge for 18 years, had previously held
high office in the Luxembourg Ministry of Foreign
Affairs and helped to found the Institute of European
Legal Studies at the University of Liège. At some stages
of their earlier careers, Catalano, Delvaux, Lecourt and
van Kleffens all practised law or acted as legal counsel
to commercial or public institutions. Also significant as
a group are those who had an academic career: Monaco
and Trabucchi occupied Chairs of Law in the Universities of Rome and Padua, Sørensen a Chair of Law in

the University of Aarhus, and Donner a Chair of
Constitutional and Administrative Law in the Free
University of Amsterdam; Riese taught in the University of Lausanne from 1932 to 1951 before returning to
Germany as judge of the Federal Supreme Court. The
previous Italian judge, Bosco, combined a long career
in Italian Universities with political service in various
ministerial appointments and as head of the Italian
delegation to the U.N. General Assembly; and Catalano
and Hammes combined professorial appointments with
their other functions. Chloros, the first Greek judge,
who died in office in 1982, held the Chair of
Comparative Law at King's College in the University of
London at the time of his appointment: he had been
actively involved for his country in the negotiations
leading to the Greek accession in 1981; Everling, the
German judge until 1988, held various governmental
posts in the Federal Ministry of Economics in Bonn as
well as acting as Honorary Professor at Munster
University where he taught and wrote extensively on
Community law.

Several past judges had been active in politics. As
already mentioned, Strauss was a prominent Christian
Democrat and ran (unsuccessfully) for election to the
Bundestag. Lecourt was *Deputé* for Paris from 1945 to
1958 and was a leading member of the MRP. Delvaux
and Serrarens were both elected to their respective
parliaments. O'Dalaigh was a prominent lawyer in the
Irish Fianna Fail party, before accepting judicial office.
O'Keeffe, his successor, became Senior Counsel in
Dublin in 1951; subsequently he was Attorney-General
of Ireland (in the Fianna Fail Government), Judge of
the Supreme Court and President of the High Court.

Mertens de Wilmars, the Belgian President of the
Court from 1979 to 1984, had practised in Antwerp as
an advocate from 1935, specialising in administrative
law and later in European law, and had appeared as an
advocate before the Court. He had also been active in

political life in Belgium. Mackenzie Stuart, the recently
retired British President of the Court, was appointed
judge in 1973 upon the accession of the United
Kingdom. After war service he graduated in law from
Cambridge and Edinburgh and practised as an Advocate
at the Scots Bar. His first judicial appointment was as
Sheriff Principal in 1971, and in the following year he
was elevated to the Court of Session.

This varied background, ranging far beyond the
narrowly legal, is well designed to serve the needs of
the Court, whose jurisdiction, as we shall see, touches
economic, social, fiscal, administrative and even political
issues lying beneath the surface of Community law. The
American commentator, Werner Feld, has perceptively
remarked:

> "The broad knowledge possessed by some of the
> justices in the field of economics, finance, and
> administration may be a significant factor in
> arriving at decisions which transcend narrow judi-
> cial considerations and which reflect an application
> of the Treaties with a keen eye on the purpose of
> the Communities and with an appreciation for the
> future. The assumption is justified that the diversity
> of interests, experiences, and values represented in
> the deliberating sessions of the Court may have
> stimulated a fertile interchange of concepts and
> ideas and thus broadened the views of the
> participants."

When we turn to the present judges, a similar
diversity is evident. *Due*, the President of the Court,
held various posts in the Danish Ministry of Justice; he
also directed courses in Community law for practitioners
and civil servants. *Schockweiler*, who succeeded Pescatore as Luxembourg judge in 1985, read law at Paris
University before embarking on a governmental career
in the Ministry of Justice of the Grand Duchy. *Joliet*,
the Belgian judge, followed a doctorate in law at Liège

University by postgraduate studies at Northwestern University, Chicago; he held the Chair of European Community Law at Liège and specialised in competition law. *Kakouris* became the Greek judge in 1983; he was previously a senior member of the Greek Council of State and had been an outspoken critic of the dictatorial regime of "the Colonels." *Koopmans* had pursued an academic career as Professor and Dean in the University of Leyden before becoming in 1978 a Judge of the Netherlands Supreme Court. *O'Higgins*, the Irish judge, was called to the Bar in 1938; he was a Member of the Dail for many years and served as Minister of Health; in 1973 he was appointed a Judge of the High Court and in 1974 was appointed Chief Justice; on two occasions, in 1966, and again in 1973, he was elected a candidate for the Presidency of the Irish Republic. The French judge, *Grévisse*, was *Président de la Section des Travaux publics* in the *Conseil d'Etat* at the time of his appointment in 1988; he had previously been detached from the *Conseil* to serve as the additional French judge from 1981 to 1982. The *Conseil d'Etat*, France's supreme administrative court, has supplied several members of the Court, whether as judges or advocates general. For the French pattern of appointments to the Court strives to maintain a balanced representation from the "administrative" and "judicial" hierarchies of the dual system of courts in France. Thus, Grévisse's colleague at Luxembourg, Advocate General Marco Darmon, was previously a member of the *magistrature*, moving between service in the Ministry of Justice and various judicial appointments, including that of President of Chamber in the *Cour d'appel* of Paris. Likewise, their immediate predecessors as judge and advocate general were, respectively, Galmot of the *Conseil d'Etat* and Simone Rozès, a past President of the Paris *Tribunal de grande instance* (and subsequently First President of the *Cour de cassation*—France's senior *magistrat*). *Slynn*, who was previously the British advocate general, became judge in succession to Mackenzie Stuart in October 1988; this was the first time there had been this particular change of roles, although judges of the Court had on two occasions become advocates general (see Chapter 4, p. 56). Before appointment to the Court in 1981, he had been Junior Counsel to the Crown, High Court Judge, and President of the Employment Appeal Tribunal. As he will retain the seniority in office attributable to his earlier appointment, he will rank in precedence before those fellow judges appointed since 1981. *Mancini*, the previous Italian advocate general, also switched roles to become judge in succession to Bosco in October 1988. Before his appointment as advocate general in 1982, he had spent most of his previous career as an academic lawyer in Bologna and Rome. *Moitinho de Almeida*, the Portuguese judge, entered the career judiciary after graduating in law at Lisbon University; following service as Assistant Public Prosecutor at the Lisbon Court of Appeal he became a senior official in the Ministry of Justice, with special responsibility for Community law. *Rodriguez Iglesias*, the Spanish judge, studied law at the Universities of Oviedo and Freiburg; he taught at various Spanish Universities before being appointed to the Chair of Public International Law at the University of Granada in 1983. Prior to his elevation to the Court he occupied the Chairs of European Law at both Granada and Madrid Universities. *Zuleeg*, the German judge appointed in 1988 to succeed Everling, had also followed an academic career, holding the Chair of Public Law at Frankfurt University from 1977 and publishing extensively on Community law. The additional judge to complete the team of 13 has, after unseemly wrangling in the Council (see above), been allotted to Spain: he is *Diez de Velasco Valleja*, whose long career in Spanish Universities culminated with the Chair of Public International Law in Madrid; he had also been a member of the Spanish Constitutional Court and the Council of State.

Chapter 4

ADVOCATES GENERAL

While the functions of a judge are universally understood, the role of the advocate general in the Court is less easily grasped, especially in countries where the legal system has no precise equivalent. His title, too, is something of a misnomer, since he is really no more an advocate than he is a general. On the contrary, he is a member of the Court. But that term is itself ambiguous, being sometimes restricted to the judges alone, as in the first paragraph of Article 166 EEC, which provides (as amended) that "The Court of Justice shall be assisted by six Advocates General." This ambiguity may reflect a certain ambivalence, in the minds of the authors of the Treaties, about the role of the advocate general: although a member of the Court, he acts as its independent adviser. Unlike however his counterpart in the French *Conseil d'Etat,* the *commissaire du gouvernement,* he does not attend the judges' deliberations (see p. 232, below), even in a consultative capacity. On the other hand, the advocates general do join the judges and vote in parity with them on all procedural issues and matters of administration of the Court, *e.g.* to appoint a new Registrar (Art. 168 EEC).

In 1982 the Court assumed the practice (despite the spelling adopted in the Treaties) of omitting the hyphen in written references to the advocate general, thus complying with the English usage commended by the great Fowler, although a hyphen should still be used in the possessive case. For ease of expression, the advocate general is referred to in this chapter in the masculine gender; the authors intend no disrespect to the first woman advocate general, Mme Simone Rozès, or the other Portias who will follow her on the Kirchberg.

The advocates general serve in turn for one year as "First Advocate General." As each case arrives at the Court, it is assigned to one of the advocates general. While the President of the Court designates the "judge-rapporteur" (below, p. 226), it is the First Advocate General who allocates the cases among the corps of advocates general (including himself). Judge-rapporteur and advocate general are designated on similar principles, the aim being to achieve a balanced work-load but not to produce any particular specialisation by way of subject-matter. There is however one difference in the designation of the advocate general: the unwritten rule that the judge-rapporteur should not be a judge from a Member State concerned in the case does not apply to the advocate general, no doubt because the latter performs his function in public so that there can be no suspicion of his opinion being influenced by political considerations.

It is the main task of the advocate general, again according to Article 166, "acting with complete impartiality and independence, to make, in open court, reasoned submissions on cases brought before the Court of Justice, in order to assist the Court in the performance of the task assigned to it in Article 164." This he does by delivering what is termed an "opinion," (in French, *"conclusions"*), after the case has been heard and normally at a later hearing, in which he gives the judges his view of the case and seeks to help them to reach their judgment. Usually in his opinion he will review the facts of the case, deal with the submissions of the parties and of any others who have taken part in the proceedings, review the law, and finally express his own opinion on how the judges should decide the case. He takes no further part in the case and does not attend the private meetings at which the judges deliberate. He also advises the Court, in private, on questions of procedure before the case comes up for hearing; more will be said of this in Chapter 12.

The position of the advocate general is symbolized by his physical position at Court hearings: he sits on the Bench, together with the judges, but apart from them, to the side of the Court, and opposite the Registrar. After the case has been argued by the parties, and usually after an adjournment to enable him to prepare his opinion, he delivers it from the Bench, but standing, and addresses it to the judges.

To the English lawyer the closest analogy to the advocate general might be an institutionalised *amicus curiae* or a Queen's Proctor, who intervened in every case, but as will be apparent neither analogy is at all exact. The advocate general may also see himself as in effect delivering a reserved first instance judgment in a case taken on appeal, but his opinion, while it may have authority in future cases, does not of course decide the instant case, even provisionally. The parties may not comment on his opinion, which closes the oral procedure. In continental legal systems, such as the French, the institution of a legal representative for the public interest is well established before the higher courts. Thus, in France the *ministère public* may interpose its view ("*conclusions*"), distinct from that of the parties, in civil cases before the *Cour de Cassation, Cours d'appel* and *Tribunaux de grande instance*; and in the *Conseil d'Etat*, the *commissaire du gouvernement* is often regarded as having provided the model for the advocate general, although the former (unlike the latter) retires with the judges and may participate in their deliberations, whilst having no vote in the ultimate decision.

The status of the advocate general as a member of the Court is illustrated by the fact that his appointment, and the terms and conditions of his office, are governed (as we saw in the previous chapter) by the same provisions as those of the judges, and that according to the Rules of Procedure judges and advocates general rank equally in precedence according to their seniority in office. On two occasions, a judge has changed roles to become advocate general, Mr. Trabucchi taking this step in 1973 and Mr. Capotorti, another Italian judge, in 1976; the reverse has now occurred, Advocates General Mr. Mancini and Sir Gordon Slynn becoming judges in 1988. The First Advocate General ranks equally with the Presidents of Chambers, the other five taking precedence between themselves according to their respective personal seniorities.

An advocate general enjoys, in a sense, a greater independence than a judge since he is free to speak his mind in public (and in his own language), and is not bound by the collegiate character of the Court's judgments. He can also range beyond the questions for immediate decision. In addition to presenting his own view on those questions, he can also comment on the circumstances in which the case has arisen, on the way in which it has been presented, on any irregularities or special features of the procedure, and can deal generally with other matters beyond the purview of the Court's judgment with its more formal style (see Dashwood (1982) *Legal Studies* 202, at 208). As Lord Mackenzie Stuart once observed in a tribute to Maurice Lagrange, it is as if the advocate general held a professorial Chair of Community Law.

The advocate general, as well as setting out the facts, expounding the law, and (in a reference under Article 177 EEC) proposing the reply which the Court in his view should give to the question referred, may also comment on other matters, such as the compatibility with Community law of the actions of the national authorities (see, *e.g.* the opinion in *Import Gadgets* [1976] ECR 1371, above, p. 44)—matters which are outside the scope of the Court's judgment.

Similarly, the opinion often ranges more widely in setting out the sources of law, referring for example in some detail to relevant previous decisions of the Court, to decisions under national law from the courts of the Member States where national law is relevant, and also occasionally to the opinions of legal writers ("doctrine"). The Court's judgment, by contrast, is less free and less full, usually setting out only those propositions which are necessary to its decision, and often not seeking to justify or substantiate them.

The advocate-general's opinion is normally written in advance of delivery and translated as necessary, by the Court's translation department, into the language of the case and into the working language of the Court, but he is free to deliver it in his own language and commonly does: the version in his own language should be looked to in case of doubt on any point. Subsequently it will be translated into the other official languages for publication in the European Court Reports (see p. 21, above), where it now appears immediately *before* the judgment to which it relates, thereby facilitating citation from it as persuasive authority (see Chapter 16). Up to 1984 the opinion followed the judgment in the European Court Reports. In the Common Market Law Reports it has always appeared before the judgment, according thus with the actual sequence of events.

Although the advocate general may have started work in preparing a case before the oral hearing of the parties, he will normally write his opinion in the week or fortnight following that hearing. He will work closely with his legal secretaries, whose role has been mentioned in Chapter 2; in some respects, his relationship with his legal secretaries may be closer than that of the judges with theirs, since the judges will be able to discuss the case among themselves, while the advocate general is on his own. Usually he will not want to know too much of the minds of the judges, so that he can preserve his independent viewpoint.

About three weeks after the oral hearing, when the opinion has been prepared and translated as necessary,

it will be delivered in open court. This is something of a
formality, since the judges will often have the written
text, and the parties, as has been mentioned, have no
right to comment on the opinion, so that there is no
need for them to attend. The reading by the advocate
general of his opinion closes the oral procedure,
although there is a rarely used provision, in the Rules of
Procedure, for the oral procedure to be re-opened
before the Court gives judgment (see p. 232, below).
Judgment itself is always reserved, so that there is a full
opportunity for the judges to consider the advocate-
general's opinion.

The judges are of course in no way bound to follow
the opinion and indeed they not infrequently depart
from it. It is not now customary for the judgment to
refer directly to the opinion at all. It has often been
asked why there is any need for the advocate-general's
opinion. Yet even when the judges disagree with him,
they may derive much assistance from his opinion, if
only because it provides a single coherent picture of the
complexities of the whole case and a starting-point for
their own deliberations. Its value may be greater the
larger the Court, and especially with one whose judges
come from different legal systems and speak, at least
metaphorically, no common language.

In some respects, the assistance which the Court is
given by the advocate general may be compared with
that which an English or Scottish court obtains from the
Bar. The standard of counsel appearing before the
Court of Justice is extremely varied, the right of
audience being very wide, as will be seen in Chapter 13,
and forensic traditions varying considerably among the
Member States. To take one illustration only, there is
no convention, as in Britain, requiring counsel before
the Court to cite authorities which are against him.
Thus the advocate general may fill a considerable gap.

Apart from the immediate practical utility of their
opinions, the advocates general have contributed over

the years to the development of Community law, and are frequently cited on questions which the judges have not found it necessary to decide. The authority of such pronouncements is a question to which we shall return when we come to the subject of precedent in the Court. But in developing the law, and in guiding the Court in its early years over the uncharted terrain of the Community Treaties, the first advocates general, Maurice Lagrange of France and Karl Roemer of Germany, made a remarkable impact which can still be seen in the reports of the latest cases. For illustrations of their respective contributions one need look only at the opinion of Maurice Lagrange in the first reference to the Court under Article 177 EEC (Case 13/61 *Bosch* [1962] ECR 45), or his dicta on the subject of interpretation of Community law (see for example Case 8/55 *Fédéchar* v. *High Authority* [1954–1956] ECR 245); or, in the case of Karl Roemer, at many of the early cases on judicial review under the ECSC Treaty (see for example Cases 7 and 9/54 *Groupement des Industries Sidérurgiques Luxembourgeoises* v. *High Authority* [1954–1956] ECR 175).

An incidental advantage of the institution of advocate general, as was pointed out in the previous chapter, is that the opinion, which is printed in full as part of the report of the case, often provides a clearer introduction to a case than the judgment itself, and so is best read first.

Comments are sometimes made on the proportion of cases in which an advocate general is or is not followed by the Court. But it seems doubtful whether any reliable statistics could be assembled on this question. Frequently the Court will agree with the advocate general on some aspects of the case but disagree on others; or it may arrive at the same result but on grounds which diverge to a greater or lesser extent from his reasoning. Some suggestions of the advocate general may be passed over in silence, so that it is not possible to state with certainty whether the Court accepts them or not. It is true, however, that in some of the cases which represent the most striking advances in its jurisprudence, the Court has gone against the views of the advocate general. Examples of such landmarks can be found in cases like *Van Gend en Loos* (p. 183), *Continental Can* (p. 287), and the ERTA case (p. 98), of which more will be said in later chapters. The explanation of this phenomenon may lie partly in the fact that the advocate general often regards it as one of his principal functions to remind the Court of its previous case-law and to emphasise the virtue of a consistent and harmonious development of the law; it may also simply be easier for the judges collectively to advance further than an individual advocate general. Although it may only be a matter of impression, it does not seem that an advocate general, despite his more exposed position, is more influenced by his national background or is any less "Community-minded" than the judges. Indeed, Rasmussen suggests that the opinions of the advocates general over the years "have provided a powerful and steady pro-Community input into the Court's process" (in *On Law and Policy in the European Court of Justice*, 1986, p. 273).

The number and national origins of the advocates general have been determined by somewhat arbitrary factors. In the original Community of the Six there had to be seven judges in order to ensure that there was an uneven number of judges and not less than one from each Member State. As the larger Member States were considered entitled to a second member of the Court, there were from 1952 to 1972 a French and a German advocate general, with Italy, towards the end of that period, having two judges. (Earlier, there had been two Dutch judges.) After the first enlargement of the Communities to nine, there was one judge from each Member of State and an advocate general from each of the "big four," France, Germany, Italy and the United

Kingdom. Following the second enlargement, a Greek judge was added, as well as a second French judge in order to preserve an uneven number; by way of concession to the smaller Member States, a fifth advocate general was added, drawn initially from the Netherlands. Upon the accession of Spain and Portugal in 1986 a sixth advocate general was added; it was agreed that both the fifth and sixth advocates general should be drawn from the eight smaller Member States (*i.e.* including Spain) by rotation: so far, from Belgium, Luxembourg, Netherlands and Portugal.

Following Maurice Lagrange, advocate general from 1952 to 1964, a succession of French advocates general was drawn from the *Conseil d'Etat*, appropriately enough since the *commissaire du gouvernement* in that institution is probably the closest model for the Court's advocate general. Indeed one has the impression, in reading the opinions of a French advocate general, that he sees his function in Luxembourg as the same as that of his counterpart in Paris. Maurice Lagrange was succeeded in turn by Joseph Gand, Alain Dutheillet de Lamothe, and Henri Mayras. However, with the appointment of Simone Rozès, this pattern was broken, although, as we have seen, the second French judge was drawn from the *Conseil d'Etat*. For, before being appointed to the Court, Mme Rozès had risen through the career judiciary to the presidency of the *Tribunal de grande instance de Paris*, the most important court of first instance in all France. Her successor, Marco Darmon, had also risen to senior judicial office in the Paris *Cour d'appel* (see previous chapter, p. 51). The first German advocate general, Karl Roemer, who served from 1952 to 1973, was succeeded by Gerhard Reischl, who had combined judicial and political experience in Germany and had been a member of the European Parliament. In 1984 he was succeeded by Otto Lenz, a German constitutional lawyer and practising notary, who had had a long parliamentary career, holding several senior posts in the Bundestag. Of previous Italian advocates general, Francesco Capotorti, achieved eminence in his own country as a professor of international law; both he and his immediate predecessor as advocate general had previously been judges of the Court, a change of role to which we have already made allusion. Capotorti's successor as advocate general, Federico Mancini, became, as we have seen (above, p. 52), judge at the Court in 1988. His successor as advocate general is Giuseppe Tesauro, who combined appointments as Professor and Director of the International Law Institute at Rome University with practice as an *avvocato* in the Italian *Corte di Cassazione*.

The fifth post as advocate general was, until 1986, occupied by a Dutchman, Verloren van Themaat, who had held a chair of law at the University of Utrecht and co-authored a widely used treatise (in both Dutch and English) on Community law. His successor is the Luxembourg lawyer Mischo, who, after postgraduate studies in international law at the Universities of Paris and Cambridge, spent five years in the Legal Service of the Commission; later, he returned to the Grand Duchy to play a prominent part in the Luxembourg Ministry of Foreign Affairs.

The sixth post of advocate general was first held by a Portuguese lawyer, da Cruz Viliça, who had combined an academic career at the University of Coimbra with political activity, becoming a Member of Parliament in 1980 and Secretary of State for European Integration in 1982. Under the rotation principle he was succeeded in 1988 by a Belgian, Walter van Gerven, who had pursued an academic career and at the time of his appointment presided over the Belgian Banking Commission.

The first British advocate general, Jean-Pierre Warner, had been Junior Counsel to the Treasury in Chancery matters from 1964 to 1972. After distinguished service in Luxembourg from 1973 to 1981, he became a Judge in the Chancery Division of the High Court. He was succeeded as advocate general by Sir Gordon Slynn, who had previously been Junior Counsel to the Treasury in common law, Senior Counsel to the Crown, High Court Judge, and President of the Employment Appeal Tribunal. His successor is Francis Jacobs who participated in the preparation of this edition until his appointment to the Court in September 1988 (see Preface, p. vii above). A legal secretary at the Court from 1972 to 1974 (for this function, see p. 17, above), he was then appointed to the Chair of European Law at King's College in the University of London. A member of the Bar (Middle Temple) he took silk in 1984 and frequently appeared as an advocate before the Court.

But the diverse backgrounds of the advocates general seem to have influenced the style rather than the substance of their opinions. One may read more like the reserved judgment of an English court; one may read more like the *conclusions* of a *commissaire du gouvernement*; one may be more clearly marked by a particular national legal system; but taken as a whole the opinions are as much the product of a Community view, and of the *esprit de corps* which characterises the Court as a whole, as are the judgments themselves.

Chapter 5

THE COURT OF FIRST INSTANCE

The year 1989 saw the appearance of a new Community Court. At the suggestion of the Court of Justice itself, the Single European Act amended the Treaties (see now Article 168A EEC) to allow for the establishment of a Court of First Instance "attached" to the Court of Justice, to try certain classes of case brought by natural or legal persons (but not cases brought by Member States or by Community institutions, nor references for preliminary rulings). There was to be a right of appeal, on points of law only, to the Court of Justice. The Court of First Instance was duly established by a decision of the Council, on a proposal from the Court of Justice, taken in October 1988 and is expected to start work in 1989: see Tom Kennedy, "The Essential Minimum: The Establishment of the Court of First Instance" (1989) 14 E.L.Rev. 7.

Proposals for a First Instance Tribunal in staff cases (Chapter 9) had long been made and were approved in principle in 1974 but were not adopted, although they could have been implemented merely by amendments of the Staff Regulations. As the case-load of the Court of Justice continued to grow, it was thought appropriate to extend the jurisdiction of any new tribunal to certain other types of case, such as appeals against competition decisions of the Commission, which often involve complex factual issues. The new tribunal, it was thought, would both relieve the Court of Justice of the task of examining questions of fact and improve the quality of judicial review in the Community legal system. However the creation of such a tribunal required amendments to the founding Treaties, and the

64

negotiation of the Single European Act provided the opportunity for such amendments.

As finally constituted, the jurisdiction of the Court of First Instance extends, under Article 3(1) of the Council Decision, to three categories of case. The first category, and by far the largest, consists of staff cases. The second category comprises actions brought against the Commission by undertakings or associations of undertakings under the ECSC Treaty in relation to levies, production, prices and competition. The third category comprises competition cases brought by natural or legal persons under the second paragraph of Article 173 EEC and the third paragraph of Article 175 EEC.

Where such actions are accompanied by claims for damages, Article 3(2) of the Decision provides that the Court of First Instance shall have jurisdiction to decide those claims also. However, other claims for damages will not be heard by the Court of First Instance.

The Council was unable to agree to the proposal of the Court of Justice that anti-dumping cases should also be heard by the Court of First Instance. The omission is unfortunate, since such cases, often raising complex factual issues, would seem ideally suited to the new tribunal. However, Article 3(3) of the Decision provides that the Council will review this matter after two years of operation of the Court of First Instance.

The Court of First Instance is to consist of 12 members; in practice therefore it can be expected that one member will come from each Member State. The members are to be chosen "from persons whose independence is beyond doubt and who possess the ability required for appointment to judicial office" (Article 168A(3) EEC); like the members of the Court of Justice, they are appointed by common accord of the Governments of the Member States for a renewable term of six years. The Court of Justice in its proposal had envisaged only seven members but it may be that no Member State was willing to forego an appointment of one of its nationals. Cases before the Court of First Instance may be heard by a chamber of three or five judges or exceptionally by the plenary court. While 12 members may initially prove too many, the Council Decision envisages, in contrast to the proposal of the Court of Justice, that the judges will be assisted by an advocate general (who may give his opinion in writing—not "in open court" as required by Article 166 EEC before the Court of Justice). However there is to be no separate corps of advocates general; instead, members of the Court of First Instance may be called upon to perform the task of an advocate general. Nor will there be an advocate general in every case; the advocate general will give an opinion in "certain cases," and the criteria for selecting such cases, as well as the procedures for designating the advocate general, will be laid down in the Rules of Procedure of the Court of First Instance.

In accordance with Article 168A(4) EEC, the Rules of Procedure will be drawn up by the Court of First Instance in agreement with the Court of Justice, and the rules will require, like the rules of the Court of Justice, the unanimous approval of the Council. The adoption of the rules may be a lengthy process, and to avoid delay Article 11 of the Decision provides that until their entry into force the Rules of Procedure of the Court of Justice shall apply *mutatis mutandis*. Thus initially the procedure will be the same as that for direct actions in the Court of Justice as described in Chapter 12 below.

Decisions of the Court of First Instance may be the subject of appeal to the Court of Justice within two months of their notification. The right of appeal is stated by Article 168A(1) EEC to be "on points of law only and in accordance with the conditions laid down by the Statute." The EEC Statute is amended by Article 7 of the Council Decision to provide, by a new Article 51, for three grounds of appeal. These are:

1. Lack of competence of the Court of First Instance;
2. A breach of procedure before it which adversely affects the interests of the appellant;
3. The infringement of Community law by the Court of First Instance.

These grounds, which reflect in part the grounds of annulment under Article 173 EEC (below, p. 116), seem sufficiently broad to cover all possible points of law, while leaving open the question in what circumstances (if any) a mistaken characterisation of the facts might constitute an error of law. Further guidance on that difficult question (which in the French *Conseil d'Etat* has been resolved by the doctrine of *erreur manifeste d'appréciation*) will doubtless be provided in the course of time by appellate decisions of the Court of Justice.

The Rules of Procedure of the Court of Justice itself have been amended by the addition of a new Title IV governing appeals against decisions of the Court of First Instance. Under the amended Statute, such appeals may be brought within a period of two months from the notification of the decision appealed against, either by any party which was unsuccessful, in whole or in part, before the Court of First Instance, or, except in staff cases, by a Member State or Community institution which did not take part in the proceedings before the Court of First Instance. There is also provision for certain interlocutory appeals, *e.g.* against decisions of the Court of First Instance on interim measures or on applications to intervene.

Where an appeal is brought, a notice of the appeal is served on all the parties to the proceedings before the Court of First Instance. The procedure on appeal departs on many points from the current procedure in other cases before the Court of Justice. Any party may lodge a response within two months of the appeal being served; this time limit cannot be extended. The appeal

and the response may be supplemented by a reply and a
rejoinder only where the President expressly allows it.
The Court may at any time dismiss an appeal which is
manifestly inadmissible or manifestly ill-founded. The
Court may also decide to dispense with the oral
procedure unless one of the parties objects. In these
respects the procedure on appeal is designed to be more
expeditious.

In accordance with the language of Article 168A EEC
which describes the Court of First Instance as
"attached" to the Court of Justice, the new court is not
a separate institution but is organically linked to the
older Court (and will occupy offices in the new annexe
(above, p. 30) physically linked to the older building
by an underground tunnel). It will appoint its own
Registrar, but will share the existing administrative
services, library and other facilities, and such staff as it
needs of its own are likely to be seconded from the
Court of Justice.

The preamble to the Decision of the Council
establishing the Court of First Instance justifies its
establishment on the ground that "in respect of actions
requiring close examination of complex facts, the
establishment of a second court will improve the judicial
protection of individual interests in the Community"
and also that "it is necessary in order to maintain the
quality and effectiveness of judicial review in the
Community legal order, to enable the Court [of Justice]
to concentrate its activities on its fundamental task of
ensuring uniform interpretation of Community law." As
pointed out above, the Court of First Instance may
initially not have sufficient work to justify the full
complement of 12 members; however, with the likely
development of new forms of jurisdiction, such as the
creation of a Community trademark office, the decisions
of whose organs will have to be subject to judicial
review, it is likely that in the long term the Court of
First Instance will prove a busy as well as a vital part of

the Community's judicial machinery. It will enable the Community legal system fully to respect the emerging principle, not yet explicitly stated in any decision of the Court of Justice, that all decisions both on law and on fact, must be subject to effective judicial review. The Court of First Instance will be an essential means of securing the proper implementation of that principle.

APPENDIX

First appointments of Judges of the Court of First Instance

Donal BARRINGTON, Judge of the Irish High Court

Jacques BIANCARELLI, Director of Legal Services, Crédit Lyonnais, Paris; former legal secretary at the Court of Justice

Cornelis BRIET, Vice-President of the District Court of Rotterdam

José Luis DA CRUZ VILACA, former Portuguese advocate general at the Court of Justice

David EDWARD, Salvesen Professor of European Institutions, University of Edinburgh

Rafael GARCIA-VALDECASAS Y FERNANDEZ, Head of the Community Legal Service of the Spanish State

Christos GERARIS, Councillor of the Greek Council of State

Heinrich KIRSCHNER, Director in the Ministry of Justice of the Federal Republic of Germany

Koen LENAERTS, Professor at the University of Leuven; former legal secretary at the Court of Justice

Antonio SAGGIO, Judge of the Italian Court of Cassation, former legal secretary at the Court of Justice

Romain SCHINTGEN, General Administrator in the Luxembourg Ministry of Employment

Bo VESTERDORF, Director in the Danish Ministry of Justice

PART TWO: FUNCTIONS AND JURISDICTION

Introductory

In the Community legal order the Court of Justice has a crucial role. It has to see that the Council and the Commission, as the decision-taking and policy-making organs of the Community, keep within their powers under the Treaties. It has to restrain Member States who act in breach of the Treaties. It has also a legislative function, inasmuch as it often falls to the Court to fill gaps in the legal system arising from the political impotence of the Council—impotence which the Single European Act now seeks to correct.

For these important and varied tasks the Court is armed by the Treaties with an extremely wide jurisdiction. Indeed, the Court is vested with powers which in most continental countries lawyers would expect to find shared between a number of specialised courts. But in the Community legal order the Court of Justice has had to serve as a judicial maid of all work, at least until the creation in 1989 of the Court of First Instance.

Thus, the Court acts as an administrative court to impose judicial control on the other institutions of the Community. Again, in certain circumstances, an individual may bring before the Court an action for annulment of a Community act or a suit for damages against an institution of the Communities. Until 1989 it also acted as would a continental administrative court by providing a tribunal to which the public servants of the Communities might appeal in disputes relating to their terms of service; but since 1989, as we saw in the last chapter, this head of jurisdiction, which used to constitute about one third of the Court's business, has now passed to the Court of First Instance and may only reach the Court on appeal on a point of law.

71

The Court exercises powers of judicial review not only over administrative acts but also over Community legislation, such as regulations or directives of the Council or Commission. The Court may also rule upon the conformity with the Treaties of any international agreement entered into by the Communities. In this respect, the Court resembles a constitutional court such as that of the German Federal Republic or the Supreme Court of the United States.

If the Court in these respects resembles the administrative or constitutional courts familiar to continental lawyers, it also serves, in a sense, as an international court by hearing suits brought against a Member State for an alleged violation of the Treaties. Such suits may be brought by another Member State but are usually instituted by the Commission in the exercise of its watchdog function.

Among the Court's functions, mention must be made of its jurisdiction to give preliminary rulings when requested to do so by a court of a Member State. Preliminary rulings may be given upon a question of the interpretation of Community law or of the validity of Community legislation. This head of the Court's jurisdiction has proved in the event to be much the most influential for the development of Community law and will be fully discussed in Chapter 10. From a procedural point of view preliminary rulings may be contrasted with the other heads of the Court's jurisdiction. For, whereas a reference for a preliminary ruling can only be made by the national court and not by the parties themselves, all other cases are brought directly before the Court by the party initiating the proceedings, whether this be a Member State, a Community institution, a legal person such as a firm or company, or a private individual.

In an Appendix to this part (below, p. 209) are included various Judicial Statistics concerning the work of the Court from its inception up to January 1, 1989.

There (Table 1, p. 210) the term "Direct actions" is used in contrast with "Staff cases," on the one hand, and "Preliminary Rulings" on the other. Direct actions may conveniently be divided into (A) actions against Member States (which will be the subject of Chapter 6) and (B) actions against Community institutions (which will be the subject of Chapters 7 and 8). Category (B) corresponds to what we have termed above the administrative and constitutional jurisdiction of the Court; category (A) to its international jurisdiction.

This last expression must be treated with caution. To receive and decide suits against States is the characteristic function of an international tribunal; contemporary examples are the International Court of Justice at The Hague or the European Court of Human Rights at Strasbourg. In this sense one may speak of the Luxembourg Court's international jurisdiction, for under various provisions of the Treaties the Court may be seised of complaints that a Member State is failing to fulfil its treaty obligations, including the failure to implement obligations arising under regulations or directives.

Nevertheless, this jurisdiction of the Court differs in significant respects from that of a traditional international tribunal. Thus, it differs from the Hague Court in that the breaches by Member States with which it is concerned are breaches primarily of Community law, not of international law (except in so far as they stem from a treaty infringement). The concern here of the Luxembourg Court is with upholding and enforcing the Community legal order, whereas that of the Hague Court is the settlement of international disputes. Again, suits against Member States are usually brought to Luxembourg not by another State but by the Community's own policeman or watchdog, the Commission. A somewhat similar relationship exists at Strasbourg between the European Court and the European Commission of Human Rights, but such a filtering device is not characteristic of international tribunals. Furthermore, preliminary references to Luxembourg from courts in Member States have, as we shall see later, the same effect as certain direct actions in putting a particular Member State in the dock there for a treaty infringement with the watchdog role of the Commission being played by the individual plaintiff; but such references are not normally thought of as falling within the international jurisdiction of the Court.

The last head of jurisdiction to be considered in this part does have an international aspect. Under Article 228 EEC the Court may be asked its opinion on whether an international agreement which the Community is contemplating entering into is compatible with the provisions of the Treaty. This jurisdiction was exercised for the first time in 1975 and, although exercised infrequently, has recently acquired enough significance to warrant a separate chapter (Chapter 11).

The six chapters which form this part will cover then the main categories of cases falling within the Court's jurisdiction. But this manifold jurisdiction also extends to a few exceptional types of case not dealt with below, such as the power of the Court under Article 13 of the Merger Treaty compulsorily to retire a member of the Commission who no longer fulfils the conditions required for the performance of his duties or if he has been guilty of serious misconduct: this power has been used only once, in 1976, when a Commissioner was permanently incapacitated by a stroke.

Potentially more significant, but rarely exercised, is the jurisdiction of the Court under Article 95 ECSC to give an opinion if it is found necessary to amend, subject to certain limitations, the provisions of the ECSC Treaty. Other heads of jurisdiction can be found in Articles 180 to 182 EEC. Frequently contracts concluded by the Community with outside bodies include an arbitration clause conferring jurisdiction on the Court pursuant to Article 181 EEC (or Article 153

Euratom: an instance of this jurisdiction is mentioned below, p. 133).

Article 182 EEC confers upon the Court jurisdiction in any dispute between Member States which relates to the subject matter of the Treaty, if the parties agree to submit their dispute to the Court. Moreover, Member States whose disputes concern the interpretation or application of the Treaty are bound by Article 219 not to submit their dispute to any other method of settlement than those provided by the Treaty.

From 1989 one further task will now fall to the Court by virtue of the creation of the Court of First Instance. This will be to act as an appellate jurisdiction from the latter. In this capacity, it will also have to resolve any conflicts of jurisdiction arising between itself and the lower court.

Chapter 6

ACTIONS AGAINST MEMBER STATES

Introduction

Proceedings may be brought in the Court of Justice against
Member States to establish that they have infringed their
Community obligations. Under the EEC Treaty such direct
actions against Member States arise, principally, under
Articles 169 and 170. They may also be brought under
Article 93 in the special context of "State aids." In the
ECSC Treaty, as we shall see, it is the Commission which
acts, in effect, as a jurisdiction of first instance to determine
the infringement and issue a decision addressed to the
Member State in breach of the Treaty.

Articles 169 and 170 EEC provide two distinct but
inter-related procedures. Under the former Article it is
the Commission which brings the action against the
Member State, whereas under the latter the action is
brought by another Member State.

While actions under Article 170 remain very rare
(only one to date taken to judgment), enforcement
actions by the Commission under Article 169 have
become increasingly frequent in the last decade; for
instance, directives to harmonise VAT have led to many
such actions: see, *e.g.* the judgments of June 21, 1988 in
Cases 414/85 *Commission* v. *Ireland*, 416/85 *Commission*
v. *United Kingdom*, 257/86 *Commission* v. *Italy* and 283/
86 *Commission* v. Belgium; Case 353/85 *Commission* v.
United Kingdom ("VAT on spectacles") *The Times*,
February 24, 1988. The Table appended to this chapter
shows a total of 166 actions for the 28 years 1953 to
1981 but towards 50 actions each year from 1981: in
1987 there were 64 and in 1988 73.

Criticism has been expressed that the Commission should be more selective in its resort to the big stick: not every peccadillo by a Member State warrants the diversion of precious time and manpower which Commission proceedings entail; it should exercise sparingly the discretion to "prosecute" which, as we will see, Article 169 allows it (see Audretsch, *Supervision in European Community Law*, 2nd ed., 1986). Moreover, as will be seen below (p. 92), infringements of Community law may be the subject of proceedings before a national court in the Member States by virtue of the doctrine of direct effect.

Procedure under Article 169

An action by the Commission under Article 169 involves three phases. The formal procedure however is invariably preceded in practice by the Commission writing a letter to the Member State warning it of its breach and inviting its comments. If this does not settle the matter, and in two cases out of three it does so, then the first formal step is for the Commission to invite the State formally to submit its observations on the alleged breach, after which the Commission will deliver a reasoned opinion. This pre-contentious phase may well result in a settlement of the matter by the State recognising its breach and correcting it. In practice, a high percentage of the cases terminate at this stage.

If the State is recalcitrant, the second phase in the procedure is for the Commission to bring the matter before the Court. Settlements are also sometimes reached at this stage. The third and final phase is for the Court to give judgment. Under Article 171 this judgment is only declaratory: there are no sanctions for non-compliance. Article 171 simply declares that the State shall be required to take the necessary measures to comply with the judgment. Yet the violation of a treaty obligation by a Member State is a serious matter which must carry political consequences in its relations with other Member States. The Commission has also indirect means of bringing pressure upon the defaulting State through its powers to grant (or withhold) various authorisations which the State may seek from it under numerous Articles of the Treaty. To date, almost every judgment against a Member State has been complied with, although in a few instances only after considerable delay.

Again, in some Member States it has been accepted that it may be possible for an individual with a sufficient interest to sue the Government for damages in respect of its breach of Community law; see, for example, in France *Avilar* (*Conseil d'Etat* March 23, 1984) and *Steinhauser* v. *City of Biarritz* (*Tribunal Administratif de Pau*, November 12, 1985), and in the Netherlands *Roussel Laboratories* (Hague District Court, July 18, 1984): these and other cases are discussed by Green and Barav in 1986 *Yearbook of European Law* pp. 54 *et seq.* In English and Scots law the question is moot and straddles the uncertain boundary between public and private law. In *Garden Cottage Foods* v. *Milk Marketing Board* [1985] 2 All E.R. 770 there were dicta in the House of Lords in favour of a remedy in damages against the Board for breach of statutory duty. But in *Bourgoin* v. *Ministry of Agriculture, Fisheries and Food* [1985] 3 All E.R. 585 the Court of Appeal (Oliver L.J. dissenting) reversed the decision of Mann J. at first instance who had awarded damages in tort to a French producer of turkeys whose imports to the United Kingdom had been illegally embargoed by the Ministry in breach of Article 30 EEC. Before a further appeal could come before the House of Lords, the case was settled (see Steiner, "How to Make the Action Suit the Case: Domestic Remedies for Breach of EEC Law" (1987) 12 E.L.Rev. 102).

Under Article 88 ECSC the procedure is different. Thus, under the first phase the Commission reaches a *decision* whether the State is in breach: it does not merely deliver an *opinion*. In the second place it is therefore the State which must bring the matter before the Court by way of a challenge to the Commission's decision. Finally, in the third phase, if the State does not challenge the decision or if the Court upholds it, then the Commission is empowered to impose certain sanctions, provided the Council supports this by a two-thirds majority. The sanctions include the suspension of payments otherwise due to be paid by the Commission to the State in default or the taking of discriminatory measures which would normally be proscribed under Article 4 ECSC (*e.g.* a ban on imports from the State in question).

In practice, Member States have generally come to heel. The two most notorious instances to date of reluctance to conform concern, respectively, Italy and France. The Italian Government imposed a tax, pursuant to a Law of 1939, on the export of art treasures, which it was only prevailed upon to repeal as a tax on exports contrary to Article 16 EEC, after having been declared in breach in three different proceedings before the Court (Case 7/68 *Commission* v. *Italy* [1968] ECR 423; Case 18/71 *Eunomia* v. *Italian Ministry of Education* [1971] ECR 811, Case 48/71 *Commission* v. *Italy* [1972] ECR 527).

In the so-called Lamb War between France and the United Kingdom (1978–80), a French ban on the import of mutton and lamb from the United Kingdom was declared by the Court, in proceedings under Article 169 EEC, to be an infringement of Articles 12 and 30 EEC (Case 232/78 *Commission* v. *France* [1979] ECR 2729). When France did not comply with this judgment, the Commission began a second action under Article 169 (Case 24/80, lodged in January 1980), based upon France's infringement of Article 171, which (as we have seen) requires a State to take the necessary measures to comply with any judgment of the Court. Before this case was heard, the Commission, in March 1980, lodged a further action (Case 97/80) against France under Article 169 in respect of an illegal charge upon mutton and lamb imports and of the continuing defiance of the first judgment. Cases 24/80 and 97/80 then proceeded as joined cases, in the course of which the Commission, pursuant to Article 186 EEC and Article 83 of the Rules of Procedure, made an application for the adoption of "interim measures" in which it invited the Court "to order the French Republic to desist forthwith from applying any restriction and/or levying any charge on imports of mutton and lamb from the United Kingdom." For reasons which will be discussed below (p. 237) when interim measures are explained, the Court refused the order requested. Nevertheless, in September 1980 a compromise was reached in the Council of Agricultural Ministers by the adoption of a sheepmeat regime (long demanded by France) which induced the latter to remove the charge on imports, thus ending this twentieth century "War of Jenkins' ear."

By contrast with the earlier dispute with Italy over the art treasures tax (above) or the later dispute with the United Kingdom over an import ban on potatoes (Case 231/78 *Commission* v. *United Kingdom* [1979] ECR 1447 and Case 118/78 *Meijer* v. *Department of Trade* [1979] ECR 1387), in the Lamb War no challenge to the French action was brought in the French courts, though this might have proved more effective.

An illustration of Article 169 procedure is provided by the *Pigmeat* case (Case 7/61 *Commission* v. *Italy* [1961] ECR 317). By a Decree of June 1960 the Italian Government decided to suspend the import of certain pigmeats from all countries until August 31, 1960. This suspension was subsequently extended a number of times. In October 1960 the Commission told the Italian Government that in its opinion the suspension was contrary to Article 31 EEC whereby Member States should refrain from introducing between themselves any new quantitive restrictions upon imports. After giving the Italian Government an opportunity to present its observations, the Commission wrote a letter on December 21, 1960 requesting the Italian Government to put an end to the alleged infringement within one month and repeating its view that the Italian measures stopping import of pigmeat were contrary to Article 31 EEC. This letter did not contain a full review of the economic situation in the Italian market for pigmeat nor a discussion whether this situation might justify the Italian measures.

In a letter of January 1961 the Italian Government informed the Commission that it had decided to extend the measures once more until March 31, 1961 and requested the Commission to authorise them under Article 226 EEC. This Article provides that if serious economic difficulties arise, Member States may apply to the Commission for authorisation to take protective measures in order to rectify the situation. The Commission replied that, while prepared to consider the request for special authorisation, this could not affect the continuation of the Article 169 proceedings. In fact, the Commission proceeded to bring a suit against Italy in the Court on March 20, 1961. Before the Court gave judgment on December 19, 1961, the Italian Government had, as from July 1, 1961, repealed the import measures and substituted a system of minimum prices, which system had been recommended by the Commission.

Before the Court the Italian Government raised three preliminary objections to the admissibility of the action (for admissibility, see p. 225). First, it argued that the letter from the Commission of December 21, 1960 was not a 'reasoned opinion' within the terms of Article 169 so as to satisfy the first phase of procedure under that Article. In particular, it claimed that the letter did not examine the relevance of the Government's arguments regarding the grave crisis in the pigmeat market and the need for temporary measures to deal with that crisis. Secondly, it argued that the Commission should have postponed action under Article 169 until it had decided whether the Italian measures could be authorised under Article 226. Thirdly, it argued that the suit should have been discontinued after July 1, 1961, from which date the Italian Government had repealed the disputed measures: in effect, the suit had then lost its object and become merely academic.

All three arguments were rejected by the Court. The Commission's letter was sufficiently reasoned because it had presented a coherent statement of the reasons that had led the Commission to believe that Italy had failed in one of its obligations under the Treaty. The fact that the Commission was considering a special authorisation under Article 226 did not prevent it believing, rightly or wrongly, that Italy was in breach of its obligations so as to justify proceedings under Article 169. And it was still proper for the Court to declare whether or not a Member State had failed in its obligations, even though, subsequent to the bringing of the action, the State may have put an end to its infringement of the Treaty.

On this last point, the Court appears to have changed its position in the later decision of Case 26/69 *Commission* v. *French Republic* [1970] ECR 565, and will now examine whether a sufficient interest can be shown by the Commission for seeking a judgment on a matter which has become moot. In the later case, the Commission succeeded in showing a sufficient interest by reason of the fact that the Court's decision would govern a number of similar cases then pending.

In Cases 2 and 3/62 *Commission* v. *Luxembourg and Belgium* [1962] ECR 425, the Court re-affirmed its view that a subsequent request for special authorisation does not operate to suspend Article 169 proceedings; to decide otherwise would deprive the Article of its effectiveness.

A different line of defence to Article 169 proceedings was attempted in Cases 90 and 91/63 *Commission* v. *Luxembourg and Belgium* [1964] ECR 625 (the *Dairy Products* case). Here the two Governments argued that the action against them was inadmissible because the Council was itself in default in having delayed the setting up of a common organisation for dairy products, although it had resolved that it would do so by regulation before July 31, 1962. The Governments therefore argued that their own protective import duties would have been unnecessary if the Council had done its job by the date it had itself proposed and made a regulation governing dairy products generally. They argued that under the theory of interdependence of obligations in international law a party which is affected by the failure of another party to fulfil its obligations has the right not to fulfil its own obligations. The Court roundly rejected this plea as having no place in Community law: the Treaty created a new legal order whose structure, except for cases expressly covered by the Treaty, involved the prohibition of Member States taking justice into their own hands. Hence, the Council's failure to fulfil its obligations could not excuse the defendant Governments from carrying out their own obligations. Furthermore, self-help was not an appropriate remedy where an agency (namely, the Commission) existed for law enforcement. Accordingly, the import duties were declared contrary to Community law.

Although the Belgian Government then abolished the duties, the recovery of duties already paid was prohibited by statute. This led to further proceedings in the Belgian courts, culminating in the landmark decision of the Court of Cassation upholding in Belgium the supremacy of Community law over conflicting national law: *Minister for Economic Affairs* v. *Fromagerie Franco-Suisse "Le Ski"* [1972] CMLR 330.

Consistent with the *Dairy Products* case is the later case of *R.* v. *Kirk*, Case 63/83 [1984] ECR 2689, where the United Kingdom Government took unilateral action to impose a ban on fishing in British waters, arguing that this was justified by the failure of the Council to agree a new Common Fisheries Policy. A Danish skipper defied the ban, was caught and fined £30,000 by North Shields Magistrates; he appealed to the Crown Court, who sought a preliminary ruling under Article 177 EEC: the Court of Justice declared the British ban to be contrary to Community law; consequently, the fine was quashed.

It is well established that a Member State may not rely upon provisions, practices or situations in its internal legal system in order to justify a failure to fulfil obligations arising under Community law. Thus, in Case 58/81 *Commission* v. *Luxembourg* [1982] ECR 2175, the Grand Duchy was held in breach of a directive on equal pay despite its plea that it needed time to enact implementing legislation and to study the budgetary consequences of the directive.

In Case 167/73 *Commission* v. *French Republic* [1974] ECR 359 the long-standing rule of French law was challenged under which a certain proportion of the crew of French merchant ships had to consist of French nationals. The Commission argued that this was contrary to Community law, in particular Article 48 EEC enshrining the principle of free movement of workers. The French Government did not agree that this principle automatically applied to transport, especially transport by sea in view of the terms of Article 84(2) EEC; but it did indicate its intention to amend the offending provision of the *Code du Travail Maritime*, although not accepting that it was under any treaty obligation to do so. The Court held that the basic principle of free movement of workers was not subject to any qualifications in relation to sea transport and that consequently France was in breach of Article 48, nor had France in any way atoned for this breach by its declared intention to amend its ways. Moreover, the principle of legal certainty required the removal from the French statute book of a provision contrary to Community law.

Procedure under Article 170

The alternative procedure to Article 169 is that under Article 170 which permits any Member State to bring another Member State before the Court if it considers the latter has failed to fulfil an obligation under the Treaty. This form of action has rarely been used. Like the procedure under Article 169, Article 170 procedure is in successive phases. The first phase requires the complaining State to bring the alleged infringement before the Commission. The Commission must then deliver a reasoned opinion, as under Article 169, after allowing the States concerned to submit their observations. Only then (or if the Commission has not delivered an opinion after three months) may the complaining State bring the defaulting State before the Court.

That procedure under Article 169 is preferred to that under Article 170 is readily understandable. Direct confrontation between Member States as litigants at Luxembourg is better avoided by leaving it to the Commission to initiate any suit. In any event, the Commission has still to be involved whichever alternative procedure is used, although under Article 170 a Member State could commence an action in the Court even if the Commission's opinion was that no treaty infringement had occurred. Under the corresponding Article of the ECSC Treaty (Article 89) only one action was begun, by Belgium against France, but it was not pursued. Under the EEC Treaty actions have occasionally been threatened but only rarely pursued. Thus, Italy threatened to proceed against France during the "Wine War" of 1975–76. Only one case to date has proceeded to judgment: Case 141/78 *France* v. *United*

Kingdom [1979] ECR 2923, where the United Kingdom was adjudged in breach of its obligations under the EEC Treaty by adopting a national measure governing the minimum size of mesh for fishing nets used in British territorial waters. As required by Article 170(3), the Commission gave a reasoned opinion, which was in support of the French application; it also intervened in the proceedings (for such interventions, see p. 239 below).

Procedure under Article 93

In addition to the general enforcement procedure available to the Commission under Article 169 EEC, certain categories of infringements by Member States may be the subject of a more expeditious procedure which dispenses with the requirement of the Commission delivering a reasoned opinion. Instead, the Commission may proceed directly to the taking of a binding decision. Such derogation from the general procedure under Article 169 EEC is permitted by Articles 93 and 225: the latter Article concerns improper use by a Member State of the powers given it by Articles 223 and 224 to disregard the provisions of the EEC Treaty in the essential interests of its security, where these involve arms production or the withholding of information; the former Article concerns State aids to industry and has proved the more important in practice.

Under Article 93, where a State aid distorts or threatens to distort competition within the common market, the Commission, after giving notice to the parties concerned to submit their comments, may proceed to decide that the State concerned shall abolish (or alter) such aid within a prescribed time: if the State does not comply with this decision within the time prescribed the Commission (or any other interested State) may refer the matter to the Court of Justice direct. Of course, the decision (unlike the reasoned

opinion under Article 169 EEC) is open to challenge by
the State as a binding act under Article 173 (see
Chapter 7, below).

The special procedure under Article 93 resembles
therefore the enforcement procedure under Article 88
ECSC in that the Commission (erstwhile, the High
Authority) takes a decision that the State is in breach of
the ECSC Treaty; as we have seen (p. 78 above), it
does not merely deliver an opinion. It differs, however,
from Article 88 in that under Article 93 it is the
Commission which must seise the Court of the fact that
the offending State has not complied with the decision,
whereas Article 88 leaves it to the State to challenge the
decision before the Court. For, if not challenged, or if
challenged but upheld, the decision under Article 88
ECSC carries with it certain sanctions for non-
compliance, though none have ever in fact been
imposed. No such (theoretical) sanctions attach to a
decision under Article 93, although, as we shall see,
when brought before the Court, it may be the subject of
interim measures, and although not enforceable in the
national courts, it will render Article 93 directly
effective.

An example of the special procedure under Article 93
is provided by the *Pig Producers* case (Cases 31/77 and
53/77R *Commission* v. *United Kingdom* [1977] ECR
921). The British Government introduced a subsidy for
United Kingdom pig producers to help them compete
with Dutch and Danish imports subsidised by the
Community. The Government had informed the Commission of its intention to introduce the subsidy, but
before the Commission had decided whether the subsidy
was compatible with the common market within the
terms of Articles 92 and 93, it brought the subsidy into
operation, thereby infringing the clear prohibition in
Article 93(3).

The Commission thereupon took a decision on
February 17, 1977 which required the United Kingdom

to terminate the pig subsidy "forthwith." As the British Government did not comply, the Commission began an enforcement action under Article 93(2) on March 11, 1977. And it went further, for on May 12, 1977 it asked the Court to make an interim order requiring the United Kingdom to stop paying the subsidy. As we will see later, the power for the Court to grant what are, in effect, interlocutory injunctions is contained in Article 186 EEC, which states:

> "The Court of Justice may in any cases before it prescribe any necessary interim measures."

Despite advice to the contrary by the advocate general in his opinion, the Court in a laconic order on May 21 directed the United Kingdom to end the subsidy, again "forthwith." In fact, payment of the subsidy did cease towards the end of June, so that the enforcement action was not pressed to judgment.

What sanctions, other than political, could have been applied if the Member States had remained recalcitrant is a question discussed in the next section.

Effect of Judgments against Member States

It may be helpful to summarise the effects of a judgment delivered in proceedings brought under Articles 169, 170 and 93. Such judgments, unlike those to be discussed in the next chapter, are not made against a Community institution, but against a Member State. They touch, therefore, the tender nerve of national sovereignty.

In contrast with Article 88 ECSC, a judgment under any of these three Articles is only declaratory: it has no executory force, no sanctions are provided, nor are any national measures thereby annulled. Essentially, it is left to the defaulting Member State to recognise the error of its ways and to comply with its treaty obligations.

Nevertheless, it is in the nature of the proceedings under these Articles that the Commission will have specified the acts which have given rise to the breach. If the Court finds the charges made by the Commission proved, then the Member State is left in no doubt as to what it must do, and, as the Court pointed out in Case 314/81 *Procureur de la République* v. *Waterkeyn* [1982] ECR 4337, the courts also of the Member States are bound, by virtue of Article 171 EEC, "to draw the necessary inferences from the judgment of the Court." Thus, in Case 70/72 *Commission* v. *Germany* [1973] ECR 813 Germany had provided State aids for certain mining regions which the Commission alleged was an infringement of Article 92. In an enforcement action under Article 93 the Commission invited the Court to declare not only that Germany had infringed the Treaty but also that it should be required to obtain repayment of the aids from the recipients. For the German Government it was submitted that such a ruling for repayment could be neither requested by the Commission nor made by the Court. The Court did not accept this submission, although, on the merits of the case, it dismissed the action: had it found against Germany, it could not formally have ordered the repayment of the aids, but it could have achieved the same result, in substance, by an appropriate wording of its declaratory judgment. Moreover, the Court made clear that its approach would be no different in proceedings brought under Articles 169 and 170: under these Articles as under Article 93, the Commission may specify what measures must be taken by the Member State concerned to meet its treaty obligations, and, in the event of non-compliance, the Court may grant a declaration in no less specific terms.

Likewise, where the breach consists of the enactment (or retention) of legislation contrary to Community law, the Court has no power to annul the offending national measures. It will confine itself to condemning such

measure as conflicting with Community law. The
Member State concerned should then be in no doubt
how it must amend its own law. Thus, in Case 167/73
Commission v. *France* [1974] ECR 359, as we have seen
(above p. 84) the successful action under Article 169
induced the French Government, albeit reluctantly, to
amend its *Code du Travail Maritime*. The Court brushed
aside the Government's plea that, even if its own law
did conflict with Community law, it would therefore be
inapplicable and so not require to be repealed: the
Court made clear that the unamended Code would
leave Community seamen uncertain of their rights to
seek employment on French ships; nor was it a
sufficient answer that the French Government no longer
applied the offending provision of the Code.

In enforcement actions under Articles 169, 170 and 93
the Court of Justice has no power to award damages
against a Member State in favour of those who may
have been prejudiced by the infringement: this follows
from the declaratory nature of the judgment. Moreover,
such actions are normally brought, not by the parties
prejudiced, but by the Commission acting in the
Community interest. Nevertheless, an ingenious attempt
may have been made in the *Lamb War* cases (Cases 24/
80 and 97/80 R [1980] ECR 1319) to achieve indirectly
what could not be done directly. Thus, the British
Government is reported to have proposed to the
Commission that it should invite the Court to make a
declaration that France was in further breach of the
Treaty by reason of its failure to pay compensation to
British meat exporters prejudiced by the import ban
which the Court had already declared illegal in the
previous proceedings (Case 232/78 [1979] ECR 2729).
The British Government considered, presumably, that
the language of Article 171 was wide enough to permit
the Court to do this. The Commission, however, did not
adopt the British proposal, and the claim for compensation was dropped once the dispute over lamb was

settled. Accordingly, it remains a moot question whether an appropriately worded declaration could be issued by the Court if the Commission (or another Member State) proved that the particular breach consisted in the State's failure to pay compensation or damages to an injured party.

As we have seen above (*e.g.* in the *Lamb War* cases) proceedings under Article 169, 170 or 93 culminate in a judgment under Article 171. Under this Article the State is required to take the necessary measures to comply with the judgment: it is required to do so by the Treaty, it is not *ordered* to do so by the Court. We have also seen that the failure to comply with the judgment may constitute a further treaty infringement by the Member State, this time of Article 171, for which a new enforcement action may be brought under Articles 169 or 170. We shall see later how to such proceedings under Articles 169 and 170 may be attached a request for interim measures to be prescribed by the Court under Article 186; we shall see too that an interim measure may be couched as an actual *order* by the Court to the offending State that it shall desist from certain conduct on its part, pending judgment in the principal action (see Case 45/87R *Dundalk Water Scheme* [1987] 2 CMLR 197 and 536).

We have already noted in the previous section how the general enforcement procedure available to the Commission under Article 169 EEC is replaced, for certain categories of treaty infringement by a Member State, by a more expeditious procedure, notably under Article 93 EEC relating to impermissible State aids. Where the offending State fails to comply with the Commission's decision requiring the abolition or alteration of the aid, the Commission may refer the matter to the Court, which may then prescribe any necessary interim measures pursuant to Article 186 (see *Pig Producers* case, Case 31, 53/77R [1977] ECR 921).

It will now be appreciated that the Court enjoys wider powers in interim proceedings under Article 186 than it has when giving final judgment in enforcement actions (an anomaly justifiable by the interim or interlocutory nature of the relief), although it may be most reluctant to use these powers, where it has already given judgment against a Member State, to seek to compel the State to comply. The Court dislikes merely beating the air, so that when it has a discretion (as it has under Article 186), it may well refuse the interim measures sought for fear of further undermining respect for the authority of the Court by provoking disobedience of its specific order: a recalcitrant child who disobeys its parent's first request is just as likely to disobey the second or third.

In the last resort, a Member State complies only when it has the political will to do so. Defiance, however, puts in jeopardy the whole future of the Community.

In recent years the European Parliament has followed closely the issue of enforcement of Community law against Member States; the Commission now submits to the Parliament an annual report on "monitoring of the application of Community law." In its Draft Treaty establishing the European Union (below, p. 328), the Parliament proposed that the European Council should be empowered to impose certain sanctions on Member States wherever there was a "serious and persistent violation" of the provisions of the Treaty: Draft Treaty, Article 44, *e.g.* suspending the offending State's rights under the Treaty.

Even if there is no completely effective remedy in the Court of Justice, a remedy may lie in the national courts of the Member State in breach. For, as the Court ruled in its landmark decision in Case 26/62 *Van Gend en Loos* [1963] ECR 1 at 13 (see p. 162), "The vigilance of individuals concerned to protect their rights amounts to an effective supervision in addition to the supervision

entrusted by Articles 169 and 170 to the diligence of the
Commission and of the Member States." Furthermore,
as the Court has constantly held, the individual will
have such a right of action in the national court
whenever the Community provision in question is
categorised by the Court of Justice as having direct
effect. However, the remedies available to the individual will vary according to the way in which the issue
comes before the national court. Thus, in Case 88/77
Minister for Fisheries v. *Schoenenberg* [1978] ECR 473 a
Dutch fisherman was acquitted by the Irish court on a
charge of illegal fishing in Irish waters because he
established, as his defence, that the Irish Government
had imposed restrictions which were contrary to
Community law. Community law may afford not only,
as here, a shield, but also a sword. Thus, a Dutch
potato exporter successfully sought a declaration in the
English High Court that the United Kingdom's ban on
potato imports infringed Community law and was,
therefore, invalid (Case 118/78 *Meijer* v. *Department of
Trade* [1979] ECR 1387). In both these cases Community law was effectively upheld in the national courts of
the Member State concerned in its breach. Both cases
involved references to the Court of Justice for preliminary rulings that Community law was being infringed.
Parallel actions under Article 169 were brought by the
Commission against the infringing State in both cases
(Case 61/77 [1978] ECR 417; Case 231/78 [1979] ECR
1447); but such enforcement at Community level should
not conceal the important function of the national
judiciary in sanctioning breaches of Community law by
their own Governments. While the Article 169 procedure is an effective method of bringing Member States
into line for the future, an action in the national courts
coupled with a reference for a preliminary ruling under
Article 177 may provide, as we shall see in Chapter 10,
an immediate remedy for the individual in the instant
case.

APPENDIX

ENFORCEMENT ACTIONS AGAINST MEMBER STATES
(The figures given are for cases introduced in the years stated)

	1982	1983	1984	1985	1986	1987	1988	1953–1988
Belgium	9	4	5	23	16	7	10	103
Denmark	1	3	1	2	1	—	3	15
France	8	12	15	14	8	8	10	101
Germany	4	4	7	9	11	3	8	54
Greece	—	2	4	10	11	12	14	53
Ireland	3	1	3	9	2	3	8	35
Italy	14	13	12	31	18	22	14	193
Luxembourg	3	—	3	6	4	2	2	28
Netherlands	2	3	2	5	—	4	3	27
Portugal	—	—	—	—	—	—	—	—
Spain	—	—	—	—	—	1	1	2
United Kingdom	2	1	4	5	1	2	—	23
TOTAL :	46	43	56	114	72	64	73	634*

* For the period 1953 to 1982 there were 166 enforcement actions.

94

Chapter 7

JUDICIAL REVIEW OF COMMUNITY ACTS

Introduction

In national constitutions, limits are normally set to the powers exercisable by the agencies of government. Thus, in the United Kingdom there are legal limits upon the powers of the central government and local authorities; these limits are one of the main topics falling within the subject of English administrative law and are found under such headings as "the doctrine of *ultra vires*" or "the judicial review of administrative authorities." In all the Member States of the European Communities the powers of governmental bodies are confined within prescribed limits and so, in Dicey's sense, subject to the rule of law. In some, the policing of these limits is the task of a separate system of administrative courts. This is the case, for instance, in France where there is now a three-tier system, comprising the *tribunaux administratifs* of first instance, five regional *Cours administratives d'appel and the Conseil d'Etat* as the supreme administrative court.

Again, in some countries the constitution sets limits upon the permissible extent of legislation, and the legislature may then be subject to control by a constitutional court exercising judicial review of the constitutionality of its enactments. The United States and the Federal German Republic provide examples of such courts. In the United Kingdom, on the other hand, the doctrine of Parliamentary sovereignty prevails absolutely, at least south of the Scottish border.

In the Community legal order, the administrative (or executive) agencies are the Commission and, to some

95

extent, the Council, although the function of the latter is, first and foremost, that of the legislature. As in the Member States, so in the Communities the administrative agencies have only limited powers of rule-making and individual decision. The Treaties serve as constitutional documents to define those powers, including those of the Council when acting as a legislature. The Treaties also vest in the Court the necessary jurisdiction to control the lawful exercise of such power. Hence, Valentine refers to the Court, neatly, as a Conseil d'Etats (Valentine, *The Court of Justice of the European Communities* Vol. 1. 1965). Hence also we might adopt the heading "administrative jurisdiction" under which to describe this part of the Court's jurisdiction. Nevertheless, the jurisdiction may also be regarded as "constitutional" in so far as the Court reviews the legality of legislation by the Council or Commission. For, as we have seen in Chapter 1, many regulations and directives of these institutions are better regarded as Community legislation than likened to delegated or subordinate legislation as that term is used in English law.

In the EEC Treaty the relevant Articles to be considered first are 173 and 175; these are the counterpart of Articles 33 and 35 of the ECSC Treaty and deal respectively with actions to annul an act of the Council or Commission and actions for inactivity, or the failure to act, on the part of those institutions.

But it must be borne in mind that, in addition to the action for annulment, there are various ways in which the legality of Community measures may be the subject of indirect challenge. First, there is the "plea of illegality," considered later in this chapter (p. 184). Secondly, an action for damages (Chapter 8) may put in issue the legality of a measure alleged to have injured the applicant: and in practice actions for damages have frequently led the Court to examine the legality of Community legislation. Thirdly, a reference from a national court to the Court of Justice for a preliminary ruling (Chapter 10) may be directed to the validity of any measure adopted by a Community institution, so that an aggrieved person may be able to obtain, not by a direct action in the Court of Justice but by proceedings originating in a national court, a ruling by the Court of Justice that a Community measure is invalid.

A. *Actions to Annul (Article 173)*

Our discussion will consider in sequence the following questions:

(1) What acts can be attacked?
(2) Who can attack?
(3) Within what time limit?
(4) On what ground?
(5) What effect has annulment?

1. *What acts can be attacked?*

Article 173(1) states: "The Court of Justice shall review the legality of acts of the Council and the Commission other than recommendations or opinions."

Having regard to the terms of Article 189, which lists the acts of the Council and the Commission as "regulations, directives, decisions, recommendations or opinions" one might expect that only the first three were subject to review under Article 173(1). The Court however has adopted a more liberal interpretation. What is required is an act binding in law, and the Court has always been prepared to look behind the label of an act to its substance. Thus, under the ECSC Treaty, in Cases 1 and 14/57 *Saar Tubes* [1957 and 1958] ECR 105 it was argued by the applicants that what was in form an opinion did in fact impose binding obligations, and the Court accepted that it had a duty to consider whether the act complained of, though in form and name an opinion, did constitute a disguised decision. In the event, it held that it was only an opinion and that consequently the action to annul was inadmissible (under Article 33 ECSC).

However, in Cases 8 to 11/66 *Cement-Convention* [1967] ECR 75 a "communication" issued by the Commission under Regulation 17, Article 15, to remove protection from certain cartels was held by the Court to constitute not a mere opinion but a decision (and consequently to be binding in law); the plea of inadmissibility under Article 173(1) raised by the Commission was accordingly rejected, and the Court proceeded to review the legality of the communication in issue.

On the other hand, the Court has not accepted as a reviewable act the "statement of objections" which, under the regulation governing competition proceedings, the Commission is required to send to a firm whose marketing practices are under investigation: Case 60/81 *IBM* v. *Commission* [1981] ECR 2639. Similarly, in Case 7/61 *Pigmeat* [1961] ECR 317, the Court made clear that the reasoned opinion which is required under Article 169 proceedings (discussed at p. 80, above) cannot be the subject of review for illegality under Article 173.

The *ERTA* case (Case 22/70 *Commission* v. *Council* [1971] ECR 263) well illustrates the bold approach of the Court to the interpretation of the term "acts" in Article 173(1). In this case the Commission challenged the action of the Council in laying down guidelines for Member States to follow in the negotiations to revise the European Road Transport Agreement, such action being allegedly a usurpation by the Council of a function reserved to the Commission by the EEC Treaty. The Court, although deciding against the Commission on the merits, held the action to be admissible: the Commission had *locus standi* (see below), and the Council's action in laying down guidelines did amount to an act having legally binding consequences for the Member States and one therefore reviewable under Article 173. On this last point the Court disagreed with the advocate general in whose view the Council's discussion of the guidelines could not constitute an act of the Council open to review under Article 173(1). The Court did not accept that the Article was confined to the category of acts (regulations, directives and decisions) enumerated as legally binding in Article 189. It held that "an action for annulment must...be available in the case of all measures adopted by the institutions, whatever their nature or form, which are intended to have legal effects."

Was there significance in the words "measures adopted by the *institutions*," when Article 173 refers only to "acts of the Council and the Commission..."? The question was raised ten years later whether acts of the European Parliament can be challenged under that Article. The fact that the question could arise may surprise the English lawyer, since the question seems excluded by the clear terms of Article 173—a point which illustrates the very different approach of Community law to constitutional texts. The first case, Case 230/81 *Luxembourg* v. *European Parliament* [1983] ECR 255 was inconclusive: Here the Government of Luxembourg challenged a resolution of the European Parliament purporting to decide that future sessions of the Parliament should be held in Strasbourg (and not, as previously, in either Strasbourg or Luxembourg). The Government argued that, under the Treaties, it was for the Member States to fix the seat of the Community institutions. The action was based in part on Article 38 ECSC which does provide for annulment (at the suit of a Member State or the Commission) of a measure adopted by the Parliament, but there is no corresponding provision in the EEC and Euratom Treaties and it was open to question whether a provision in the ECSC Treaty can confer jurisdiction in respect of acts common to the three Communities. It was easier to contend that the EEC Treaty governs such common acts. The difficulty then is that Article 173 does not refer to the Parliament. The action was also based on Article 173: it was argued that, by analogy with the *ERTA* decision, that Article provides a remedy against any measure of any institution having legal effects. The Court was content (typically) to allow the action under Article 38 ECSC.

The example set by Luxembourg was followed by the Council itself, which in 1982 brought proceedings under Article 173 (the Council having no standing under Article 38 ECSC) against the Parliament (Case 72/82) for annulment of the act of the President of the European Parliament declaring that the general budget of the European Communities for the financial year 1982 had been finally adopted. Here it could be argued that, although the gap in Article 173 can be explained historically by the fact that the Parliament had no legally binding powers when the EEC Treaty was drawn up, nevertheless with the development of the Parliament's budgetary powers the Treaty should be interpreted dynamically to avoid the development of a hiatus in the system of judicial protection. However the budgetary dispute was settled on the political level and the Council's action withdrawn.

Another case was brought by the Council (and by several Member States) against the Parliament in 1986 over the 1986 budget. Here it was alleged that the Parliament, which is empowered to increase, within certain limits, some heads of Community expenditure, had exceeded those limits and that the entire budget adopted by the declaration of the President was consequently void. The Council's action was expedited by the Court because of its urgency but before the action was heard and before the issue of admissibility

under Article 173 was decided the United Kingdom
obtained an interim order (see on interim measures
below, p. 237) from the President of the Court
suspending the implementation of the budget, the
United Kingdom having convinced the President that it
would otherwise suffer irreparable damage: Case 23/
86R, *United Kingdom* v. *European Parliament* [1986]
ECR 1085.

The Council's action against the Parliament was
successful: Case 34/86 [1986] ECR 2155, but by the
time the Court gave judgment it had already resolved
the issue of admissibility in yet another case brought
against the Parliament; Case 294/83 *Partie Ecologiste
'Les Verts'* v. *European Parliament* [1986] ECR 1339.
The Parliament had allocated funds from its own
budget to the political parties for an "information
campaign" leading up to the direct elections to the
Parliament to be held in 1984. The new French
environmentalist or "green" party complained that by
reserving only a limited proportion of funds to parties
putting up candidates for the first time in 1984 the
Parliament was discriminating in favour of parties
already represented in Parliament.

The Court held, in a judgment of great constitutional
significance, and in which it clearly had the budget case
in mind, that proceedings could be brought against the
Parliament under Article 173. The Court emphasised
that "the European Economic Community is a Community based on the rule of law, inasmuch as neither its
Member States nor its institutions can avoid a review of
the question whether the measures adopted by them are
in conformity with the basic constitutional charter, the
Treaty." Although Article 173 refers only to acts of the
Council and the Commission, the "general scheme" of
the Treaty is to make a direct action available against
"all measures adopted by the institutions ... which are
intended to have legal effects" (the *ERTA* case). The
Parliament is not expressly mentioned, according to the

Court, because, in its original version, the Treaty merely granted it powers of consultation and political control rather than the power to adopt measures intended to have legal effect *vis-à-vis* third parties. An interpretation of Article 173 which excluded measures adopted by the Parliament from those which could be contested would lead to a result contrary both to the spirit of the Treaty as expressed in Article 164 and to its system:

> "Measures adopted by the European Parliament in the context of the EEC Treaty could encroach on the powers of the Member States or of the other institutions, or exceed the limits which have been set to the Parliament's powers, without its being possible to refer them for review by the Court. It must therefore be concluded that an action for annulment may lie against measures adopted by the European Parliament intended to have legal effects *vis-à-vis* third parties."

The Court went on to find that the measures challenged by the Green Party in this case did have such effects and to declare them void. The judgment is of interest on other points to which we shall return below.

2. *Who can attack?*

(1) *Member States and Institutions* (*privileged applicants*)

In the first place Article 173(1) enumerates a Member State, the Council or the Commission as competent to bring an action to annul: they are accepted as having a sufficient legal interest to give them *locus standi* for such an action, and for this reason they are sometimes referred to as "privileged applicants." It does not matter that the Member State is attacking some act of a Community institution which relates to another Members State. Thus, in Case 6/54 *Netherlands* v. *High*

Authority [1954 to 1956] ECR 103, the Court permitted the Netherlands to seek annulment of a decision of the High Authority relating to German coal companies: not only Germany but the other Member States had a sufficient interest in the legality (or otherwise) of that decision. And in Case 41/83 *Italy* v. *Commission* [1985] ECR 873 the Italian Government challenged a competition decision of the Commission addressed to British Telecom. In recent years Member States have frequently challenged measures of the Council and Commission, and often with success.

Again, the Council has *locus standi* in relation to the acts of the Commission, and *vice versa*. Suits of this kind are not infrequent: one example is the ERTA case (22/70, discussed above).

Another is the pair of *Staff Salaries* cases (Case 81/72 *Commission* v. *Council* [1973] ECR 575; Case 70/74 *Commission* v. *Council* [1975] ECR 795). These cases concerned the Staff Regulations governing Community civil servants, which provide for an annual review of salaries by the Council after a report by the Commission. The Council is required to take into account various factors, including inflation, the rise in salaries of civil servants in the Member States, etc. How to quantify these factors had led to disagreement with the staff associations, to resolve which a scheme was eventually negotiated and embodied in a Council decision. The decision was expressed to be applicable for three years, but at the next annual review the Council made a salaries regulation which the Commission alleged to be in breach of the scheme. Accordingly, it sought to annul the regulation. The main issue before the Court was whether the decision of the Council was legally binding or a mere statement of policy, a "policy decision." The Court, declining to follow the view of Advocate General Warner, held the policy decision to be binding on the ground, first, that it laid down basic principles for reviewing salaries and, secondly, that it was announced as applicable for three years and consequently the Community staff were entitled to rely upon it. It followed that the salaries regulation was invalid in that it conflicted with the policy decision; the Council had therefore to devise new arrangements. These were in turn the subject of proceedings to annul brought by the Commission (Case 70/74, above). Staff salaries came before the Court again in Case 59/81 *Commission* v. *Council* [1982] ECR 3329, where the Council's measures were again declared unlawful.

Other examples are cases brought by the Commission against the Council where the Commission has challenged the legal basis of the measure adopted by the Council: *e.g.* Case 45/86 *Commission* v. *Council* [1987] ECR 1493 (the *GSP* case discussed below, p. 118).

A question which has arisen only recently is whether the European Parliament, although not named as a potential plaintiff, can bring proceedings under Article 173. The text of the Article seems decisively to exclude the possibility, and the notion of Parliament as a plaintiff before the Court is at first sight strange. Possibly the point would not have occurred to anyone if proceedings had not been taken *against* the Parliament, from 1981 onwards, as described above. But the Court accepted, in 1980, that the Parliament could intervene in proceedings before the Court (on such interventions, see below, p. 239); and in 1985 the Parliament's entitlement to bring actions under the more widely drafted Article 175 was upheld (below, p. 123). Once the Court had accepted, in 1986, as described above, that the Parliament could be sued although not named as a potential defendant under Article 173, the Parliament seems to have considered that justice or even symmetry required that it should equally be able to sue. Indeed, the Parliament's Draft Treaty establishing the European Union, adopted in 1984 (p. 328), had already proposed, in Article 43, equal rights of appeal and equal treatment for all the institutions before the Court of Justice; but the Inter-Governmental Conference which led to the adoption of the Single European Act rejected a proposal to amend Article 173 in the sense desired by the Parliament.

Not discouraged, the Parliament launched its first proceedings under Article 173 against the Council in 1987 (Case 302/87 *European Parliament* v. *Council The Times*, October 11, 1988) and contended that Article 173 must be interpreted extensively in favour of the Parliament, as it had been against the Parliament in *Les Verts* (Case 294/83 above) and in the 1986 budget case (Case 34/86 above). But the analogy is not complete. The Parliament can be sued because that is necessary to ensure the availability of judicial review of all Community acts: to secure the rule of law. There is no corresponding justification for giving the Parliament an unqualified right to sue.

The Court, in a carefully reasoned judgment, firmly rejected any right of the Parliament to sue under Article 173. It was not impressed by the argument either of symmetry or of justice: Parliament had its own political machinery for making its voice heard. Nor did the Court favour the compromise suggested by Advocate General Darmon who, while not contending that the Parliament had an unqualified right of action under Article 173, argued that it should be entitled to sue where its own interests or prerogatives are directly affected by a measure of the Council or Commission: otherwise, it would be in an uniquely unfavourable position compared not only with other institutions and Member States but even with private parties.

(2) *Natural and legal persons (non-privileged applicants)*
If the Parliament's standing to sue under Article 173(1) has been a vexed question, the most troublesome question has certainly been the defining of the sufficiency of interest requisite for natural and legal persons under Article 173(2) to challenge a measure not

addressed to them. The Court has not pursued a consistent policy, being anxious, on the one hand, to allow individuals or companies an opportunity to seek annulment of acts of the Council or the Commission, yet on the other hand fearful of finding itself overwhelmed by a flood of such suits. Accordingly, it is difficult to reconcile the conflicting cases. One conclusion is clear: it is now exceedingly difficult for an individual or company to satisfy the test of "direct and individual concern" as prescribed under the second limb of Article 173(2).

That limb allows only a decision to be attacked, not a (true) regulation: Case 789/79 *Calpak* [1980] ECR 1949. If the decision is addressed to the applicant, no problem arises. A common instance is where the Commission has issued a decision declaring the applicant to be infringing the competition law of the Community: landmark cases in which the applicants have then challenged such decisions include Cases 56 and 58/64 *Consten and Grundig* v. *Commission* [1966] ECR 299; Case 6/72 *Continental Can* [1973] ECR 215; Case 17/74 *Transocean Marine Paint Association* v. *Commission* [1974] ECR 1063. If however the decision is in the form of a regulation or is addressed to some other person, the applicant has then to establish that it is of direct and individual concern to him.

Anti-dumping regulations, inevitably, present special problems under Article 173(2), since they involve elements of both regulation and decision. Dumping, typically, is where an exporter in a third country sells goods into the Community at a lower price than he charges on his home market. To protect the Community against this form of unfair competition, the Council has adopted legislation under Article 113 EEC which enables duties to be imposed on such imports to counter the effects of dumping. After an investigation conducted by the Commission, provisional duty may be imposed by regulation of the Commission and definitive duty by

regulation of the Council. The procedure has elements
of a decision since the Commission will investigate
individual exporters and importers and base its finding
of dumping on those investigations. But the regulations
will be general in nature, will often extend to all
imports of the product from the third country in
question, and will affect importers generally, all of
whom are liable to pay the duty.

In the first anti-dumping case, *Japanese Ball-Bearings*
(Case 113/77 *NTN Toys* [1979] ECR 1185) the Court
accepted that the Japanese exporters could challenge
the Council regulation, but that was a somewhat
unusual regulation which named the exporters concerned. In Joined Cases 239 and 275/82 *Allied Corporation* v. *Commission* [1984] ECR 1005 the Court
accepted that exporters could challenge the regulations
regardless of whether they were named provided that
they were "concerned by the preliminary investigations," *i.e.* took part in the Commission investigation. A
similar test is applied, as we shall see, to complainants,
i.e. the Community industry seeking protection against
dumping. As for importers, if they are independent of
the exporter and are members of an open class, they
cannot challenge the regulation directly in the Court
under Article 173: their only remedy will be in the
national court, with the less satisfactory avenue of a
reference under Article 177 on the validity of the
regulation. It seems that only an importer who is
commercially related with an exporter, and whose resale
price is used as a basis for determining the export price,
can bring proceedings under Article 173: see most
recently the Order in Case 279/86R *Sermes* v. *Commission* [1987] ECR 3110.

By this complex series of decisions, the Court has
sought to reconcile, within the terms of the second
paragraph of Article 173, the need to avoid opening its
doors to an unlimited category of applicants with the
requirement to afford the possibility of direct judicial

review to those most immediately affected by anti-dumping measures.

Dumping apart, in relatively few cases have applicants succeeded in satisfying the Court of their direct and individual concern. In Cases 106 and 107/63 *Toepfer* v. *Commission* [1965] ECR 405, the Commission addressed to the German Government a decision authorising it to impose a levy on the import of maize. The applicants were two of the largest maize importers and sought to have the decision annulled. On the question of admissibility the Court held that the applicants were *directly* affected by the decision addressed to their Government, since a decision authorising protective measures of this kind was to be regarded as directly applicable. The applicants were also individually concerned because at the time of the decision the Commission knew that there were only 27 importers (of which the applicants were two) whose import applications could be affected by the decision in issue.

The Court here applied a formula which it had first propounded in the *Clementines* case (Case 25/62 *Plaumann* [1963] ECR at 107) where it stated:

> "Persons other than those to whom a decision is addressed may only claim to be individually concerned if that decision affects them by reason of certain attributes which are peculiar to them or by reason of circumstances in which they are differentiated from all other persons and by virtue of these factors distinguishes them individually just as in the case of the person addressed."

Plaumann, an importer of clementines, was held not to satisfy this test.

The *Plaumann* formula was again applied by the Court in Case 62/70 *Bock* v. *Commission* [1971] ECR 897, where the applicant was one of a limited category of importers of Chinese mushrooms who would be affected by a decision of the Commission addressed to the German Government authorising it to prohibit such mushroom imports, a prohibition which that Government had already made clear it wished to impose. At the date of the decision the number and identity of the importers concerned was already fixed and ascertainable, and this factor differentiated them from all other persons in accordance with the *Plaumann* formula, distinguishing Bock and his fellow importers individually just as in the case of the person addressed. Accordingly, the application was held admissible.

The *Apples* case (Cases 41 to 44/70 *International Fruit Company* v. *Commission* [1971] ECR 411) concerned not a decision but a regulation. The Commission had introduced a system whereby it issued licences for import of dessert apples into the EEC, on the basis of weekly data which Member States supplied setting out the licences applied for in each State; the Commission gave its decision by means of regulations. At the moment when the regulation was adopted, the number of applications was fixed and no new applications could be added. It was on the basis of the global amount applied for that the Commission decided what percentage of each individual application should be allowed. A Dutch apple importer objected to the reduction of its application and challenged the relevant regulation under Article 173. The Court held that the regulation had to be regarded as a bundle of individual decisions taken by the Commission, each of which, although in the form of a regulation, affected the legal position of one of the applicants. Thus, the decision was of individual concern to the Dutch importer within the terms of Article 173(2). As the decision directly affected the applicant, it was also of "direct concern" to him.

The Court did not attempt to reconcile this decision with the earlier case of *Compagnie Française Commerciale et Financière* v. *Commission* (Case 64/69 [1970] ECR 221) where it refused to accept Advocate General Roemer's view that the regulation in question was really a decision since the persons affected by it were a closed category whose identity was ascertainable. But in the later case of *C.A.M., SA* v. *Council and Commission* (Case 100/74 [1975] ECR 1393) the Court disregarded (*sub silentio*) the *Compagnie Française* case and followed its approach in the *Apples* case: since the applicant was one of a fixed and identifiable category he was individually concerned; and the Court also found that he was also directly concerned. It followed that the application was admissible.

The Court also seems to have felt driven to adopt a more liberal view of individual concern in the case of *Les Verts* (above, p. 101). There the decision in issue affected all political groupings which might decide to present candidates at the 1984 elections, a class whose members could not be identified at the date when the decision was taken. In its judgment the Court emphasised the uniqueness of the situation, in which those political groupings which were represented in the Parliament took part in the adoption of a decision dealing both with their own treatment and with that of rival groupings which were not represented. To regard only the former as individually concerned would give rise to unequal protection. The latter would be unable to prevent the allocation of funds before the beginning of the campaign: they would be able to challenge only the individual decisions refusing to reimburse sums greater than those provided for by the decision. The Court ultimately decided that the Parliament had no power to allocate funds for this purpose at all; and the Court seemed anxious to avoid a legal hiatus in which the Parliament could adopt a decision which the political groupings within Parliament would have no interest in challenging and which those outside Parliament would be debarred from challenging. Accordingly the Court did not insist on a strict definition of individual concern in this case. At bottom, the Court seems to have been guided in its decision by a sense of what Community public policy required.

As we have seen, Article 173(2) refers to "a decision addressed to another person" being open to challenge if the claimant can show the necessary direct and individual concern. In most cases the decision has been addressed to a Member State government, but the Court from the first saw no difficulty in interpreting "person" to include a government (*e.g. Toepfer*, above). A further and novel point of interpretation arose in Case 26/76 *Metro* v. *Commission* [1977] ECR 1875.

Here the Commission had addressed a decision to SABA, a German producer of electronic equipment. The decision followed a complaint lodged with the Commission by Metro, who operated as self-service wholesalers of such goods. SABA had refused to recognise Metro as distributors of their products because Metro was unable (or unwilling) to comply with their usual conditions of sale. Metro then asked the Commission to strike down these conditions as in restraint of competition and so contrary to Article 85 EEC; they invoked the procedure under Council Regulation 17 under which anyone with a "legitimate interest" may complain to the Commission of infringements of Article 85 and 86.

The Commission, after an investigation, concluded that, subject to some minor modifications, the SABA conditions did not infringe Article 85 and it addressed to SABA a decision to this effect. It also informed Metro of its decision.

Metro challenged the decision addressed to SABA. The Court upheld the action as admissible under Article 173(2). In a somewhat cryptic judgment, illuminated by the opinion of Advocate General Reischl, who invoked the *Plaumann* formula (above p. 108), the Court simply ruled that it was in the interests of a satisfactory administration of justice that a person lodging a complaint with the Commission should be able to institute proceedings before the Court to protect its legitimate interests; accordingly, Metro must be considered to be directly and individually concerned. Certainly, by complaining the applicants had "distinguished themselves individually" and "differentiated themselves" from self-service wholesalers generally (all of whom were affected by the conditions of sale in issue). As for directness, the judgment appears to endorse *sub silentio* the argument of the advocate general that, although the decision merely empowered SABA to maintain their sale conditions, it was a commercial certainty that they would embrace the decision in order to keep the system complained of by Metro.

The Court has adopted a similar approach in other proceedings analogous to competition proceedings. A complainant in anti-dumping proceedings can challenge a regulation it considers inadequate: Case 264/82 *Timex* v. *Council and Commission* [1985] ECR 849, or a refusal by the Commission to initiate a proceeding: Case 191/82 *FEDIOL* v. *Commission* [1983] ECR 2913. Similarly, where the Commission takes a decision under the treaty provisions governing State aids or subsidies (Articles 92 to 94), although there is no formal status for private complainants in the proceedings, and although an indefinite category of persons might be affected by an aid which distorted competition, the Court considered that a person who takes a part in the procedure comparable to that of a complainant was entitled to challenge the Commission's decision if that person's position in the market was significantly affected by the aid. Thus where the Commission decides that there is no aid incompatible with the common market and terminates the proceeding, the "complainant" can challenge that decision before the Court: Case 169/84 *COFAZ* v. *Commission* [1986] ECR 391.

As the above cases demonstrate the Court has laid more emphasis on the requirement of individual concern than that of direct concern: if the more difficult obstacle of the former can be overcome, the latter seems almost at times to be assumed. Nevertheless, the Court has sought to define direct concern and has done so by analogy to the doctrine of direct effect. Thus, if the addressee of the decision is left no margin of discretion as to how the decision is to be applied, then that decision will be of direct concern to the applicant. As we saw above, in *Toepfer*, the Commission's decision addressed to the German Government was one falling within the doctrine of direct effect: since the applicant could have invoked that doctrine in relation to the decision, the latter was also of direct concern to him. Likewise, in the *Japanese Ball-Bearings* cases direct concern was accepted because the national measures implementing the Community provisions in question were purely automatic. On the other hand, in Case 69/69 *Alcan* [1970] ECR 385, the applicant was not directly concerned because the two Member States to whom the decision (refusing them a certain import quota) was addressed retained a complete discretion how (if at all) to allocate any quota granted to them. Moreover, quite apart from the question of direct effect, direct concern is established if it can be shown (as in *Bock* above) that the addressee has already tied his own hands in advance of the decision; for there is then a close causal connection between the eventual decision and the application of that decision by the addressee with regard to the applicant. The same reasoning was extended, as we have just seen, in the *Metro* case.

On *locus standi* Article 33 ECSC differs in several respects from Article 173 EEC. In the first place, only undertakings (*entreprises*, in the French text) can sue and not individuals: and the right of action is further limited to undertakings engaged in production in the coal and steel industries (Article 80 ECSC). Secondly, the undertaking must show *either* that the challenged decision or recommendation (the term used in the earlier Treaty for a directive) is "individual in character" *or* that the decision or recommendation, although general in character, involves a misuse of power affecting that undertaking. Thirdly, there is no requirement under Article 33 ECSC of *direct* concern: no doubt because, under the scheme of the ECSC Treaty, the High Authority is the hub of the Community, decisions radiating directly from the High Authority to the undertakings without the mediation of the national authorities.

In the early decisions on this Article the Court adopted a liberal interpretation: the floodgate which the Court has hesitated to open too wide under Article 173 EEC could at most under Article 33 ECSC only admit the limited number of coal and steel undertakings. Thus, in Cases 7 and 9/54 *Groupement des Industries Sidérurgiques Luxembourgeoises* v. *High Authority* [1954–1956] ECR 175 the applicants brought proceedings under Article 33 ECSC against the implied refusal of the High Authority to declare illegal a Luxembourg levy on coal imports. The Luxembourg Government intervened in the proceedings to argue that the applicants had no *locus standi* as they were a steel-producing, not coal-producing firm. The Court had little difficulty in rejecting this plea. The Court agreed with the advocate general that there was no provision in the Treaty which required that the particular product made by the producer should be connected with the subject-matter of the dispute and that the silence of the Treaty on this point could not be interpreted in any manner which would be detrimental to companies. The Court also appeared to accept that the act being challenged (namely, the implied refusal of the High Authority to declare the levy illegal) was a decision "individual in character," that is, that it did apply to the applicants individually. This was hardly surprising as the Group represented the main consumers of coal in the Grand Duchy.

The absence of any reference to direct, as distinct from individual, concern in Article 33 ECSC reflects the quite different system of the earlier Treaty, in which the High Authority, true to its name, was to be the real source of power rather than the Member States. Hence, its relationship with the coal and steel enterprises was necessarily assumed to be direct, being almost that of overlord to vassals.

Under the EEC Treaty, covering as it does the entire economy, the Community's functions are normally exercised through the Member States; and it was therefore considered appropriate that anyone seeking to challenge a Community measure directly before the Court should have to show both individual and direct concern. In its earlier decisions on Article 173 EEC, however, the Court of Justice, perhaps conditioned by its experience under the ECSC Treaty, laid more emphasis on the first of these two requirements, as we have seen.

3. *Within what time limits?*

Article 173(3) EEC lays down a time limit of two months for bringing proceedings to annul. This period is calculated from the publication of the measure in issue, or from its notification to the applicant, or, in the absence of publication or notification, from the date when it came to his knowledge. Under Article 33 ECSC the corresponding time limit is one month.

So short a time limit as one or two months, while desirable in the interests of legal certainty, can give rise to problems. As we shall see below (p. 184) Article 184 (Article 36 ECSC) may provide a partial solution, and, as we have already noted (p. 96), other forms of challenge to validity escape such stringent time limits. Moreover, in Cases 6 and 11/69 *Commission* v. *French Republic* [1969] ECR 523 the Court was prepared to entertain a plea by the French Government that the Commission had reached a decision in a field reserved by the EEC Treaty to the Member States, even though the time limits to challenge under Article 173 had expired, for in the Court's words, "if this allegation were valid, the above-mentioned decision would lack all legal basis in the Community legal system." It seems possible that the Court was here adopting from French administrative law the notion, well developed there, of the *inexistence* of an administrative act taken wholly without legal authority: such an act may be declared non-existent even outside the normal French time limit (of two months) for annulment proceedings.

4. *On what grounds?*

Article 173 EEC sets out four grounds for annulment. These are:

    (a) lack of competence (or authority)
    (b) infringement of an essential procedural requirement
    (c) infringement of the EEC Treaty or of any rule of law relating to its application
    (d) misuse of powers

All four grounds appear to raise only questions of law, not of fact nor of the merits of the challenged act. But the Court may be led inevitably into a review of the facts as found by the Council or Commission if, for example, the issue is whether there is such a manifest error of fact as to constitute a violation of law. The lines between the four grounds are fluid and one or more may be pleaded in the alternative or in combination. The Court is always at pains to avoid undue formalism in proceedings brought before it.

Historically, the grounds are derived from French administrative law where the *Conseil d'Etat* has elaborated in its case law the precise meaning of the corresponding French terms: *incompétence, vice de forme, violation de la loi, détournement de pouvoir.* Community law, however, has a life of its own, and reference to French decisions would, at best, be only persuasive authority in the Court of Justice. Moreover, German and, latterly, English administrative law have influenced the development of the grounds of review at Luxembourg.

The grounds in Article 173 EEC, with certain limited exceptions, correspond to those in Article 33 ECSC. Some of the illustrative cases now to be discussed derive from the ECSC Treaty.

Thus, Case 9/56 *Meroni* v. *High Authority* [1958] ECR 133 is a useful example of both lack of competence and an infringement of the ECSC Treaty. The High Authority imposed certain levies on scrap iron on the basis of decisions taken by a subordinate body (the Scrap Bureau) to which the Authority had purported to delegate its powers. The Court quashed the levies on the grounds, first, that the Treaty had been infringed inasmuch as it did not permit the Authority to delegate its decision-making powers (*delegatus non potest delegare*), and secondly, that there was a lack of competence on the part of the Authority to proceed as it had.

Procedural infringements are commonly invoked, and it is then for the Court to assess whether the infringement is of an *essential* requirement. Thus, in Cases 8 to 11/66 *Cement-Convention* case [1967] ECR 75, it was pleaded that the failure to give sufficient reasons for the decisions in question constituted the infringement of an essential procedural requirement, namely, the general rule in Article 190 that decisions of the Commission shall state the reasons on which they are based. The same Article was successfully invoked in Case 24/62 *Germany* v. *Commission* [1963] ECR 63, when the Commission partially rejected Germany's application to import a large quantity of wine from outside the Community for blending into "Brennwein" for domestic consumption. By way of reasons the Commission simply stated that its decision was based on "information that has been gathered indicating that the production of wines of this nature within the Community is amply sufficient."

The Court explained the purposes of the requirement of reasoning as follows:

> "In imposing upon the Commission the obligation to state reasons for its decision, Article 190 is not taking mere formal considerations into account but seeks to give an opportunity to the parties of defending their rights, to the Court of exercising its supervisory functions and to Member States and to all interested nationals of ascertaining the circumstances in which the Commission has applied the Treaty".

To attain these objectives a decision must set out, in a concise but clear and relevant manner, the principal issues of law and of fact upon which it is based.

In the *GSP* case (Case 45/86 *Commission* v. *Council* [1987] ECR 1493) the Commission challenged two Council regulations which, under the Generalised System of Preferences (GSP), granted favourable tariffs to developing countries. The Commission had no objection to the substance of the regulations but complained that the regulations did not specify their treaty basis as Article 190 of the Treaty requires. The Commission had taken the view that such regulations could be based on Article 113 (and could therefore be adopted by majority vote) while the Council's position was that such regulations went beyond the scope of Article 113 and could be adopted only by the use of Article 235 (and therefore unanimously). The Court held that it was essential in such a case to specify the legal basis of the measures, that the failure to do so infringed the requirement of a statement of reasons, and that the regulations should have been adopted on the basis of Article 113.

Another instance of an "essential procedural requirement" is the requirement that the Council should consult the European Parliament on proposals for legislation when the Treaty so prescribes. Thus in Cases 138 and 139/79 *Roquette* and *Maizena* v. *Council* [1980] ECR 3333 and 3393 producers of isoglucose sought the annulment of a Council regulation imposing a levy on isoglucose, contending that the requirement of consultation of the European Parliament had not been observed as the Parliament, although asked for its opinion, had not given its opinion when the regulation was adopted by the Council. The Parliament intervened to support the applicants (see p. 240) and the Court annulled the regulation.

The third ground of annulment includes, as we have seen, both treaty infringements and an infringement of any rule of law relating to the application of the relevant Treaty. This last expression has been liberally construed by the Court. Thus, it includes all legislation made pursuant to the Treaties (*e.g.* regulations or directives) and such general principles as are recognised in international law, or such "general principles common to the laws of the Member States" as the Court deems to be applicable in the particular case.

The expression "general principles common to the laws of the Member States" is only expressly referred to in Article 215 EEC where these principles are declared the basis of the non-contractual (below, p. 134) liability of the Community. The principles, however, have been extended beyond this narrow but important context and may be invoked under other Articles, such as Article 173. Moreover, despite the absence of any reference to such general principles in the ECSC Treaty, the Court has in several ECSC cases (some prior to the EEC Treaty) invoked these principles. Examples include the principle of proportionality of administrative acts (in Case 8/55 *Fédéchar* v. *High Authority* [1954–1956] ECR 245), and the principles of legal certainty and of due process (in Cases 42 and 49/59 *SNUPAT v. High Authority* [1961] ECR 53). More recently, there has been an important extension of this doctrine of general principles to embody fundamental rights, as in Case 29/69 *Stauder* v. *Ulm* [1969] ECR 419, the *Internationale Handelsgesellschaft* case (Case 11/70 [1970] ECR 1125), and the Second *Nold* case (Case 4/73 [1974] ECR 491) in which the Court roundly declared that "fundamental rights form an integral part of the general principles of law, the observance of which it ensures" (below, p. 303). But whereas, in the cases mentioned, the Court finally concluded that there had been no breach of the principles invoked, more than lip service was paid to the principles in the *Transocean Marine Paint Association* case, in which the Court decided, at the prompting of Advocate General Warner, that the Commission had acted in breach of the principle of natural justice as embodied in the maxim *audi alteram partem* (Case 17/74 [1974] ECR 1063).

General principles of law have proved of great importance in the review by the Court of legislation and decisions, both under Article 173 and in references on validity (below, p. 197) under Article 177. They also provide a striking example of the creative development of the law. For these reasons they warrant treatment in a separate chapter (Chapter 15), where the Court's role as law-maker is explored, and which illustrates the use of general principles to challenge Community measures.

The remaining ground for review under Article 173 EEC is misuse of powers. This is a well developed notion in some continental systems of administrative law: the French text speaks of *détournement de pouvoir*, a notion familiar in French administrative law. English law variously acknowledges the same notion under such labels as abuse of power, misuse of power or bad faith. As interpreted by the Court, the term includes not only the use of a power for an unlawful purpose but also its use for a purpose, itself lawful, but not the one contemplated in conferring the power in question. An early decision to explore this ground under Article 33 ECSC was Case 1/54 *French Republic* v. *High Authority* [1954–1956] ECR 1.

In this case the High Authority had taken three decisions purportedly on the basis of Article 60 ECSC so as to prevent discrimination in prices. The French Government argued that the real object of the Authority had been to secure a general reduction in prices and the prevention of price agreements: for these objects the Authority should have exercised the powers conferred upon it by Articles 61 and 65. Accordingly, it was argued, there had been a misuse of powers. The Court held that there was no misuse of powers where (as in the case) the act complained of has as its dominant or primary object the purpose for which that power is conferred, even though the act achieves incidentally some other object which is not properly the object of the power in question.

By contrast with the EEC Treaty, under Article 33 ECSC misuse of powers may be invoked by undertakings to challenge general, as distinct from individual, decisions or recommendations. This point arose in Case 8/55 *Fédéchar* v. *High Authority* [1954–1956] ECR 245. The applicants were an association of Belgian collieries. They challenged the validity of a decision of the Authority fixing lower prices for coal as a result of which three collieries within the Association would receive lower compensation payments. The Authority contested the argument of the Association that the decision was on that account individual in character and so open to review on any of the four grounds. The Authority maintained that the fact that a decision might have different effects for different collieries was not relevant in determining the nature of the decision: a decision was general or individual according to the scope of its application, and the decision in question had a general character as it was intended to be general in effect and to apply to all the firms falling within its scope. The Court accepted this argument, with the consequence that the applicants were limited to establishing a misuse of powers as the only ground for annulling the decision, and this they failed to show on the facts.

5. *What effect has annulment?*

Article 176 states that the institution whose act has been declared void shall be required to take the necessary measures to comply with the Court's judgment. Article 34 ECSC is in similar terms.

The Court has accepted the principle that a challenged act, like the curate's egg, may be bad in part only. Thus, in Cases 56 and 58/64 *Consten and Grundig* v. *Commission* [1966] ECR 299, C and G had entered into an agreement whereby C was to be sole agent for G in France. Competitors wishing to sell G's products in France complained to the Commission that the agreement infringed Article 85 EEC. The Commission agreed with the complainants and issued a decision declaring an infringement of Article 85. This decision was challenged by C and G under Article 173. The Court held that the decision was partly valid and partly invalid inasmuch as the agreement in part infringed Article 85 but in part did not. The Court followed in this respect its earlier decision in Case 6/54 *Netherlands* v. *High Authority* [1954–1956] ECR 103, under the ECSC Treaty, where part only of a decision was annulled for lack of adequate reasons. Not all the national laws of the Member States permit such severability of the good from the bad.

Where a regulation is annulled, Article 174(2) expressly provides that the Court may, if it considers this necessary, state which of the effects of the void regulation shall be considered as definitive. Thus, as we have seen above in Case 81/72 *Commission* v. *Council* [1973] ECR 575, a Council regulation laying down a scale for staff salaries within the Community institutions was declared void, but in order that salaries could continue to be paid the Court ordered that the regulation should continue in operation until the Council could pass a new (and valid) regulation. Similarly in the *GSP* case the Court ruled that, having regard to the circumstances of the case and the requirements of legal certainty, the effects of the annulled regulations must be treated as definitive.

B. *Actions for Inactivity (Article 175)*

The authors of both the ECSC and the EEC Treaties recognised that a remedy should be available not only where an institution had acted illegally but also where it had failed to act. Article 175 EEC and Article 35 ECSC seek to fill this gap.

Article 175(1) states:

> "Should the Council or the Commission, in infringement of this Treaty, fail to act, the Member States and the other institutions of the Community may bring an action before the Court of Justice to have the infringement established."

And Article 175(3) confers upon individuals and companies the right to complain to the Court that an institution has failed to address to the complainant any act other than a recommendation or an opinion.

It should be noted that Article 175 permits the European Parliament, as one of "the other institutions of the Community," to bring the Council or Commission before the Court for a failure to act.

The Parliament, having threatened to do so on several previous occasions, exercised this right for the first time in proceedings which it introduced against the Council in 1983 complaining of the latter's failure to adopt an adequate transport policy as required by the EEC Treaty (Article 74 *et seq.*): Case 13/83 [1985] ECR

1513. The Court rejected various objections by the Council to the admissibility of the action and upheld the action in part.

An action under Article 175 is only admissible if the institution in default has first been called upon to act. If then, within two months of being so called upon, the institution has not defined its position, the action may be brought within a further period of two months. This procedure is prescribed by Article 175(2).

There are two further obstacles to success in proceedings under Article 175 which are more difficult to overcome. The first arises from the requirement that the applicant (if not a Member State or a Community institution) must apparently show that the desired act would have been addressed to him, when it will often be the case that he wanted the defendant (normally the Commission) to take a decision in respect of someone else: for example against another undertaking which he alleges is infringing the EEC competition rules. It would be more consistent with the purpose of Article 175 if the same test of *locus standi* were applied as under Article 173, namely that the desired act would have been of direct and individual concern to him: see the advocate-general's opinion in Case 15/71 *Mackprang* v. *Commission* [1971] ECR 797 at 807–808.

Secondly, the defendant will be able to meet the complaint of failure to act if it has "defined its position." As the cases show (see for example Case 48/65 *Lütticke* v. *Commission* [1966] ECR 19 and Case 125/78 *GEMA* v. *Commission* [1979] ECR 3173), the Commission may be able to "define its position" without adopting a measure which can be challenged under Article 173. In contrast, under the ECSC Treaty, the decisions of the Court establish that a complaint of inactivity (under Article 35) can be met only by a binding act, which will itself be liable to challenge under Article 33. There is therefore an apparent gap in the protection afforded under the EEC Treaty, although the existence of such a gap has been ingeniously disputed (see T. C. Hartley, *The Foundations of European Community Law* (2nd ed., 1988), pp. 406–409). The fact remains that, with the exception of the *Transport* case brought by the European Parliament, no action brought under Article 175 EEC has to date succeeded, and the remedy has proved ineffective for private litigants.

C. *Plea of Illegality (Article 184)*

This (to English ears) curiously named remedy is derived from French administrative law where it is known as *l'exception d'illégalité*. A close parallel in English procedure is where a challenge is raised collaterally to the validity of a statutory instrument or byelaw in a prosecution for its infringement. In Community law it is a means of challenging an illegal act, even after the lapse of the time limit imposed by Article 173. The plea, if successful, renders the act, not void, but "inapplicable." This is made clear by the language of Article 184: "Notwithstanding the expiry of the period laid down in the third paragraph of Article 173, any party may, in proceedings in which a regulation of the Council or of the Commission is in issue, plead the grounds specified in the first paragraph of Article 173, in order to invoke before the Court of Justice the inapplicability of that regulation."

The remedy under Article 184 is an important supplement to that given under Article 173. In the first place it mitigates the effect of the very short time limit under the latter Article. For, although the regulation in issue may now have become immune from annulment by lapse of time, a decision based upon that regulation may be challenged by the person affected through the plea of illegality. This will permit a party to have the decision set aside upon satisfying the Court that the "parent" regulation is tainted with illegality on one or more of the grounds set out in Article 173. The Court will then hold the regulation "inapplicable" in the particular case, so that the decision becomes without legal foundation.

Whereas Article 173 may be invoked, as we have seen, against a wide category of acts, the plea of illegality only lies, on a strict reading of Article 184, against a regulation. But in Case 92/78 *Simmenthal* v. *Commission* [1979] ECR 777, the Court of Justice interpreted Article 184 as giving expression to a general principle conferring upon any party to proceedings the right to challenge, for the purpose of obtaining the annulment of a decision of direct and individual concern to that party, the validity of previous acts of the institutions which form the legal basis of the decision that is being attacked, but which that party lacked *locus standi* to challenge under Article 173.

Thus, in *Simmenthal,* the applicant was allowed to bring the plea against a general notice of tender issued by the Commission for the purchase, by importers such as Simmenthal, of meat held by an intervention agency. The general notice, though not in form a regulation, was held to be analogous in effect and normative in character: it could therefore be challenged by way of the plea of illegality although the applicant was directly and individually affected only by the consequent decision of the Commission which fixed the price for tenders from Italian importers at a price above that offered by Simmenthal, thereby leading to the rejection of the tender.

The plea of illegality reconciles two otherwise conflicting policies of Community law. On the one hand, there is the policy, in the interest of legal certainty (*sécurité juridique*), of making the acts of Community institutions unimpeachable after short time limits; on the other, there is the countervailing policy, exemplified in Article 184 (Article 36 ECSC), of not allowing an illegal act, although perfected by lapse of time, to "father" further illegal acts: a party affected

thereby may challenge the offspring as illegal because
of the original illegality of the parent regulation.
If the challenge succeeds, the regulation is rendered
inapplicable in the particular case. To that extent,
one may speak of the "relative nullity" of the
regulation, that is, relative to the particular party who
has invoked the plea. But the regulation is not thereby
rendered absolutely null and void: in the unlikely
event of it being invoked again to found a further
decision, a party affected by that decision will be
obliged, in turn, to invoke the plea: otherwise the
decision will be valid.

The plea is also important in another respect. We
have seen that the rules of *locus standi* under Article
173 are very restrictive so far as actions by individuals
or companies are concerned. In particular, a private
party cannot challenge a regulation, unless it is in
substance a decision of direct and individual concern to
him. The plea, however, permits the private party to
plead the illegality of any regulation (or a general
decision or recommendation under the ECSC Treaty)
which is now being applied in a specific decision
affecting him.

It should be emphasised that the plea does not
provide an independent cause of action but can only be
invoked where proceedings are already properly before
the Court under some other Article of the Treaties. The
Court has made this clear in the *Wöhrmann* and *Dalmas*
cases relating to Article 184 EEC and Article 36(3)
ECSC respectively (Cases 31 and 33/62 [1962] ECR 501
and Case 21/64 [1965] ECR 175). Commonly, the plea is
made in conjunction with an action to annul under
Article 173 (or Article 33 ECSC). But in Cases 42 and
49/59 *SNUPAT* v. *High Authority* [1961] ECR 53, it was
invoked in an action for inactivity under Article 35
ECSC. It could also arise in a staff case under Article
179 EEC (see Case 20/71 *Sabbatini* v. *European
Parliament*, p. 165, below).

An illustration of the plea is provided by Case 9/56 *Meroni* v. *High Authority* [1958] ECR 133, a case arising under the ECSC Treaty and involving, *inter alia*, Article 36(3) which states:

> "In support of its appeal, a party may, under the same conditions as in the first paragraph of Article 33 of this Treaty, contest the legality of the decision or recommendation which that party is alleged not to have observed."

M was appealing against a decision of the High Authority of October 24, 1956 which imposed a pecuniary obligation and was accordingly enforceable pursuant to Article 92 ECSC. By the decision the Authority requested M to pay a levy on scrap bought by M for its steel production. This decision was based upon two general decisions (No. 22 of 1954 and No. 14 of 1955) which founded the general system of levies on scrap imports, a system administered by a special "Scrap Bureau." To support its action (under Article 33 ECSC) challenging the decision of October 24, 1956, M alleged (under Article 36(3) ECSC) the illegality of decisions Nos. 22/54 and 14/55 on grounds which we have previously discussed. The Authority argued that M's case should be dismissed as the time limit of one month under Article 33 had long expired so that the question of the illegality of decisions Nos. 22/54 and 14/55 was out of time and statute-barred.

The Court held that the plea of illegality could be raised by M under Article 36(3). For, although the language of Article 36 is limited to appeals against pecuniary penalties, the Article is the application of a general principle, namely, the plea of illegality, and this can be raised at any time to challenge the irregularity of general decisions or recommendations upon which the individual decision is based. The plea, however, cannot lead to the annulment of the general decision but only to the annulment of the individual decision based upon it.

The Court went still further in its bold interpretation of Article 36(3). For it proceeded to hold that, notwithstanding the words "under the same conditions as in the first paragraph of Article 33," the scope of the plea was not limited to misuse of powers, despite this being the sole ground upon which a private party could challenge a general decision under Article 33: rather, all the four grounds could be invoked in support of the plea. As we saw in the previous discussion of this case, M successfully pleaded the grounds of both lack of competence and infringement of the Treaty.

Having considered the nature of the plea, we must now examine by whom it may be made. The plea may not be invoked by a Community institution, for the apparent purpose of this remedy is to protect the interests of a private party against the threatened application of an illegal general act, such as a regulation. Moreover, Community institutions are not subject to the restrictive rules of *locus standi* applicable to private parties in annulment proceedings: the Council or Commission have an unrestricted opportunity to challenge general acts under Article 173, subject only to the two months time limit.

So far as concerns private parties, an individual or a company can rely upon Article 184, but under Article 36(3) ECSC the plea of illegality may be invoked only by the limited class of undertakings having *locus standi* under Article 33 ECSC (above, p. 113).

Under Article 184 EEC the extent to which a Member State may invoke the plea is not entirely settled. In Case 32/65 *Italy* v. *Council and Commission* [1966] ECR 389 the Court impliedly accepted that a Member State could do so when challenging a regulation under Article 173: Italy there invoked Article 184 to extend its challenge to earlier (and related) regulations. The justification for this is questioned by some authors on the ground that a Member State has the same opportunity as the Council or Commission to

challenge any act, including regulations, directly under
Article 173. The Court went some way to recognise the
point in Case 156/77 *Commission* v. *Belgium* [1978]
ECR 1881 where, in the course of enforcement
proceedings brought against Belgium by the Commission under Article 93 in respect of a prohibited State aid
(above, p. 86), the Belgian Government sought to
invoke the plea against a specific decision addressed to
it which it had failed to challenge directly and timeously
by an action under Article 173. The Court ruled that
the plea "can in no case be invoked by a Member State
to whom an individual decision has been addressed." If,
then, a Member State may invoke the plea against a
regulation, but not against an individual decision
addressed to it, the question remains open whether it
may do so against a directive, which may not be
individual in character but may be addressed to it.

For the comparative lawyer the plea is a particular
illustration of the insertion into the Treaties by the
founding Member States of a concept well known in
civil law systems but one which the common lawyer of
the United Kingdom or the Irish Republic hardly
recognises as a form of judicial review, although in
practice it is common enough for the substantive or
procedural validity of byelaws, regulations or executive
action to be raised as a defence in proceedings taken to
enforce administrative decisions.

Chapter 8

PLENARY JURISDICTION

Introduction

The title of this chapter calls for explanation, especially for common lawyers. In French administrative law a broad division is made, in suits brought to the administrative courts, between actions to annul and *recours de pleine juridiction*, that is, actions where the court is asked to exercise its fullest powers, for example by awarding damages against the administration or by itself revising (as distinct from merely quashing) the administrative act submitted to it. This notion of plenary jurisdiction was carried over into the EEC Treaty as one familiar to French and other continental systems of administrative law. It appears, for instance, in Article 172 EEC where, in the English text, the Court is given "unlimited jurisdiction" in regard to penalties provided for in the regulations made by the Council pursuant to the Treaty. This means that the Court can not only cancel such a penalty but also alter its amount. This is made explicit in Article 17 of Regulation 17/62 of the Council (relating to competition) which states:

"The Court shall have unlimited jurisdiction within the meaning of Article 172 of the Treaty to review decisions whereby the Commission has fixed a fine or periodic penalty payment; it may cancel, reduce or increase the fine or periodic penalty payment imposed."

The Court's plenary jurisdiction in the above sense includes, or used to include, the following categories of actions:

(a) Actions to review penalties (Article 172 EEC, Article 36(2) ECSC);
(b) So-called "staff cases" involving disputes between the Communities and their staff in relation to their terms of service (Article 179 EEC);
(c) Actions for damages based upon the non-contractual liability of the Communities (Article 178 EEC, Article 40 ECSC).

Category (b) has now been transferred into the jurisdiction of the Court of First Instance and may only reach the Court of Justice on appeal (see Chapter 5, above); this category is the subject of a separate chapter below (Chapter 9). Category (a) has already been briefly referred to (above, p. 131). The present chapter will be concerned with category (c). But first reference must be made to the contractual (as distinct from the non-contractual) liability of the Communities.

Contractual liability of the Communities

Liability on the part of the Communities may obviously arise in contract as well as in tort: such is the wide range of their activities and functions. In the EEC Treaty, Article 215 draws a distinction, in the terminology more familiar to continental lawyers, between contractual and non-contractual liability, although the latter term, because of its residuary character, could extend beyond tort into the field, for example, of restitution. Under Article 215(1) contractual liability is governed by the law applicable to the contract in question. The law referred to will be whichever national law governs that contract as its proper law, and any litigation arising on the contract will come before the relevant national court.

The jurisdiction of the national courts is exclusive; for the jurisdiction of the Court of Justice arises only where it is expressly conferred by the Treaties, and there is no provision conferring jurisdiction on the Court in these cases, as there is (under Article 178 EEC) in cases of non-contractual liability. Only where the contract contains an arbitration clause conferring jurisdiction in any dispute upon the Court of Justice (as Article 181 EEC and Article 153 Euratom permit) will a question of contractual liability come before the Communities' own Court: *e.g.* Euratom research contracts usually contain such clauses.

Articles 181 EEC and 153 Euratom are applicable whether the contract in question be categorised as "public" or "private"—a distinction derived from French administrative law and embodied in the terms of the Articles.

For a case involving such a contract with Euratom, see Case 23/76 *Pellegrini* [1976] ECR 1807, where the contract included an arbitration clause conferring jurisdiction upon the Court; it also provided that the contract was to be governed by Italian law: the Court accepted jurisdiction and resolved the dispute in accordance with Italian law. Similarly, contracts made between the Commission and universities in the Member States for the provision of various technical services usually embody an arbitration clause and provide for the contract to be governed by the national law of the university in question or of the seat of the Community institution concerned (in the case of the Commission, Belgium). In such cases the Court may find itself determining substantive questions of national law and treating such questions as ones of law (of which it has judicial notice) and not of fact (for which it would require expert evidence). Moreover, such cases in contract are the only instances in which a private individual may find himself the defendant before the Court in a direct action brought by the Community: in Case 426/85 *Commission* v. *Zoubek* [1986] ECR 4057 the Commission invoked Article 181 EEC to recover, under an arbitration clause, an advance paid to a journalist who had failed to produce a report which it had commissioned.

For avoidance of doubt, Article 183 EEC makes explicit that the Communities may be a party to a dispute brought before a court or tribunal of a Member State. Thus, "should the Court of Justice purchase some stationery in Luxembourg from a Luxembourg supplier and then, to imagine the unimaginable, default on the purchase price, the supplier would have his remedy in the Luxembourg courts according to Luxembourg law" (Lord Mackenzie Stuart, "The Non-Contractual Liability of the European Economic Community," Maccabaean Lecture in Jurisprudence 1975, 4).

Special considerations apply to contracts of employment entered into by Community institutions with their officials and other servants. As we shall see in the next chapter, such staff disputes were previously a separate head of the Court's jurisdiction under Article 179 EEC and so fell outside the sphere of application of Articles 178 and 215 EEC: Case 9/75 *Meyer-Burckhardt* [1975] ECR 1171: they now come within the jurisdiction of the Court of First Instance. The law applicable to these contracts will be that laid down in the official Staff Regulations or Conditions of Employment or, in default, "the general rules of administrative law": see, for this phrase, Cases 43, 45, 48/59 *Von Lachmüller* v. *Commission* [1960] ECR 463; also Case 1/55 *Kergall* v. *Common Assembly* [1954–1956] ECR 151.

Non-contractual (including tortious) actions against the Community

This clear-cut pattern in contract contrasts with the Communities' non-contractual liability. Here Article 178 EEC confers exclusive jurisdiction on the Court, by virtue of Article 183.

Why there should be this fundamental divergence in the treatment of contractual and non-contractual liability of the Communities is an interesting question. M. Lagrange, a former advocate general of the Court, suggests an historical explanation (M. Lagrange in [1965–66] 3 C.M.L Rev. 32). The framers of the ECSC Treaty saw that an independent legal order required special provision to be made for the legal liabilities of the Community arising from contract or of a non-contractual character. Contractual liability could be left to be governed by the more or less uniform principles found in the national laws of the original Member States. But non-contractual liability raised questions of delicacy and importance involving the activities of the Community as a "public authority": the rules governing the liability of public authorities differed considerably in the national laws of the various Member States, nor might they have been wholly appropriate to apply unchanged to the liability of the Community. Accordingly, a conscious choice was made to vest in the Court of Justice exclusive jurisdiction over the non-contractual liability of the Community and to entrust the Court with the fashioning of an independent Community law to govern such liability, guided only by the broad terms of Article 40 ECSC (and later Article 215(2) EEC, Article 188(2) Euratom).

M. Lagrange points out that the terms of Article 40 ECSC were borrowed directly from French administrative law. For that system was felt the most appropriate, since, unlike the systems prevailing in the other five Member States, France had entrusted jurisdiction over the tortious liability of public authorities exclusively to its administrative courts (in particular the *Conseil d'Etat*); moreover, that liability was governed by its own public law principles, elaborated in praetorian fashion by the *Conseil d'Etat* in complete independence of the private law principles enshrined in the Civil Code: see the landmark decision of *Blanco* in the *Tribunal des Conflits* February 1, 1873.

The ECSC Treaty therefore adopted the French solution of vesting in one and the same jurisdiction actions for the annulment of official acts and suits for damages arising from the tortious liability of public authorities. In this way, the Court of Justice would be fully equipped to exercise the most effective judicial control over Community institutions. This solution had the added advantage of excluding the national courts from sitting in judgment upon the administrative activities of Community institutions. To have permitted this would have threatened, it was thought, the Community's independence.

Subsequently, the principles in this respect embodied in the ECSC Treaty were carried over without substantial modification into the EEC and Euratom Treaties.

In the result, Articles 178 and 215(2) EEC, read together, render unnecessary any recourse to the principles of private international law so far as the Communities' non-contractual liability is concerned. For Article 178 settles categorically the question of which court shall have jurisdiction, and Article 215(2) determines what principles of substantive law shall govern that liability. In effect, for such liability the *lex causae* is to be the *lex fori*: the Community Court is to apply Community law. What, however, Article 215(2) offers as the Community law governing non-contractual liability is a mere reference to "the general principles common to the laws of the Member States." This vague formula has been left for the Court itself to elaborate in a series of cases. Dependent on the accidents of litigation, the working out of a consistent body of principles is still far from complete. Moreover, the Court has shown itself properly cautious in not wishing to expose the Communities to a flood of speculative claims in damages. The account which follows is therefore necessarily tentative, but the dearth of clear principle does not mean that the subject is not of vital importance as completing the armoury of remedies which the individual needs for his legal protection within the Communities.

Parenthetically, we may observe that the Court has also invoked the same concept of general principles, by way of analogy, in cases not involving liability under Article 215. This wider development of the concept, outside the context of non-contractual liability, calls for separate consideration (Chapter 15).

So far as non-contractual liability is concerned, "the general principles common to the laws of the Member States," to which Article 215(2) refers, provide no certain guide in this matter. There does not exist within the 12 countries of the Communities a common *corpus* of legal principles governing State liability in tort. Comparative study of the 12 national laws (or rather 13, as the Scottish law of reparation is distinct from the English law of tort) is a regular exercise of the Court in the preparation of cases and of the advocates general in their opinions; but, as Professors Kapteyn and VerLoren van Themaat well remark (*Introduction to the Law of the European Communities* (1973), p. 94):

> "This use of the comparative technique is not governed by an *a priori* intent to find the greatest common denominator; rather is it governed by an intent to trace elements from which such legal principles and rules can be built up for the Community as will offer an adequate, fair, and fruitful solution for the questions with which the Court is confronted."

In this free-ranging enquiry the Court has established certain essential elements for Community liability: there must be damage, an illegal act on the part of the Community, and a causal link between the damage and the act complained of. A number of leading cases illustrate these elements.

In Cases 5, 7 and 13–24/66 *Kampffmeyer* v. *Commission* [1967] ECR 245, a group of cereal importers, K and others, sued the Commission for damages in respect of its decision to authorise the German Government to take certain "safeguard measures" in the cereal market. Such measures could only be taken legally if there was a threat of "serious disturbances" in the market. In the earlier case of *Toepfer* (Cases 106 and 107/63, p. 108 above) the Court had held that this particular decision of the Commission must be annulled as the Commission had had no grounds to expect serious disturbances. K and the other importers proved that they had been prejudiced by the illegal decision and claimed damages accordingly. The Court found there was liability in principle on the part of the Commission arising from what it categorised as a *"faute de service."* But the Court deferred a decision on the amount of damages until the plaintiffs had exhausted any remedy they might have against the German Government in the German courts (this latter aspect of the case is returned to later).

As this case shows, although Article 215(2) EEC refers simply to the Community making good any damage caused by its institutions or by its servants in the course of their duties, the practice of the Court appears to require a finding of fault on the part of the Community. The importation of the concept of *faute* into the interpretation of Article 215(2) was no doubt influenced by the fact that the corresponding Article in the earlier ECSC Treaty (Article 40) specifically based liability upon fault. The Court has usually adopted the distinction known to French administrative law between a *faute de service* and a *faute personnelle*, that is a fault in the functioning of the system as distinct from a purely personal fault by the individual Community servant not linked with his official functions. The former concept of French law is wide enough to overlap with what an English lawyer would regard simply as maladministration, to be redressed, if at all, through the

Parliamentary Commissioner for Administration: the more narrow English rules which curtail the scope of actions for damages against administrative authorities are therefore little guide to the French-inspired principles governing Community liability.

What constitutes a *faute de service* so as to impose liability on the Community was further examined in Case 4/69 *Lütticke* v. *Commission* [1971] ECR 325. There the Court held that under the general principles referred to in Article 215(2) the liability of the Community presupposed the combination of a number of conditions relating to (a) the reality of the damage, (b) the existence of a causal link between the injury relied upon and the behaviour of the institution complained of, and (c) the illegality of this behaviour. L complained that they were being required by the German Government to pay a tax on imports of powdered milk at too high a rate. After recourse to various remedies without success, they sued the Commission for damages under Article 215(2) on the ground that it had a duty to intervene with a Member State who (allegedly) was imposing a tax offending Community law; accordingly, the Commission had defaulted in its duty. On the facts, the Court held that the Commission had done all that could be expected of it in its extensive negotiations with the German Government: there had been no failure in its duty. Accordingly, the action was dismissed on the merits, no *faute de service* being established.

By contrast, a *faute de service* was established by the applicants in Cases 19, 20, 25, 30/69 *Richez-Parise* v. *Commission* [1970] ECR 325. The applicants were Community officials who, on the basis of incorrect information given by the Commission concerning their pensions, had resigned from the service and elected to take their pensions in a certain form; subsequently, the Commission discovered that their advice was misleading but did not immediately inform the applicants to this effect. The Court held that, while the initial information supplied did not constitute a wrongful act, the failure to correct it as soon as the Commission discovered their mistake was a *faute de service*.

The series of misfortunes which befell Stanley Adams provided the grounds for a successful action for damages against the Commission, based in this case on a breach of the duty of confidentiality which it owed him: Case 145/83 *Adams* v. *Commission* [1985] ECR 3539. A was employed by the company Hoffmann-La Roche in Switzerland and supplied the Commission with information which led to the company being fined in competition proceedings for breaches of Article 86 EEC. Due to the carelessness of the Commission, the company identified A as the informant. He had now left the company and set up his own business in Italy. On a later visit to Switzerland he was arrested for economic espionage, an offence under the Swiss Penal Code, and held in solitary confinement. His wife was interrogated by the Swiss Police and committed suicide. He was released on bail and returned to Italy. In his absence he was convicted under Swiss law and given a one year's suspended prison sentence. This conviction destroyed his creditworthiness so that his business failed. Not surprisingly, the Court held the Commission liable in damages both for the breach of confidentiality and for failing to warn A of the risk of prosecution in Switzerland, a threat of such prosecution having been made by the company's lawyer on a visit to the Commission. But if the Commission had been at fault, so also, in the Court's view, had A, who had been careless of his own interests: the agreed damages had therefore to be reduced by half. In the event, for this public-spirited act, A received £200,000 as compensation, with a further £200,000 as costs: see March Hunnings (1987) 24 C.M.L. Rev. 65.

Liability arising from legislation

Liability under the terms of Article 215(2) can extend to liability in respect of legislation—what has been referred to in the context of Community law as "normative injustice." Normative is here used to describe an act such as a regulation, laying down a rule, as opposed to an individual decision. The notion that administrative rule-making may give rise to an action for damages is a novelty in English law, but Lord Wilberforce did canvass the possible need for such a remedy in *Hoffmann-La Roche & Co.* v. *Secretary of State for Trade and Industry*, [1975] A.C. 295 (H.L.) at 359. Case 5/71 the *Zuckerfabrik Schöppenstedt* case [1971] ECR 975 explored the nature of this normative injustice in Community law. It arises where a Community institution (in this case the Council) has taken a measure of a legislative or normative character, such as a regulation, which measure is subsequently proved to be in breach of the Treaties or other provisions of Community law. But the Court requires, as it stated in the case, "a sufficiently flagrant breach of a superior rule of law protecting individuals." This stringent test was held not to be satisfied in this case. It is enough however that the provision allegedly violated was for the protection of individuals generally rather than for the protection of the particular plaintiffs: there is no equivalent under Article 215 of the requirement of "direct and individual concern" under Article 173. At least the balance of cases appears so to decide (compare *Vloeberghs*, p. 149, above, *Meroni*, p. 117, above, *Kampffmeyer*, p. 138, above, *Zuckerfabrik Schöppenstedt*, above, and *Compagnie d'Approvisionnement*, p. 147, below).

The *Schöppenstedt* formula cited above was applied by the Court in Cases 83, 94/76, 4, 15, 40/77 Bayerische *HNL* v. *Council and Commission* [1978] ECR 1209 (part of a series of *Skimmed-Milk Powder* cases).

Over-production of milk in the Community had led to the creation of a skimmed-milk powder "mountain," to reduce which the Council made a regulation requiring animal feed producers to buy skimmed-milk powder from the intervention agencies; the powder would be mixed with the feed to supply protein in place of soya. But as the powder was more expensive than soya, livestock farmers had to pay more for their animal feed.

The farmers brought various actions to challenge the legality of the Council regulation. One group of actions was brought in the national courts, and the question of the validity of the regulation was referred to the Court of Justice under Article 177 (*e.g.* Case 114/76 *Bergmann* v. *Grows-Farm* [1977] ECR 1211; Case 116/76 *Granaria* [1977] ECR 1247). Another group was actions for damages brought directly before the Court of Justice under Article 215(2) EEC: the *HNL* case was in this category.

Judgment was given first in the cases under Article 177. The Court ruled the regulation to be invalid as offending the principle of proportionality and as producing discrimination between the different agricultural sectors contrary to Article 40(3) EEC.

In the action by *HNL* under Article 215(2) the Court had no difficulty in finding that there had been an infringement of a superior rule of law: the previous ruling under Article 177 had established that the regulation infringed the principles both of proportionality and non-discrimination. The principles were also intended for the protection of individuals. But had there been a sufficiently flagrant breach to justify an award of damages? In the circumstances, the Court held that there had not: where the Community institution was charged, as here, with wide discretionary power to legislate on matters involving choices of economic policy, it would not be liable unless it had manifestly and gravely disregarded the limits on the exercise of its powers. In the Court's view the Council had not shown such disregard, nor was the effect of the invalid regulation upon *HNL* sufficiently serious.

Subsequent cases falling on either side of the line are exemplified by the so-called *Quellmehl*, *Gritz* and *Isoglucose* cases, all involving Council regulations ruled invalid as discriminatory. In the *Quellmehl* and *Gritz* cases the Court found the Council's violation sufficiently flagrant and awarded damages under Article 215(2) EEC (Cases 64, 113/76, 167, 239/78, 27, 28, 45/79 *Dumortier* [1979] ECR 3091; Case 238/78 *Ireks-Arkady* [1979] ECR 2955; Cases 241, 242, 245–250/78 *DGV* [1979] ECR 3017; Cases 261, 262/78 *Interquell* [1979] ECR 3045); on the other hand, this test was held not to be satisfied in the *Isoglucose* cases (Cases 116, 124/77 *Amylum and Tunnel Refineries* [1979] ECR 3497; Case 143/77 *KSH* v. *Council and Commission* [1979] ECR 3583), in which a gloss appeared to be added to the *Schöppenstedt* formula, the Court stating that liability thereunder could only arise "in exceptional cases where the institution concerned has manifestly and gravely disregarded the limits on the exercise of its powers"; and grave meant "conduct verging on the arbitrary."

Limitation period

As well as being more generous in matters of *locus standi*, actions under Article 215 (or its equivalent in the other Treaties) are subject to a limitation period of five years (Article 43 of the Statute of the Court). This may be compared with the very short period of two months allowed for actions to annul under Article 173 EEC. Article 43 of the Statute makes the period of five years run from the occurrence of the event giving rise to the alleged liability; the period is interrupted if an application for relief is made to the Community institution concerned, in which case, if the institution has not defined its position (*e.g.* by accepting liability) the applicant will have two further months in which to commence proceedings (see Article 175, p. 123, above).

Case 51/81 *De Franceschi S.p.A. Monfalcone* v. *Council and Commission* [1982] ECR 117 concerned these provisions. The applicant suffered loss through the operation of a Council regulation, published on March 4, 1975 and abolishing certain refunds, which was held invalid by the Court on October 19, 1977 in Joined Cases 124/76 and 20/77. The present action was commenced on March 9, 1981. The defendants argued that proceedings were time-barred, the five-years limitation period having begun to run on March 4, 1975. The Court, however, agreed with the applicant that the period only began to run from the moment when the damage became known: the injurious effects of the regulation were produced only with effect from October 19, 1977, on which date the measure was adjudged unlawful. Similarly, in Case 145/83 *Adams* v. *Commission* (above, p. 140), the limitation period did not begin to run until the injured party became aware of the event giving rise to his claim, namely the visit of the company's lawyer to the Commission; he only learnt of this visit when it was disclosed in the Commission's pleadings.

Distinctive nature of the remedy

The distinctive nature of the remedy under Article 215 was blurred in the earlier decision of Case 25/62 *Plaumann* v. *Commission* [1963] ECR 95. There the Court pronounced that an administrative act which had not been annulled could not amount to a wrong founding liability in damages. This view has been rejected in several more recent cases: the Court now acknowledges that the two Articles have different objectives; Article 173 seeking to annul a particular act *erga omnes*; Article 215 providing compensation to the individual who has sustained damage through the faulty exercise of its functions by a Community institution. Thus, in *Zuckerfabrik Schöppenstedt* the plaintiffs sought damages for the loss they had suffered in consequence of a regulation of the Council fixing sugar prices. The Court was prepared to entertain the claim under Article 215 without action also being brought under Article 173, observing (at p. 984) that "in the present case, the non-contractual liability of the Community presupposes at the very least the unlawful nature of the act alleged to be the cause of the damage."

Subsequently, in Case 43/72 *Merkur* [1973] ECR 1055, the Court made explicit its readiness to rule on the illegality of an act in an action brought for damages. Thus, the two-months limitation period in Article 173 may be circumvented either by way of an action under Article 215(2) (subject to a five-years limitation period), or by resort to the plea of illegality under Article 184, or by a reference for a preliminary ruling as to validity made by a national court under Article 177 (neither Article 184 nor Article 177 being subject to any period of limitation).

Nevertheless, in several staff cases, claims for damages have been rejected on the ground that the plaintiffs could, by timely proceedings, have sought annulment of the allegedly illegal regulations; having failed to do so, they could not then complain of the damage caused them by such illegality: Case 4/67 *Muller-Collignon* [1967] ECR 365; Cases 15–33, etc.,/73 *Schots-Kortner* [1974] ECR 177. The cases seem to illustrate a wider principle: the Court will not usually entertain a claim for damages by a plaintiff who could have sought annulment of the normative act in issue— *vigilantibus non dormientibus iura subveniunt.*

Damage, causation and liability without fault

The Court has avoided laying down firm principles as to the categories of damage which may be claimed or on what basis the actual damages will be calculated. Thus, it has admitted claims for such financial damage as loss of profit or loss due to currency fluctuations (see Cases 5, 7 and 13–24/66 *Kampffmeyer*, above; Case 74/74 *CNTA*, below); and in staff cases, damages may be claimed for anxiety and injured feelings by Community employees wrongfully dismissed or unfairly treated (*e.g.* Case 7/56, 3–7/57 *Algera* [1957 and 1958] ECR 39).

Actual damage must be proved, or at least imminent damage which is foreseeable with sufficient certainty (Cases 56–60/74 *Kampffmeyer* [1976] ECR 711). A mere expectation or likelihood of damage in the future will not suffice. Nor must the damage be too remote: the Court speaks of the need for there to be a causal link between the damage and the act complained of (Case 4/69 *Lütticke*, above).

This causal link was present in Case 74/74 *CNTA* [1975] ECR 533, where an exporter relied, as he claimed that he was entitled to do, on the fact that a payment from Community resources to offset the effects of the devaluation of the dollar would not be discontinued without due notice and, in such reliance, entered into certain binding contracts; the Commission suddenly suppressed the payments, thereby causing the exporter to sustain a quantifiable loss. The Court held him entitled to recover: in the absence of an overriding public interest, the Commission could not abolish the right to these payments without notice but must either provide transitional measures to cushion the effects of suppression or render itself liable in damages. In later proceedings, however, he failed to establish any damage.

Damage may be adjudged to be non-existent where the plaintiff is able to pass on the loss sustained to his customers: the Court so held in the *Quellmehl* and *Gritz* cases (Cases 64, 113/76, 167, 239/78, 27, 28, 45/79 *Dumortier* [1979] ECR 3091; Case 238/78 *Ireks-Arkady* [1979] ECR 2955; Cases 241, 242, 245–250/78 *DGV*

[1979] ECR 3017; Cases 261, 262/78 *Interquell* [1979] ECR 3045), but for criticism of this view, see Rudden and Bishop (1981) 6 *European Law Review* 243.

Lord Mackenzie Stuart, speaking extra-judicially, has expressed the view that in the Court's more recent decisions "there can be detected a change of emphasis from the culpability of the administration to the protection of the legitimate interests of the administered," and he raises the question whether Community liability can arise without fault and without illegality. "Can a normative act competently made under the powers contained in the Treaties and justifiable in the Community interest form the basis of a claim for damages if injury has been sustained as its consequence?" (Maccabaean Lecture in Jurisprudence 1975, 20). Two cases touch on this important question.

In Cases 9 and 11/71 *Compagnie d'Approvisionnement* v. *Commission* [1972] ECR 391, certain French importers alleged not only fault on the part of the Commission in that it had acted illegally in fixing certain payments at too low a level, but also that, even in the absence of any illegality on its part, the Commission was liable to them in damages as they had suffered "abnormal and special loss" in comparison with Dutch and German importers. The Court rejected their argument on the ground that the measures in question had been taken in the general economic interest to reduce the consequence of devaluation for the whole body of French importers. Nevertheless, Advocate General Dutheillet de Lamothe left open the possibility that the principle of "equality in the face of public burdens," to which, in effect, the plaintiffs were appealing, might be applied in Community law, as it undoubtedly has in French administrative law, to cover an appropriate case (which this was not).

It should be pointed out, however, that if the French analogy were adopted, breach of the principle would constitute the violation of a general principle of law and, as such, amount in French eyes to an illegality. The *Compagnie d'Approvisionnement* case therefore does not resolve the problem whether the Community can be liable without fault and without illegality.

No less ambiguous in this respect is Case 169/73 *Compagnie Continentale France* v. *Council* [1975] ECR 117. The applicants were exporters of wheat who, in September 1972, had contracted to sell wheat to British customers for delivery in early 1973. They did so in the expectation of being entitled to certain compensatory payments for which the Treaty of Accession made provision. The amount of these payments had been fixed in advance by a draft regulation approved by the Council in July 1972; the regulation would be formally adopted after the Treaty of Accession came into force. This unusual step, as the Council explained, was taken so that dealers in the products covered by the proposed regulation should know with certainty what payments to expect from the beginning of 1973. However, the actual regulation which was adopted in January 1973 contained a modification permitted by the Treaty but having the effect of substantially reducing the value of the compensatory payments due to the applicants, a reduction made all the more substantial by the general rise in the price of wheat on the world market.

The advocate general advised the Court that, in his view, the Council's resolution of July 1972 which approved the regulation amounted to a promise to all interested parties that the text would be applied. It therefore had the consequence in law of imposing liability on the Community, because "the protection of confidence is a principle recognised in the Community legal system."

The Court rejected the applicants' claim for want of the necessary causal link between the acts of the Community and the damage suffered. It differed from the advocate general by holding that Community liability might have arisen, not because of reliance upon the Council's promise, but rather because of the Council's failure to give warning that it must act in accordance with the Treaty of Accession and that the application of the Treaty depended upon prevailing world prices for wheat. On either view, liability would have been based upon fault, that is, a *faute de service*.

In the Coal and Steel Treaty Article 34 provides specifically that, where a decision or recommendation of the High Authority is annulled in circumstances involving a *faute de service* on the part of the Community, undertakings which have suffered direct and special harm in consequence have the right to damages. As the Article is not limited to individual decisions, liability appears to extend to normative injustice, provided that the legislative measure has been annulled. The undertakings referred to in the Article are the limited category of coal and steel *producers* defined in Article 80 ECSC.

In Case 9, 12/60 *Vloeberghs* v. *High Authority* [1961] ECR 197, the applicant was a Belgium firm of coal *distributors*. It claimed damages from the High Authority on the ground that the latter had refused to bring an enforcement action against France under Article 88 ECSC, although the French Government had banned Vloeberghs from bringing into France coal which it had imported into Belgium from outside the Community, thereby causing it loss. The Court rejected the High Authority's argument that Article 34 was an exhaustive statement of the right to damages in these circumstances, and that Vloeberghs, as a distributor, could sue neither under that Article nor under Article 40. The Court allowed the action under Article 40, although it rejected as inadmissible the parallel action brought by Vloeberghs under Article 35 for the High Authority's failure to act (Article 35 being only available to coal and steel *producers*).

Acts of Community servants

Often the wrongful or illegal act of a Community institution is anonymous in that it cannot be ascribed to any particular civil servant of the Communities. Sometimes, however, the fault can be laid at the door of an individual servant. In this event, EEC Article 215(2), like ECSC Article 40, limits the non-contractual liability of the Community to acts of servants in the performance of their duties. For such acts the party injured can claim damages against the Communities in the Court of Justice. If he attempted to sue the civil servant in the servant's personal capacity in the appropriate national court, he could expect to be met by a plea of immunity. For the Treaties confer upon Community servants immunity from legal proceedings "in respect of acts performed by them in their official capacity." Such official acts, however, may give rise to internal disciplinary action, which in turn may be challenged by the civil servant before the Court of First Instance (or, previously, the Court of Justice under Article 179 EEC). Only where the civil servant was acting completely outside the scope of his duties ("on a frolic of his own," as English law might express it), would he lose his immunity, and in such a case only he and not the Communities could be sued.

The exact nature of the Communities' vicarious liability (as an English lawyer would regard it) for the acts of civil servants depends upon the interpretation to be given to the phrase "in the performance of their duties."

In the two *Sayag* cases (Case 5/68 [1968] ECR 395 and Case 9/69 [1969] ECR 329) the Court had to consider this question when S, an engineer employed by Euratom, was driving in his private car to a destination in Belgium to visit an atomic plant in connection with his work. He caused an accident on the way and was the subject of both criminal and civil proceedings in the

Belgian courts. The Belgian Court of Cassation referred to the Court of Justice the question of possible immunity and of the meaning of the phrase "in the performance of their duties." The Court ruled that the use of a private car by a Community servant could only be considered as constituting the performance of his duties in the case of *force majeure* or exceptional circumstances of such compelling nature that the Community could not otherwise perform its functions. In the event, therefore, the Belgian courts had jurisdiction. It would have been otherwise, it seems, if a serious emergency at the atomic plant had required the immediate presence of the engineer at a time when neither official transport nor public transport was available.

The *Sayag* cases indicate a conservative attitude on the part of the Court of Justice. The vicarious liability of the Communities should not be extended so as to make the Community purse an insurance fund for the victims of every wrongful act of a Community servant.

The present state of the law, however, is open to several criticisms. In the first place, there is the risk of the civil servant invoking immunity for acts which are *not* committed in the performance of his duties. This risk is partly removed by the power of the Community institution which employs him to waive the immunity. If the immunity is not waived, then the Community would be impliedly admitting the official nature of the act in question. This would invite an action against it. But in such an action the Court of Justice might hold that the act fell outside the performance of the servant's duties. The aggrieved plaintiff would be left without further remedy, unless the immunity was at this stage withdrawn, which would mean the plaintiff having to recommence an action in the national court against the civil servant personally.

A second criticism is that the Community might improperly waive immunity in order to leave the civil servant, rather than itself, exposed to the action for damages. In the first *Sayag* case (above) the Court made clear that the mere waiver of immunity could not affect any possible liability on the part of the Community itself.

A third criticism arises from the lack of uniformity of the principles governing non-contractual liability in the laws of the Member States. Thus, assuming immunity has been properly waived, a plaintiff who sued the civil servant in State A might succeed in his suit, whereas in State B he might fail because of a difference, for example, in the principles of limitation of actions or remoteness of damage or contributory negligence.

Concurrent fault on part of Member States

The nature of the European Communities requires that Member States may be called upon to collaborate with Community institutions in certain tasks. In other words, the execution of Community law may be entrusted to the Member States. Without this help from national administrations the relatively small Community civil service would be overwhelmed by its work-load. Moreover, members of the public may feel themselves better served by the more accessible, more familiar officials of their own governments.

In carrying out a function on behalf of the Communities, a Member State (that is, its government, officials or civil servants) may itself commit a wrongful or illegal act. Occasionally this may be deliberate; more often it will be a case of simple error—for example, a mistaken application of Community law.

Does then the principle of vicarious liability apply where a Member State is cast in the role of an agent, so as to attach liability to the Communities? An English lawyer might well see the State's relationship as analogous to that of an independent contractor, since the Communities exercise no real control over the

Member States even when they perform Community functions; in which case, vicarious liability could not arise, although State and Communities might be joint tortfeasors. On such questions, the Treaties are silent. The problem has arisen, however, before the Court of Justice on several occasions. Thus, in a typical case, the plaintiff complains that his own government, acting on behalf of the Communities, is refusing to pay him money allegedly due under Community law, but he elects to bring his suit against the Communities in the Court of Justice rather than to sue his own government in the national court, prompted perhaps by the likelihood of a more speedy decision from Luxembourg.

Faced with this kind of problem the Court has proceeded by way of the following analysis. Firstly, is there joint liability on the part both of the Community and the Member State? If there is, then, second, is the Member State to be considered primarily liable so that it would be reasonable for it rather than the Communities to pay compensation? If so, then, third, the plaintiff must pursue his remedy in the national courts, before the Court of Justice can further entertain his claim. If, of course, he succeeds in his national court, the Member State may be entitled to recoup itself, wholly or in part, against the Communities in separate proceedings before the Court.

Thus, in *Kampffmeyer* v. *Commission* (above, p. 138), as we have seen, the Court found liability established against the Community on account of the Commission's decision, held illegal, authorising the German Government to take safeguard measures. But the Court refused to settle the amount of damages until the plaintiffs had completed proceedings against their government in the German courts: "final judgment cannot be given before the applicants have produced the decision of the national court."

Critique

The principle that normally the plaintiff should first pursue his remedy in the national courts has been upheld by the Court in a series of cases beginning with Case 96/71 *Haegeman* v. *Commission* [1972] ECR 1005. More recent cases have been Case 99/74 *Société des Grands Moulins des Antilles* v. *Commission* [1975] ECR 1531, Case 46/75 *Importazione Bestiame Carni* v. *Commission* [1976] ECR 65, and Cases 67–85/75 *Lesieur Cotelle S.A.* v. *Commission* [1976] ECR 391. Behind the very complicated facts of the three later cases was the common basic feature that, as the plaintiffs alleged, their national government was refusing them certain payments to which they believed themselves entitled under Community regulations (relating in the instant cases to cereals, cattle and meat, and colza seeds, respectively). In each case the Court decided there was a concurrent remedy in the national courts which had therefore to be pursued first before any action would be admissible against the Community.

This approach by the Court is open to criticism. In the first place, as Mr. Hartley has pointed out (T. Hartley in [1976] 1 E.L.Rev. 299–304, 396–399), the Court's own jurisdiction is made to turn on the presence or absence of a remedy under national law, and this is not a question on which the Court can give an authoritative ruling, should the parties disagree on the point. Presumably, if the Court did take the view that a remedy existed in the national court, and then, in subsequent proceedings, the national court decided otherwise, the matter would have to come back to the Court at Luxembourg—a process both dilatory and expensive. Contrariwise, where it is established there is *no* remedy in the national courts, the plaintiff may bring his claim before the Court: Cases 197–200, 243, 245, 247/80 *Ludwigshafener Walzmuhle Erling* [1981] ECR 3211.

A second criticism arises from the considerable variations in the scope of the remedy which the national laws provide to recover damages against public authorities. Differences exist on such matters as the heads of damages, the modes of assessing these, the periods of limitation, and the recovery of money paid under a mistake of law. Because of such differences an applicant in one Member State might well fare better than one in another, although both applicants were complaining, in effect, of the same fault on the part of the Community. Such lack of uniformity within the Community seems intolerable.

Again, the remedy in the Court of Justice may be more generous than that available in the national court, as, for instance, in Case 96/71 *Haegeman* (see above), where Belgian law did not permit recovery of loss of profit although this was recoverable under Community law (as held by the Court of Justice): hence the applicant was told by the Court that he could come back to the Court to obtain compensation under this head after he had sued in the Belgian court for the refund which he was claiming from the Belgian authorities (in respect of customs duties paid on imported Greek wine). This kind of circuity of actions seems also quite intolerable.

A procedure so dilatory and circuitous is hard to justify. A partial justification for it may be found in the fact that, if the Community is sued, rather than the Member State, and is then adjudged liable for the whole damages, no provision exists in the Treaties whereby the Community may recoup itself against the Member State, even though the latter bears joint liability for the plaintiff's loss. Professor Schermers suggests however that such a right of action might be deduced from the general principles referred to in Article 215(2) (Henry G. Schermers in *Legal Issues of European Integration*, 1975/1, 113).

A subsequent case suggests that the Court may be ready to relax its restrictive approach of requiring the prior exhaustion of the national remedy, at least where the action under Article 215(2) is for damages in tort rather than a claim in quasi-contract for money (such as levies) unlawfully exacted (as is alleged) by the national authorities on behalf of the Community. Thus, in Case 126/76 *Dietz* v. *Commission* [1977] ECR 2431, the applicant was a German exporter who contracted to export certain goods from Germany to Italy. After the contract was made, certain charges were introduced by the Community on the imported goods, which resulted in Dietz making an unexpected loss on the transaction. He sued the Commission under Article 215(2) for his actual loss on the ground that the sudden imposition of the charges was a violation of the principle of the protection of legitimate expectations. The Commission argued that the claim was inadmissible since Dietz should first be required to proceed in his national court against the national authority imposing the charges. In fact such an action by Dietz was pending. But the Court of Justice held the action before it to be admissible; for the alleged loss stemmed from the act of the Community itself rather than from the measures adopted by the national authorities in applying Community law. In the event, however, the action failed on the merits.

Again, in Case 175/84 *Krohn* v. *Commission* [1986] ECR 753 [1987] ECR 97, K applied to the German Intervention Agency for an import licence (for manioc from Thailand) but this was refused by the Agency acting on mandatory instructions from the Commission. When K sued the Commission for damages under Article 215(2) EEC, the Court rejected the argument of the Commission that K should first sue the Agency, holding that the Commis- sion was responsible, by its instructions, for the Agency's alleged unlawful conduct. Thus, the admissi- bility of the action before the Court was not dependent upon the prior exhaustion of the national remedies; nor was the action under Article 215(2) barred by the fact that K had not challenged the instructions by proceedings to annul under Article 173(2).

Whether the Court can work out solutions to these (and other) problems simply by way of its case-law—hanging its decisions on the peg of "general principles" provided by Article 215(2) EEC—is an intriguing question. The drastic alternative would be a revision of the Treaties so as to confer jurisdiction upon the Court of Justice in respect of actions against Member States for non-contractual liability arising out of the administration of Community law by national authorities. The Communities and the Member States could then be sued jointly in the one Community Court, which could allocate liability between them as it thought fit. If the Communities alone were sued (and the plaintiff might often prefer to proceed thus) then the Communities would be able to join the Member State as a party and claim a contribution or even a complete indemnity from it, as appropriate.

APPENDIX

METHODS TO CHALLENGE THE VALIDITY OF A REGULATION

In the light of the discussion in this and the preceding chapter, it may be helpful to gather together, in summary form, the various methods by which, directly or indirectly, the validity of a Community regulation may be called in question before the Court at the suit of the individual. These are:

(a) Action to annul the regulation as a disguised decision (Article 173 EEC);

(b) Action for damages for "normative injustice" where the regulation constitutes a sufficiently flagrant breach of a superior rule of law protecting individuals (Article 215(2) EEC);

(c) Plea of illegality in respect of the regulation (Article 184 EEC);

(d) Reference from a national court or tribunal for a preliminary ruling on the validity of the regulation (Article 177 EEC: see Chapter 10 below).

The consequences of the challenge to the validity of the regulation, even if it be successful, will vary according to which method is adopted. Thus, a successful action under Article 173 ((a) above) will result in the quashing of the regulation: it is annulled *erga omnes* and (unless the Court rules otherwise) retrospectively. The award of damages under Article 215(2) necessarily imports a decision on the invalidity of the regulation in issue: although not formally annulled by the Court, *erga omnes*, the regulation will, in practice, cease prospectively to be applied until such time as it is revoked or replaced by its authors. Similar consequences flow from an indirect challenge under Article 184 or a preliminary ruling of invalidity under Article 177 ((c) and (d) above).

Chapter 9

STAFF CASES

Introduction

"Staff cases," *i.e.* actions by employees of the Community institutions who have complaints concerning their employment, are often omitted from general works on Community law as being too specialised a topic. Dealing with such matters as salaries, pensions, allowances, promotions, and disciplinary measures, they may seem of limited interest and perhaps even unworthy of the august attention of the Court. Yet, although transferred since 1989 to the Court of First Instance, with appeals to the Court of Justice on points of law, they have constituted, as we shall see, a not unimportant aspect of the Court's jurisdiction.

Staff cases also have a special human interest and importance, since they are virtually the only cases where a private individual (as distinct from a legal person) goes directly (but now only on appeal) to the Court. In all other cases, the only access of the individual to the Court in practice is the indirect route by way of a reference for a preliminary ruling from a national court as described in the next chapter.

The fact that the Court should have been given jurisdiction in such cases is perhaps a reflection of the influence of French administrative law, since the French *Conseil d'Etat* has a similar jurisdiction in respect of the higher ranks of the French civil service. The British tradition, by contrast, has been to deny civil servants access to the courts and to favour non-judicial arbitration, through Whitley Councils, of staff disputes over pay, promotion and conditions of

159

service, although a civil servant may now sue for wrongful dismissal.

But international organisations generally have adopted the French conception of the status and conditions of service of public servants being regulated by detailed statutory provisions and subject to judicial control; thus, within the United Nations an Administrative Tribunal was set up in 1949 for the purpose of hearing staff disputes, and the Administrative Tribunal of the International Labour Organisation, set up in 1946, has jurisdiction not only over the International Labour Office but also over various specialised agencies of the United Nations (including the World Health Organisation, FAO, and UNESCO) and other international organisations. In yet other organisations, a special domestic tribunal has been established.

The Court's Jurisdiction

Within the European Community it was appropriate, in accordance with the principle of unity of jurisdiction, that the Court of Justice, rather than a special tribunal, should be the forum for staff disputes. Accordingly, Article 179 EEC gives the Court jurisdiction in any dispute between the Community and its servants within the limits and under the conditions laid down in the Staff Regulations or the Conditions of Employment. Thus the staff of the Community institutions, including for this purpose not only the four "institutions" so described in Article 4 EEC but also the Economic and Social Committee, the Court of Auditors and the European Investment Bank (p. 166), can bring their complaints against their employing institutions before the Court. The staffs of the Community institutions are very small, compared with a national civil service, ranging from about 11,000 in the Commission to a few hundred in the Court and other smaller bodies. There are two main categories of employee, the established

"officials" of the European Communities, whose status
and conditions of service are laid down in the Staff
Regulations, and "other servants," often engaged under
contract for a limited period of time, who are subject to
the "Conditions of employment of other servants of the
Communities"; both these Conditions and the Staff
Regulations are enacted by regulation of the Council on
a proposal from the Commission, and the provisions in
the Staff Regulations conferring jurisdiction on the
Court apply to all employees alike. This is one case,
therefore, where the jurisdiction of the Court can be
altered, without amendment of the Treaties, by a
decision of the Council acting by a qualified majority.
Another unusual feature of staff cases is that the Court
can adjudicate in cases brought by its own employees
against the Court itself; such cases, apparent exceptions
to the principle *nemo iudex in causa sua*, are rare but
have occasionally arisen: see *e.g.* Case 15/60 *Simon* v.
Court of Justice [1961] ECR 115 and Case 2/80
Dautzenberg v. *Court of Justice* [1980] ECR 3107. In the
latter case the Court, sitting judicially, annulled its own
administrative act refusing a promotion to a librarian at
the Court. The Court has interpreted its jurisdiction
more broadly than is suggested by the reference in
Article 179 EEC to disputes "between the Community
and its servants": it has been ready to entertain actions
brought by candidates for employment with the Community, as in Case 130/75 *Prais* v. *Council* [1976] ECR
1589.

In terms of numbers alone staff cases, until transferred to the Court of First Instance in 1989, contributed
substantially to the court's case-load, and in the first
years after the establishment of the Court, when other
business was sometimes slack, they provided grist for
the judicial mill. These early cases provided the Court
with the opportunity to start its work of building up a
body of case-law where the texts provided little
guidance. In particular, they enabled the Court to

develop the principles of Community law on the nature
and scope of judicial review of administrative action,
principles which were subsequently applied to full-scale
actions under Article 173 EEC, and despite the
specialised nature of the disputes, despite the apparent
lack of merit of some complaints which have been
entertained, and despite the fact that staff cases were
(and on appeal still are) heard by a Chamber of three
judges, rather than by the full Court, the judgments in
these cases remain authoritative and can be cited
equally with decisions given by the full Court in cases of
less parochial concern.

Thus one of the earliest staff cases, which occupies no
less than one-third of the volume of reports for 1957,
raised the constitutional issue of the balance of power
between the authorities set up under the ECSC Treaty:
Cases 7/56 and 3–7/57 *Algera and others* v. *Assembly*
[1957 and 1958] ECR 39. Legislative authority in staff
matters was originally conferred under the ECSC Treaty
on a Commission composed of the Presidents of the
four Institutions (the Court, the High Authority, the
Assembly and the Council) in order to maintain a
balance of power among the institutions. The ECSC
Assembly, the precursor of the European Parliament,
had taken certain decisions admitting the applicants to
the protection of the Staff Regulations, and appointing
them at certain grades and at certain levels of seniority.
Subsequently those decisions were revoked, and the
applicants challenged that revocation as being unlawful.
The Court's judgment laid down important principles
governing the circumstances in which an administrative
act can lawfully be revoked, referring, in the absence of
express provisions of Community law, to the laws of the
Member States as a source of general principles of law:
this aspect of the case is returned to below, p. 285. The
case was the first authority for the principle that
compensation could be given, under Community law,
for non-material damage (*dommage moral*); and also,

although with less precision, for the degree of negligence required to establish liability for damages.

The jurisdiction of the Court in staff cases is wider than that of many staff tribunals in international organisations, since it can pronounce on the legality of the Staff Regulations themselves as well as on particular decisions taken in application of those Regulations. This may arise on a plea of illegality under Article 184 EEC (p. 125, above), whereby any party challenging a particular decision before the Court may plead the inapplicability of the parent regulation. An example is a case considered more fully in Chapter 15, Case 20/71 *Sabbatini* v. *European Parliament* [1972] ECR 345. Signora Sabbatini complained of discrimination on grounds of sex, since she lost her expatriation allowance on marriage, while men in the same circumstances did not. Although the decision was taken in conformity with the Staff Regulations, it was annulled by the Court, which held that the relevant provisions of the Regulations were discriminatory and unlawful. The Regulations were subsequently amended on this point by the Council so as to apply equally to men and women. Henceforth they were entitled to the allowance under the same conditions, but subsequent attempts by other women to claim arrears of payment of the allowances were unsuccessful, the applications being rejected as out of time: Cases 15–33, etc., /73 *Schots-Kortner* [1974] ECR 177.

It is sometimes overlooked that men, as well as women, can be victims of discrimination on grounds of sex. The point is illustrated by Joined Cases 75 and 117/82 *Razzouk and Beydouin* v. *Commission* [1984] ECR 1509. The Staff Regulations provided that the widow of an official was normally entitled to a survivor's pension, while the widower of a deceased female official could receive a survivor's pension only if he had no income of his own and was permanently incapacitated. A widower's claim that he was entitled to a pension on the same terms as widows was upheld by the Court, which held that the legislation infringed the fundamental right of equal treatment. The legislation was accordingly to be amended to establish equality between the sexes; and in the meantime, the Commission was to re-examine the widower's claim, which it had rejected, and must apply to it the provisions dealing with widows' pensions. If he would have received a pension had those provisions been applicable to men, he was to receive that pension, together with arrears and interest.

As well as the jurisdiction to rule on the validity of the Staff Regulations, it will be recalled that in staff cases the Court has plenary jurisdiction in the sense described in Chapter 8 (above, p. 131). The effect of this may be illustrated by Case 32/62 *Alvis* v. *Council* [1963] ECR 49, where the applicant claimed wrongful dismissal. The facts of the case were unusual and, it might be added, uncharacteristic of the behaviour both of Community servants and of the administration. The applicant was not an established official but had been engaged under contract. He had been dismissed for alleged misconduct; among other incidents, it was said that on one occasion he had reported for duty in a state of intoxication and that on another occasion, when he was also intoxicated, glasses were thrown from the ninth floor of his office block into the street below. He claimed that he had been dismissed without being given any opportunity of submitting his defence, and had not been informed of the incidents on which his dismissal was based. The Court, applying a generally accepted principle of administrative law in force in the Member States, held that the administration must allow its servants the opportunity of replying to allegations before any disciplinary decision is taken. That had not been done. However, the Court exercised its plenary jurisdiction, and ruled that, in this case, the failure to observe this principle was not such as to render the dismissal void. Nor did the failure justify the award of damages to the applicant; but it did justify ordering the Council to pay a substantial proportion of the applicant's costs.

The Court's plenary jurisdiction thus enabled it to substitute, in effect, its own judgment for that of the administration. Although the decision to dismiss the applicant was technically vitiated by the denial of his right to be heard, it was considered that the decision should stand on its merits. Indeed the Court went on, in its judgment, to review the decision on its merits and held that the facts which had been established, with the assistance of witnesses summoned by the Court (see, p. 226 below), justified the dismissal, revealing "an attitude and conduct incompatible with the functioning of the European institutions."

Procedure in staff cases

In most respects the procedure in staff cases is similar to that described in Chapter 12 below for any other direct action; but staff cases do have a number of special features.

The complaint must first be brought before the appropriate superior in the institution concerned; in other words, domestic remedies must be exhausted. If the complainant is not satisfied by the response, or if there is no response within four months (in which case there is deemed to be an implied decision rejecting the complaint), then he can appeal to the Court of First Instance against the decision of rejection. The time-limit for the appeal is three months, as compared with two months under Article 173.

Staff cases are normally heard by a Chamber, either of the Court of First Instance or of the Court of Justice, rather than by the full Court, although the Chamber may, under Article 95(3) of the Rules of Procedure, refer a case to the full Court. Thus in one case the full Court was called upon to decide whether it could entertain an action brought against the European Investment Bank, whose officials are not subject to the Community Staff Regulations; the Court held that it could do so: Case 110/75 *Mills* v. *European Investment Bank* [1976] ECR 955.

Staff cases also differ from other types of case in that, under Article 70 of the Rules of Procedure, the defendant institution normally has to pay its own costs, even if the action is unsuccessful. However, on appeals from the Court of First Instance, that rule applies only to an appeal brought by an institution; where an official appeals unsuccessfully, he or she will normally be liable for the institution's costs also.

If the action succeeds, the decision complained of is annulled; the applicant may also be awarded damages. Thus, in the *Algera* case mentioned above, the Court awarded damages for non-material harm (*dommage moral*) although only at the modest rate of 100 units of account (approximately £50) per applicant. In other cases, more substantial damages have been awarded; in one such case the Commission was ordered to pay the applicant some 77,000 Belgian Francs (approximately £1,000), as compensation for leave which he had been unable to take "owing to the requirements of the service": Case 39/69 *Fournier* v. *Commission* [1970] ECR 267. In general, the amounts awarded for mental distress or injured feelings have been small.

A special feature of staff cases is that, as will already be apparent, the Court has frequently been confronted with disputes concerning the facts of the case. Accordingly preparatory inquiries, and the calling of witnesses, were more frequent here than in other cases; and the burden on the Court has been correspondingly greater, especially, perhaps, because the procedures available to it for the establishment of the facts of a case are not entirely satisfactory—a matter to which we return in the chapter on procedure. It was therefore appropriate to transfer staff cases to the Court of First Instance, so enabling the Court of Justice "to concentrate its activities on its fundamental task of ensuring uniform interpretation of Community law" and "relieving it of responsibility for examining questions of fact" (above, p. 68).

The problem of case-load is aggravated by the fact that very large numbers of officials may be affected by Staff Regulations, such as the provisions on pensions and related matters which were challenged by large groups of officials in 1979 and 1980: see, *e.g.* the Opinion of Advocate General Capotorti in Case 167/80 *Dunstan Curtis* v. *Commission and Parliament* [1981] ECR 1499 at 1512.

The civil service unions have no power to bring such actions on behalf of their members, because the unions are not individually concerned under Article 173 EEC (above, p. 105): see, *e.g.* Case 72/74 *Union Syndicale* v. *Council* [1975] ECR 401, where several unions together challenged a Council decision on the remuneration of their members. Occasionally, however, Council Regulations adversely affecting the Community civil service have been challenged by the Commission, acting as the guardian of the Community interest; examples have been seen in the *Staff Salaries* cases (above, p. 103). Such actions are based on Article 173 which gives the Commission a general power to challenge Council measures.

APPENDIX

RECOGNISED UNIONS AND PROFESSIONAL ORGANISATIONS OF COMMUNITY EMPLOYEES (UNDER THEIR MORE FAMILIAR FRENCH TITLES)

Fédération de la fonction publique européenne (FFPE)
Syndicat des fonctionnaires internationaux et européens (SFIE)
Union syndicale—Service public européen—Bruxelles
Union syndicale Euratom Ispra (USEI)
Union syndicale Euratom Karlsruhe (USEK)
Union syndicale Euratom Petten (USEP)

(The above were parties to an Agreement with the Commission on union relations dated September 20, 1974: for full text of this Agreement, see Megret & others, *Le droit de la Communauté économique européenne* (Brussels, 1987) vol. 15 p. 123*).

Chapter 10

PRELIMINARY RULINGS

Introduction

In many ways the most important aspect of the work of the Court is its jurisdiction to give "preliminary rulings" under Article 177 EEC and corresponding provisions of the other Treaties (Article 41 ECSC, Article 150 Euratom).

As we have seen, disputes involving Community law, between individuals or companies, or between private parties and the national authorities of the Member States, never come directly before the Court of Justice, but before the courts and tribunals of the Member States. The treaty provisions enable the Court of Justice, at the request of the national court, to rule on questions of Community law which arise in such litigation.

The preliminary ruling has proved a particularly effective means of securing rights claimed under Community law: Signora Leonesio claimed a premium for the slaughter of her cows which had been refused her under Italian law; Mme. Defrenne claimed arrears of salary from the Belgian air-line on the ground that air hostesses and male members of the cabin crew performing identical duties did not receive equal pay; Mr. Kenny claimed sickness benefit in England, notwithstanding that he had been in prison in the Irish Republic during the qualifying period; Signor Bonsignore challenged a deportation order made by the German authorities; Dr. Klopp, a Dutch lawyer who had also qualified for admission in France, asserted his right to practise as an *avocat* at the Paris Bar, whilst

retaining his Dutch chambers, despite a rule of the Paris
Bar prohibiting a second office outside Paris; Mrs Drake
could not be refused invalid care allowance simply
because she was a married woman: Case 93/71 *Leonesio*
[1972] ECR 287; Case 43/75 *Defrenne* [1976] ECR 455;
Case 1/78 *Kenny* v. *Insurance Officer* [1978] ECR 1489;
Case 67/74 *Bonsignore* [1975] ECR 297; Case 107/83
Klopp [1984] ECR 2971; Case 150/85 *Drake* v. *Chief
Adjudication Officer* [1986] ECR 1995. The type of
claim varies considerably, as does the nature of the
procedure before the national court; but in essence, in
all these cases, the mechanism is the same. The right is
claimed under Community law, despite the absence of
any provision of national law, or in opposition to
national law. The remedy is before the national court,
but the scope of the right is determined by the Court of
Justice.

Conversely, Community law may be invoked by the[1]
defendant, whether in civil or in criminal proceedings.
In an action for infringement of patent or trade mark
rights, or in a prosecution for importing medicinal drugs
without complying with requirements laid down by
national law, the defendant may rely on the treaty
provisions on the free movement of goods, Articles 30–
36 EEC: Cases 15 and 16/74 *Centrafarm* [1974] ECR
1147 and 1183; Case 104/75 *De Peijper* [1976] ECR 613.
The defence is raised in the proceedings before the
national court; its scope is determined by the Court of
Justice by means of a preliminary ruling. The Court will
of course have regard to the exceptions set out in
Article 36, *e.g.* public morality, as where on a reference
from the House of Lords the English importers of
Danish pornography from Holland, prosecuted before
the Ipswich Crown Court, pleaded unavailingly the
principle of free movement of goods: Case 34/79 *R.* v.
Henn and Darby [1979] ECR 3795; *cf.* Case 121/85
Conegate v. *H.M. Customs and Excise* [1986] ECR
1007.

The term "preliminary ruling" is something of a misnomer. The ruling is requested and given, not before the case comes to the national court, but in the course of the proceedings before it. It is therefore an interlocutory ruling, a step in the proceedings before the national court. But it is a step which may be taken, and is frequently best taken, before the case comes to trial. Thus references are commonly made in the course of interlocutory proceedings: see, *e.g.* Cases 51, 86, 96/75 *EMI* v. *CBS* [1976] ECR 811, references from English, Danish and German courts. The French *préjudiciel* is clearer: that is, the submission of an issue for *prior judgment* before determining the principal issue.

It follows from the nature of a *preliminary* reference that it cannot be made once the principal issue has been decided; thus, in *SA Magnavision* v. *General Optical Council (No. 2)* [1987] 2 C.M.L.R. 262, the Queen's Bench Divisional Court refused to refer where the judgment had already been given (although the formal order of the Court had not yet been drawn up) and leave to appeal had been refused, for a reference at this stage could in no sense be interpreted as "preliminary."

Generally, the national proceedings stand adjourned pending the outcome of the reference. However, in *Portsmouth City Council* v. *Richards* [1988] *The Times*, November 21, 1988, the English Court of Appeal upheld the granting of an interlocutory injunction restraining deliberate and flagrant breaches of the criminal law, notwithstanding a reference in the case having been made to Luxembourg.

Under the ECSC Treaty (Article 41) the Court has jurisdiction to give preliminary rulings only on the validity of Community acts; under the EEC (and Euratom) Treaty it has jurisdiction on questions of interpretation as well as validity. While Article 41 ECSC has proved virtually a dead letter (because of the readier availability of the direct action under Article 33), it provided a model for expansion in the later

Treaties, its principal architect, we are told, being Catalano (later the Italian judge on the Court) who drew on the experience of the Italian Constitutional Court (see Address at the Court's Formal Sitting on October 18, 1984).

Article 177 EEC provides:

"The Court of Justice shall have jurisdiction to give preliminary rulings concerning:

(a) the interpretation of this Treaty;

(b) the validity and interpretation of acts of the institutions of the Community;

(c) the interpretation of the statutes of bodies established by an act of the Council, where those statutes so provide.

Where such a question is raised before any court or tribunal of a Member State, that court or tribunal may, if it considers that a decision on the question is necessary to enable it to give judgment, request the Court of Justice to give a ruling thereon.

Where any such question is raised in a case pending before a court or tribunal of a Member State, against whose decisions there is no judicial remedy under national law, that court or tribunal shall bring the matter before the Court of Justice."

The effect is that any question of EEC law in issue before a national court may be authoritatively determined by the Court of Justice if that question is referred to it; that a national court is in all cases entitled, and in some cases obliged, to make such a reference; and that the Court of Justice may thus be the final arbiter on matters of Community law although the case is heard in the national forum. Moreover, a question of interpretation may also extend to the question of the direct applicability or direct effect of the Community provision in issue.

The need for a system of preliminary rulings can be seen most clearly in relation to questions of validity. Plainly it would lead to intolerable confusion if national courts were to declare Community legislation invalid: for example, to hold that a Council regulation was *ultra vires*. Under Article 41 ECSC, indeed, the Court of Justice was expressly given "sole jurisdiction" to rule on the validity of acts of the High Authority and of the Council. Although the Court is not expressly given exclusive jurisdiction on questions of validity under Article 177 EEC, it would clearly be improper for a national court to declare Community acts to be invalid, not least because a court in another Member State might come to a contrary conclusion. Thus any serious challenge in the national courts to the validity of such acts should be referred to the Court of Justice. That such self-denial is required on the part of the national judge has now been made clear beyond peradventure by the Court of Justice itself. In Case 314/85 *Foto-Frost* (1988) 13 E.L.Rev. 125 the Court interpreted Article 177 EEC as depriving the national judge of the power to declare Community acts invalid; on the other hand, unlike Article 41 ECSC, Article 177 EEC did leave the national courts competent to pronounce a Community act to be valid where there were no grounds for doubt.

Illustrations of references on the validity of Community law, as opposed to its interpretation, may be found in the legislation on the social security of migrant workers. Article 51 EEC requires the Council to "adopt such measures in the field of social security as are necessary to provide freedom of movement for workers." Hence regulations of the Council provide, for example, that periods spent in different Member States should qualify for the calculation of the worker's retirement pension. While the detailed provisions of the legislation are inevitably complex, the essential principle underlying it, derived from Article 51, is that a person who has worked successively in different Member States should not be deprived of social security benefits that he would have secured if he had always worked in the same Member State. In some cases, a claimant has been faced with a calculation, purportedly based on the regulations, which would have the result of depriving him of the benefits to which he would have been entitled on the basis of national law taken alone. Here the Court has ruled that the provisions of the regulations, to the extent to which they lead to that result, are, in effect, *ultra vires* Article 51 and void: Case 191/73 *Niemann* [1974] ECR 571; Case 24/75 *Petroni* [1975] ECR 1149. Such decisions, invalidating Community legislation and so requiring the Council to enact amending provisions, could not properly have been taken by national courts; indeed, as the Court has now ruled (*Foto-Frost*, above), it would be contrary to Community law.

A moment's reflection will show, however, that a similar line of reasoning may apply equally to questions of interpretation as well as validity. The applicability of Community law in particular situations may depend as much upon its interpretation as upon its validity. A restrictive interpretation of legislation might be tantamount to holding it invalid; or the actual validity of a provision may depend upon its precise construction. Thus the uniform interpretation of the law is necessary to secure its uniform application. As the Court itself has stated:

> "Article 177 is essential for the preservation of the Community character of the law established by the Treaty and has the object of ensuring that in all circumstances this law is the same in all States of the Community":

Case 166/73 *Rheinmühlen* [1974] ECR 33 at 38. Uniform application of the law is the basis of the common market and without it Community law, applied by the national courts, would be liable to fragment and become overlaid by the national legal systems. In the absence of a federal structure or of any Community appellate court, the preliminary ruling is the only means by which uniform application of Community law can be attained.

Moreover, the provisions of the Treaty and the measures taken by the Community institutions cannot readily be interpreted by national courts without assistance. They have to be interpreted in the light of the purposes for which they were drafted, they are often broad and general in scope, and texts in the different official languages may have to be compared. These problems of interpretation are examined in Chapter 14.

In *Customs and Excise* v. *Samex* [1983] 1 All E.R. 1042, Bingham J. explains why the Court of Justice is better equipped than any national court to decide questions of Community law:

> "Sitting as a judge in a national court, asked to decide questions of Community law, I am very conscious of the advantages enjoyed by the Court of Justice. It has a panoramic view of the Community and its institutions, a detailed knowledge of the treaties and of much subordinate legislation made under them, and an intimate familiarity with the functioning of the Community market which no national judge denied the collective experience of the Court of Justice could hope to achieve. Where questions of administrative intention and practice arise the Court of Justice can receive submissions from the Community institutions, as also where relations between the Community and non-member states are in issue. Where the interests of member states are affected they can intervene to make their views known...Where comparison falls to be made between Community texts in different languages, all texts being equally authentic, the multinational Court of Justice is equipped to carry out the task in a way which no

national judge, whatever his linguistic skills, could rival. The interpretation of Community instruments involves very often not the process familiar to common lawyers of laboriously extracting the meaning from words used but the more creative process of supplying flesh to a spare and loosely constructed skeleton. The choice between alternative submissions may turn not on purely legal considerations, but on a broader view of what the orderly development of the Community requires. These are matters which the Court of Justice is very much better placed to assess and determine than a national court."

Indeed, if the courts of each Member State were to take it upon themselves to construe Community law, it is probably not too much of an exaggeration to say that there would be as many systems of Community law as there are national legal systems within the EEC.

The need for uniform interpretation applies equally to other areas of Community law which do not fall within the categories listed in the founding Treaties. This is the case with two Conventions concluded pursuant to Article 220 EEC: the Convention of February 29, 1968 on the Mutual Recognition of Companies, Firms and Legal Persons, and the Convention of September 27, 1968 on Jurisdiction and the Enforcement of Judgments in Civil and Commercial Matters (the so-called Brussels Convention, now ratified by the United Kingdom with effect from January 1, 1987). As these Conventions are not Community acts, but treaties requiring ratification by Member States they fall outside Article 177. In each case, a separate Protocol gives the Court jurisdiction to give preliminary rulings on the interpretation of the Convention. The detailed provisions differ in some important respects from the scheme laid down by Article 177. While the Companies Convention is not yet in force, the Judgments Convention has given rise to a substantial and growing body of case law.

Provisions for preliminary rulings are also contained in the Community Patent Convention, concluded on December 15, 1975 under the title "Convention for the European Patent for the Common Market"; when in force, this Convention will establish a Community patent system, under which it will be possible to take out a single patent for the whole of the EEC, within the framework of the Convention on the grant of European patents. A draft Protocol to the Convention, agreed in December 1985 but still to be ratified, contains a radical proposal for creating a Community Patent Appeal Court (COPAC), to which patent appeals would lie from the national courts in the Member States, but from which references for preliminary rulings would be made to the Court of Justice on the interpretation of the Convention and its annexes (including the Protocol): see Wadilow in (1986) 11 E.L. Rev. 295.

In 1989 the Member States concluded two Protocols giving the Court jurisdiction to interpret the Rome Convention on the Law Applicable to Contractual Obligations (not yet in force). These Conventions are likely to be followed by others; a draft Bankruptcy Convention is at an advanced stage of negotiation, and an instrument for a Community trade mark is also in preparation. These instruments are progressively extending the jurisdiction of the Court and the implications of this increasing work-load will be considered in the concluding chapter.

The procedure on a reference is in all cases the same; it is described in Chapter 12. Here it is necessary to mention only certain points of procedure which are relevant to the subject of this chapter. Firstly it should be noted that a decision to refer can be taken only by the national court. In practice such a decision will usually be taken at the instance of the parties or of one of them; but the court may also take the step of its own motion, and even contrary to the express wishes of the parties. When a reference is made, the proceedings before the national court are generally stayed for the period, currently about 18 months, in most cases, until the ruling is given. The procedure before the Court of Justice is, as we have seen, an interlocutory step in the action before the national court; but the Community institutions concerned (that is, the Commission in all cases, and the Council if a Council act is involved, but not the Parliament) and all the Member States, as well as the parties to the action before the national court, have the opportunity of submitting observations, both in writing and at an oral hearing, before the Court of Justice. When the ruling has been given, it is sent to the national court, and the proceedings there are resumed.

The system of preliminary rulings has its origins in analogous procedures in the legal systems of the original Member States, such as the reference in France from the civil to the administrative courts, or in Germany and Italy to the Constitutional Court from other courts, and these analogies have been used where procedural difficulties have arisen. Thus, the analogies in French and German law were considered by Advocate General Lagrange in the *Bosch* case, Case 13/61 [1962] ECR 45 at 59–60, and by Advocate General Warner in the *Rheinmühlen* cases, Cases 146 and 166/73 [1974] ECR 33 at 44. In English law perhaps the closest analogies are the appeal by way of case stated and the motion for the determination of a preliminary point of law. Although these analogies with national law may sometimes be helpful, the Community system is perhaps better considered as *sui generis*.

Indeed the function of the preliminary ruling is best explained by the special character of Community law itself. Community law is by its nature a common internal law in the Member States rather than a law governing relations between them; and in the absence of a developed federal structure it is natural that Community policies should fall to be implemented primarily by the authorities of the Member States and Community

law to be applied by their courts. So it is to be expected
that, in the normal way, Community law is enforced
through the national courts, which, as mentioned above,
have an exclusive jurisdiction to apply it in disputes
between individuals, and between the individual and the
authorities of the Member States.

Conflicts of jurisdiction between a national court and
the Court of Justice can therefore rarely arise, but the
exact demarcation line may be a delicate one to draw.
The following sections illustrate the relationship
between the two courts and the limits to their respective
jurisdiction. These sections show also the pains taken by
the Court of Justice both to preserve its own jurisdiction
and at the same time to respect what is sometimes
described as the "judicial sovereignty" of the national
courts.

The decision to refer

It is for the national court alone to judge whether a
decision on the question is necessary to enable it to give
judgment. That was established in Case 6/64 *Costa* v.
ENEL [1964] ECR 585 when objections were raised to
the admissibility of the reference: it was argued that
the Court could not entertain the reference (see on
this concept of admissibility Chapter 12 below).
The argument was that the Milan court had requested
an interpretation of the Treaty which was not "necessary" for the solution of the dispute before it. The
Court of Justice simply replied to these objections
that, since Article 177 is based upon a clear separation
of functions between itself and the national courts,
it could not investigate the facts of the case or criticise
the grounds and purpose of the request for interpretation. The Court's concern was clearly to respect the
exclusive competence of the national court to decide
whether a reference should be made, and at the
same time to obviate the risk of challenge to the

admissibility of a reference. This approach is undoubtedly correct.

It will be seen from the wording of Article 177 (set out above, p. 172) that it does not require that the *reference* should be necessary, but only that the national court should consider that it cannot give judgment without deciding the point of Community law. If that condition is satisfied, then the court, unless it is a court of last instance, has a discretion whether or not to make a reference, and the exercise of that discretion is a matter for the national court alone, subject to the possibility of an appeal: Cases 146 and 166/73 *Rhein-mühlen*, (below, p. 321).

Nevertheless, the Court reserves the right not to entertain a collusive action brought in one Member State with the intention of challenging the law of another Member State as contrary to Community law. Case 104/79 *Foglia* v. *Novello* [1980] ECR 745 was a reference by the Pretore of Bra where the parties before the Italian court both contested the compatibility with Community law of a tax imposed by the French customs authorities on a consignment of Italian liqueur wine. The Court of Justice held, however, that, in the absence of a genuine dispute between the parties, it had no jurisdiction to give a ruling on the questions raised by the Pretore of Bra touching as they did the compatibility of French fiscal measures with Community law.

The holding of the Court has been criticised as introducing a kind of preliminary censorship of the motives of the parties and the judge in the national proceedings: Barav (1980) 5 E.L. Rev. 443. Certainly, the previous case law seemed to be well settled that (as was said in Case 10/69 *Portelange* [1969] ECR 309 at 315) "Article 177 does not give the Court jurisdiction to take cognisance of the facts of the case or to criticise the reason for the reference." Nor does the Court normally object to being asked to rule at the request of a judge in one Member State upon legislative measures or administrative acts in another Member State: see, *e.g.* Case 22/76 *Import Gadgets* [1976] ECR 1371; Case 261/81 *Rau* v. *De Smedt* [1982] ECR 3961. From the laconic judgment in *Foglia* v. *Novello*, read in the light of the advocate-general's opinion, it seems that the Court wished to curb what it saw as a *détournement de procédure* by the referring judge.

In a subsequent reference in the same proceedings (Case 244/80 *Foglia* v. *Novello* [1981] ECR 3045) the Pretore sought clarification of the Court's judgment in the first reference. The Court reaffirmed its authority to question of its own motion the admissibility of any reference for a preliminary ruling: it must retain what has been well described as this "valuable long-stop against abuse of process in exceptional cases" (Wyatt in (1981) 6 E.L. Rev. 449). But the Court did soften its attitude somewhat by inviting the Pretore to resubmit a reference if he could lay before the Court any new and relevant factors not present in the original reference: Article 177 being based upon co-operation between the national court and the Court of Justice, the latter could require the former to explain, where they were not obvious, the reasons why the national judge considered an answer to the question of Community law to be necessary in order to resolve the dispute.

How exceptional was the Court's attitude in declining jurisdiction in *Foglia* v. *Novello* is shown by its readiness, in a subsequent case, to accept a reference in what appeared on its face a collusive action, though no clear evidence of collusion was adduced: Case 46/80 *Vinal* v. *Orbat* [1981] ECR 77; [1981] 3 C.M.L.R. 524.

The question referred

The formulation of the question or questions referred is a matter for the national court alone. As is pointed out in the discussion on procedure in Article 177 cases (below, p. 242), a reference must usually be formulated

with considerable detail if it is to be properly
understood. But the question or questions referred will
be answered without undue formalism. Since the
proceedings in the national court will often, as we have
seen, involve a challenge to national law as being
contrary to Community law, the national court will
often ask whether the provisions challenged are indeed
contrary to Community law. Strictly such a question
involves the application of Community law rather than
its interpretation, but the Court will usually confine its
ruling to the issue of interpretation, leaving it to the
national court to draw the conclusion (which may then
be readily apparent), whether in the light of that
interpretation the national provisions should not be
applied.

Here again the Court has sought to preserve its own
jurisdiction without trespassing on that of the national
court. To put the point in a different way, it has sought
to provide an answer helpful to the national court while
remaining within the limits of its competence.

Thus in the very first Article 177 reference, the *Bosch*
case, objections were made to the jurisdiction of the
Court on the ground, among others, that the question
related not only to the interpretation but to the
application of the Treaty. The Court had been asked to
rule on the question whether the prohibition on export
imposed by the Bosch company on its customers was
void by virtue of Article 85(2) EEC as far as exports to
the Netherlands were concerned. To answer that
question would have involved not merely interpreting,
but applying, Article 85. The Court held, however,
following Advocate General Lagrange, that "...it is
permissible for the national court to formulate its
request in a simple and direct way leaving to this Court
the duty of rendering a decision on that request only in
so far as it has jurisdiction to do so, that is to say, only
in so far as the decision relates to the interpretation of
the Treaty. The direct form in which the request in the

present case has been drawn up enables this Court to abstract from it without difficulty the questions of interpretation which it contains.": Case 13/61 [1962] ECR 45 at 50. As it has frequently done in subsequent cases, the Court proceeded to extract from the material presented to it the questions of law which it was competent to answer. Thus, in Case 16/65 *Schwarze* [1965] ECR 877 72 the national judge only asked the Court to interpret a Community measure, whereas a ruling on the measure's validity was clearly required: this the Court supplied unasked.

Only where Community law has no bearing on the question referred will the Court hold that it cannot give an answer to the question referred. Thus in Case 93/75 *Adlerblum* [1975] ECR 2147, the classification under French law of a pension paid under German law to a victim of Nazi persecution was held to be a matter of national law alone. However, even in such cases the Court does not reject the reference by a preliminary decision on admissibility. Instead, the proceedings follow their normal course and result in a ruling to the effect that the Court has no jurisdiction to answer the question referred.

In the historic case *Van Gend en Loos*, where the Court for the first time held that a provision of Community law "produces direct effects and creates individual rights which national courts must protect" (Case 26/62 [1963] ECR 1 at 16) the plaintiff had challenged a Dutch law as contravening Article 12 of the EEC Treaty. The Dutch and Belgian Governments submitted, *inter alia*, that the Court had no jurisdiction to decide whether the provisions of the EEC Treaty prevail over Dutch legislation, and that the solution to this question fell within the exclusive jurisdiction of the national courts, subject to an application under Articles 169 and 170 of the Treaty. The argument was that an alleged infringement of the Treaty by a Member State could not be brought before the Court under Article

177 at the instance of an individual party to proceedings before a national court, but only in proceedings
instituted before the Court directly by the Commission
or by another Member State under Article 169 and
Article 170 respectively.

The Court rejected this argument as misconceived.
"A restriction of the guarantees against an infringement
of Article 12 by Member States to the procedures under
Articles 169 and 170 would remove all direct legal
protection of the individual rights of their nationals."
The decision is illuminating on the relation between the
Court's jurisdiction under Article 177 and its jurisdiction
in a direct action. It is plain on reading the judgment
why a remedy in the hands of the Commission and the
Member States was considered ineffective. Such an
action on their part is purely discretionary and will be
affected by political calculation. The notion of the direct
effect of Community law, coupled with the jurisdiction
of the Court to give a preliminary ruling and so to
determine the scope of the individual's rights and
obligations, is a more powerful weapon. The individual
has no direct remedy, before the Court, against the
default of a State. The remedy lies with the national
court, with the use of Article 177 where necessary. In
this way the national courts enforce, if necessary
against their own State, the rights conferred on the
individual by the Treaty

Questions of Community Law

The Court has taken a wide view, also, of the questions
of Community law which may be the subject of a
reference. It will be recalled that under the ECSC
Treaty (Article 41), the Court's jurisdiction is limited to
the validity of acts of the High Authority and of the
Council; under the EEC Treaty (Article 177) and the
Euratom Treaty (Article 150) it extends to the
interpretation of the Treaties themselves and the

validity and interpretation of the acts of the institutions. As well as the EEC and Euratom Treaties, the Court can interpret the amending Treaties such as the Merger Treaty and the three Treaties of Accession. Thus, apart from the ECSC Treaty, which by its nature is less likely to be invoked before the national courts, the Court can deal with any questions involving interpretation of the Treaties.

What "acts" of the Community institutions are subject to interpretation? The Court, as has been said, has taken a liberal view. In Case 181/73 *Haegeman* [1974] ECR 449, it interpreted certain provisions of the Agreement of Association between the EEC and Greece, on the ground that such an agreement, concluded by the Council under Articles 228 and 238 of the EEC Treaty, was an act of one of the Community institutions within the meaning of Article 177: see also Case 87/75 *Bresciani* [1976] ECR 129, Case 270/80 *Polydor* [1982] ECR 329 and Case 12/86 *Demirel* [1987] ECR 3747.

Although international agreements with non-member States can thus be interpreted by the Court, questions can of course be referred only by the courts and tribunals of the Member States, and not by the judicial bodies of other States parties to the agreements.

Courts and Tribunals of Member States

The question of what constitutes "a court or tribunal of a Member State" (in the French "*une juridiction d'un des Etats membres*") arose in *Vaassen-Göbbels* (Case 61/65 [1966] ECR 261), on a reference from a Dutch social security tribunal. The tribunal, in making the reference, suggested that it was competent to do so. It stated that although it could not be considered as a court or tribunal under Dutch law, nevertheless this did not exclude the possibility that it should be regarded as a "court or tribunal" within the meaning of Article 177.

The defendant, a social security fund set up under private law by organisations representing employers and wage-earners in the mining industry, submitted that the tribunal gave "non-binding opinions" rather than decisions and was therefore not competent to make a reference.

The Court held that the tribunal should be considered as a court or tribunal of a Member State for the purposes of Article 177. It took account of the fact that the responsible minister had to appoint the members of the tribunal, to designate its chairman and to lay down its rules of procedure; the tribunal was a permanent body which heard disputes according to an adversary procedure and was bound to apply rules of law.

This case illustrates the interaction of national law and Community law as well as the broad view taken by the Court of its Article 177 jurisdiction. The general question of what constitutes a court or tribunal of a Member State under Article 177 is a question of Community law and must be answered by reference to general criteria applicable to all Member States rather than by reference to national law. But to determine whether those criteria are satisfied in a particular case it is necessary to look at the rules of national law governing the composition, status and functions of the body in question. Thus, although the Court is normally concerned on a reference only with questions of Community law, it may have to consider questions of national law for the purposes of determining its jurisdiction.

In another Dutch case, a reference from the Dutch Council of State (*Raad van State*), Advocate General Mayras examined at some length the question whether that body, whose functions were strictly only advisory, was to be regarded as a court or tribunal; but the Court gave its ruling without adverting to this question and presumably entertained no doubts about the answer: Case 36/73 *Nederlandse Spoorwegen* [1973] ECR 1299.

In Case 138/80 *Borker* [1980] ECR 1975 the Court declined to give a ruling on a reference from the Paris *Chambre des Avocats* on the ground that the Chamber was not exercising a judicial function; and in Case 65/77 *Razanatsimba* [1977] ECR 2229 the *Cour d'appel* of Douai declared that the *Conseil de l'Ordre des Avocats* of Lille was not a tribunal which could refer questions to the Court of Justice, a view with which, in *Borker*, the Court appeared to concur.

A court does not cease to be a court for the purposes of Article 177, even though it combines other functions which are not strictly judicial in character. The Court so held in Case 14/86 *Pretore di Salo* v. *X* [1987] ECR 2565 in accepting a reference from an Italian Pretore, a magistrate who combines the tasks of public prosecutor and investigating judge; the Pretore of Salo was seised of a complaint against persons unknown regarding the pollution of a river and asked for an interpretation of a directive which he believed in point.

So far as the United Kingdom is concerned, Article 177 obviously applies, not only to the ordinary courts, but also to tribunals established by statute, *e.g.* a National Insurance Commissioner (Case 17/76 *Brack* [1976] ECR 1429) or the Special Commissioners of Income Tax (Case 208/80 *Lord Bruce of Donington* [1981] ECR 2205).

A problem might, however, arise in relation to what English lawyers term domestic tribunals. In the United Kingdom such tribunals are very numerous and diverse, ranging from the Judicial Committee of the Privy Council, exercising a disciplinary jurisdiction in relation to doctors, or a statutory body like the Solicitors' Disciplinary Tribunal, to membership or disciplinary committees of such voluntary associations as the Jockey Club or the Football Association. Would they all qualify as tribunals "of" a Member State, or does the preposition denote some relationship of the tribunal to state authority or what Mr. Hartley terms "some measure of official recognition" (in *The Foundations of Community Law* (2nd ed., 1988) p. 256)? Nor is it far-fetched to suggest issues could arise before such tribunals upon which a reference under Article 177 might be appropriate. Thus, if the facts of *Russell* v. *Duke of Norfolk* [1949] 1 All E.R. 109 had not arisen until 1973, the Jockey Club might have wished to refer to Luxembourg the question whether they could continue to deny women the right to be professional jockeys.

The approach of the Court of Justice to such problems may be illustrated by comparing Case 246/80 *Broekmeulen* [1981] ECR 2311 and Case 102/81 *Nordsee* [1982] ECR 1095. Broekmeulen was a Dutch citizen holding Belgian medical qualifications and duly authorised to practise medicine in Holland. The Dutch medical authorities refused to place him on the Dutch medical register of general practitioners on the ground of his not having had one year's experience in general practice; as a result, he was not qualified to treat patients under the Dutch social security scheme. Broekmeulen appealed to the Dutch Appeal Committee for General Practice, which body made a reference under Article 177 to ascertain whether Broekmeulen could rely on the right of establishment and the freedom to provide services conferred by Community law. On the preliminary point whether the Appeal Committee was entitled to refer under Article 177, the Court held that it was, despite its being a body set up under the rules of the Dutch Medical Association, a private association. The Court decided that the Appeal Committee was exercising a public or quasi-public jurisdiction which could affect the exercise of Community rights; it also had regard to the adversarial and quasi-judicial nature of proceedings before it. Moreover such cases did not, in practice, come before the ordinary courts.

In *Nordsee* a group of German companies made an agreement for the pooling between them of an EEC grant for the construction of new ships. They subsequently were in dispute as to how the grant should be allocated and, under a clause in the agreement, submitted their dispute to an arbitrator appointed by the Bremen Chamber of Commerce. The Chamber appointed the President of the Bremen Oberlandesgericht who decided to make a reference under Article 177 EEC on points of Community law relevant to the dispute. The Court decided, however, that the arbitration tribunal, which was established pursuant to a contract between private individuals, was not a court or tribunal of a Member State: consequently the Court had no jurisdiction to rule on the substantive issues referred to it. In reaching this decision, the Court found it significant that there was no obligation on the parties to submit their dispute to arbitration; in contrast with the position in the *Broekmeulen* case, they could have taken their case to the ordinary courts, which could also review the decision of the arbitrator and, if necessary, themselves make a reference to the Court of Justice.

Courts and tribunals obliged to refer

Under the last paragraph of Article 177, as we have seen, a court or tribunal against whose decisions there is no judicial remedy under national law is not merely entitled, but obliged, to refer a question, if it considers that a decision on that question is necessary to enable it to give judgment. A reference in such a case is not discretionary but mandatory. The question arises whether the obligation to refer is restricted to those courts and tribunals whose decisions are never subject to appeal, or whether it extends to any court or tribunal whose decision in the particular case is not subject to appeal. On the first (or "abstract") view (adopted *per incuriam* by Lord Denning M.R. in *Bulmer* v. *Bollinger* [1974] Ch. 401) only the House of Lords in England (as to Scotland, see below), and the highest courts of the other Member States, would be obliged to refer. On the second (or "concrete") view even a quite lowly tribunal would be in the same position; on this view even the Milan magistrate in *Costa* v. *ENEL* (above, p. 179) was obliged to refer since his judgment was not subject to appeal in Italian law because of the small amount involved in the claim. A literal interpretation might support the first view, since the text refers to "decisions" in the plural, but as the question is one of interpretation of the Treaty, such an approach seems unlikely to commend itself to the Court. More pertinent is a consideration of the purposes of the provision. Here the first view might be supported by the argument that the decisions of the highest national courts carry a special authority, and should therefore be subject to a special provision to ensure the uniform application of Community law at the highest level. On the other hand it could be argued that what is important is for the individual litigant to have the opportunity of a reference before a final decision is given in his case.

Here too the Court, although not expressly invited to rule on this question, has adopted the wider view, stating in *Costa* v. *ENEL* [1964] ECR 585 at 592 that the magistrate was under an obligation to make a reference in that case as there was no appeal against his decision.

In relation to the United Kingdom, the view sometimes expressed that only the House of Lords would be obliged to refer is an over-simplification even if one adopts the "abstract" view (see above). For the House of Lords is the ultimate appellate jurisdiction in the United Kingdom as a whole only for civil matters. In criminal matters, there is no appeal to the House of Lords from the Scottish criminal courts of last instance, which therefore would rank as final courts for the purpose of the last paragraph of Article 177.

A complication in determining which courts or tribunals fall within Article 177(3) arises from the

English habit of permitting an appeal, not as of right, but by leave only. Thus, an appeal from the Court of Appeal to the House of Lords requires either the leave of that court or, if it be refused, the leave of the Appeals Committee of the House of Lords. The parties therefore do not know until after the Court of Appeal has delivered judgment, and leave to appeal from that judgment has been refused, that the Court of Appeal was the court of last instance in their case. By then, it is not possible to invoke Article 177(3) and to insist on a reference: the national court has become *functus officio*, and any ruling obtained would be retrospective, not preliminary.

To this dilemma, the only logical solution and one which the spirit and intendment of Article 177(3) dictate, is to regard that court as the court of last resort from whose decisions no appeal lies as of right (but see the ingenious suggestion of T. C. Hartley, *op. cit.* p. 263). This view found support from Buckley L.J. in an obiter dictum in *Hagen* v. *Moretti* [1980] 3 C.M.L.R. 253 and was perhaps implicit in the judgments in the Divisional Court in *SA Magnavision* v. *General Optical Council (No. 2)* [1987] 2 C.M.L.R. 262 (above, p. 171).

Again, in English procedure the prerogative orders of certiorari, prohibition or mandamus, or the post-1977 application for judicial review, pose problems by reason of these remedies being discretionary in character and conducted in two stages. In the first stage, an *ex parte* application must be made for leave to apply for the order. These remedies are not therefore available as of right, and, by analogy with what was said in relation to appeals (above), a court whose judgment is final, except for possible review by way of certiorari, etc., should, logically, be considered to fall within Article 177(3). British writers differ on this question, but a National Insurance Commissioner has held himself to be outside Article 177(3) and to have a discretion whether or not to refer under Article 177(2) because his judgment, although "final," was reviewable by way of certiorari: see *Re a Holiday in Italy* [1975] 1 C.M.L.R. 184, *per* Mr. J. G. Monroe.

In practice the problem of which courts are obliged to refer will be less acute where the courts of first instance and appeal exercise correctly their discretion.

Approach of the National Courts

The success of the preliminary ruling system plainly depends on a close co-operation between the Court and the national courts. With a view to fostering this co-operation, the Court has for many years arranged regular meetings in Luxembourg with judges and lawyers from the Member States, and has also visited the courts of the Member States; on occasion, members of the Court have sat on the bench in the national courts. Individual members of the Court have also maintained contact with the Bench and Bar of their respective countries, and regularly give talks and lectures at conferences and meetings of lawyers.

Such efforts, however, must be fully reciprocal to be effective, and it cannot be said that the readiness of the Court to receive references, and to give prompt and helpful answers to the questions referred, has always been met with equal enthusiasm. Judges are generally cautious and conservative by temperament, and it was not to be expected that so radical an innovation in the European legal scene would flourish very rapidly. In the earliest years of the EEC Treaty, the Court received little but an occasional reference from a Dutch court, and subsequently only the German courts have made the fullest use of the procedure. Although it is now more widely used, there have been striking differences in the approach of the courts of different Member States, as appears from Table 7 of the Judicial Statistics (below, p. 217). In view of the importance of the preliminary ruling in the Community legal system, the approach by national courts to the exercise of their discretion to refer is crucial and has received much attention.

Those courts which have been reluctant to refer have not been very successful in their attempts to rationalise that reluctance. The French courts sought in the early days to rely on the doctrine of *"acte clair,"* so that even a final court such as the *Conseil d'Etat* could avoid Article 177 on the ground that no "question" of interpretation arose because the answer was clear; but this argument is open to abuse (see Judge Pescatore in *Legal Problems of an Enlarged European Community,* 1972, at p. 27, and *Cohn-Bendit* (below, p. 194) [1980] 1 C.M.L.R. 543, and contrast the more faithful approach of Lord Diplock in *Garland* v. *British Rail Engineering* [1982] 2 C.M.L.R. 174).

In England, when Article 177 first came before the Court of Appeal Lord Denning M.R. in *Bulmer* v. *Bollinger* [1974] Ch. 401, sought to lay down certain "guide-lines" in an apparent attempt to restrict the use of references. The attempt was marred by some confusion of thought and met a very critical reception. Broadly the chief criticism is that, while the exercise of its discretion is a matter for the national court, that discretion must be exercised in the light of the purposes of Article 177; and, as the Court of Justice itself has held, its exercise cannot be limited by any considerations of national law (the *Rheinmühlen* cases, below, p. 321). Thus the "guide-lines" have no authority as a matter of law; but emanating from so eminent a source they have had some influence in practice: see, *e.g. Concorde Express Transport* v. *Traffic Examiner Metropolitan Police,* Kingston Crown Court [1980] 2 C.M.L.R. 221; also their uncritical acceptance by the editors of *The Supreme Court Practice,* 1988 (Vol. 1, pp. 1478–79; commentary on R.S.C. Ord. 114). For a valuable corrective, however, see the views of Bingham J. cited above, p. 175). The guidelines have been expressly rejected by an Irish court: see F. Murphy, (1982) 7 E.L. Rev. 331 at 337.

Proposals have been made to remedy the problem where a final court wrongly decides not to refer; for example, a direct right of appeal to the Court could be conferred in such cases. This possibility is mentioned by the Commission in its report on European Union (below, p. 329 at para. 125. But the answer probably lies with the national courts themselves, and the statistics show that they have progressively adjusted to the system. Theoretically an action by the Commission under Article 169 would lie against a Member State whose courts were in breach of their obligation under Article 177, since the courts, although constitutionally independent, are nonetheless organs of the State for the purposes of State responsibility: see to this effect the Opinion of Advocate General Warner in Case 9/75 *Meyer-Burckhardt* [1975] ECR 1171 at 1187. But such an enforcement procedure seems inappropriate except for a flagrant breach, and even then the Commission may decide not to bring the matter before the Court for fear of exacerbating a politically sensitive situation (as, for instance, when the French *Conseil d'Etat* refused to refer on the ground that the Community law was clear, although the *Conseil's* view of that law was directly contrary to the established case-law of the Court of Justice: *Cohn-Bendit* [1980] 1 C.M.L.R. 543).

Manifestly, the *Conseil d'Etat*, in contrast with the French civil courts, is not presently imbued with that "spirit of judicial co-operation" which the Court of Justice sees as implicit in the reference procedure. Confrontation will only be avoided if national courts regard themselves also, no less than the Court of Justice, as Community courts. Encouraging in this respect is the shift of view in the German Constitutional Court (Second Chamber) between its decision in *Internationale Handelsgesellschaft* (1974) and that of October 22, 1986, *Wünsche Handelsgesellschaft* [1987] 3

C.M.L.R. 225, which now accepts the primacy of Community law. This led the Editor of the European Law Review to remark: "This happy ending provides an object lesson for those (including ourselves) who are inclined to cry havoc whenever a national court behaves inconsistently with established wisdom as to the relationship between Community law and national law" (1987) 12 E.L.Rev. 162.

Recently, in what some may see as a conciliatory gesture, the Court of Justice has conceded that the obligation to refer under Article 177(3) still leaves the national judge free not to do so where he believes the point is sufficiently clear not to require an interpretation;
the Court accepted that the *acte clair* doctrine is not limited to where the point in question has already been the subject of interpretation at Luxembourg in a previous case: Case 283/81, *C.I.L.F.I.T.* At the same time the national judge was warned against assuming that the point is clear in all the language versions of the text in issue; and the Court added a reminder that the national judge should not overlook the special features of Community law—its plurilingual versions, its own individual terminology and its particular methods of interpretation (for this last, see Chapter 14 below).

Effects of Preliminary Rulings

Firstly, we must distinguish between the effect of the ruling in the instant case and its effect in subsequent cases. The ruling is binding upon the referring court or tribunal in the sense that the interpretation or validity of the Community law in question has been authoritatively and finally determined in Luxembourg: the national judge has consulted the oracle and must accept the reply as what indeed the Treaties say it is: a ruling, not an opinion: see Case 29/68 *Milchkontor* [1969] ECR

165. It is then for the national judge to apply the Community law to the facts of the case.

The next question is whether the ruling is binding in future cases in which the same point of Community law arises; or, as an English lawyer might ask, is it a precedent? The whole question of precedent in the Court of Justice is discussed later in Chapter 16. Here we must anticipate the conclusion there reached, namely, that the Court prefers to follow its own previous decisions (including rulings) but that it does not hesitate to depart from them where necessary. Hence, the Court has held that a national court, at whatever level, is always free to seek a new preliminary ruling instead of following an old one: in Joined Cases 28–30/62 *Da Costa* [1963] ECR 31 the Dutch Tax Court put exactly the same question to the Court as it had already put in the previous case of *Van Gend en Loos* (Case 26/62 [1963] ECR 1), and the Court endorsed its freedom to do so. In practice, however, national courts frequently accept previous rulings as clarifying the question of Community law in issue now before them so as to render otiose a further reference: see, *e.g.* the *Terrapin* case before the German Federal Supreme Court [1978] 3 C.M.L.R. 102; and a United Kingdom court is bound by statute to accept not only the ruling in a case which it has referred but also the principles laid down by the Court and any relevant previous decision: see the European Communities Act 1972, s.3(1) and below, p. 320.

The doctrine of precedent is concerned with the *prospective* effect of a judgment (or ruling). Whether a ruling has *retrospective* effect is a different matter and requires us to distinguish between (1) a ruling on interpretation, and (2) a ruling on validity (or invalidity).

1. Rulings on interpretation

It is the characteristic of an oracle to make plain what has always been. Thus, when in 1963 the Court of

Justice ruled in *Van Gend en Loos* (above), that Article 12 EEC had direct effect, it was declaring what had always been the correct interpretation of that Article since the Treaty entered into force on January 1, 1958.

However, in exceptional cases where the interest of legal certainty so demands, the Court has been prepared to limit the general retrospective effect of its ruling on interpretation: see Case 43/75 *Defrenne* [1976] ECR 455, and Case 24/86 *Blaizot* v. *University of Liege, The Times*, April 4, 1988, fully discussed below, p. 289.

2. Rulings on validity

It is only common sense that provisions of Community law enjoy a presumption of validity. Rulings on invalidity, therefore, are much less frequent than rulings on interpretation: Community law is often obscure, seldom invalid.

Where the Court rules that a Community measure is valid or invalid, the ruling is binding upon the referring court in the same way as we have seen a ruling on interpretation binds that court. Similarly, the ruling has force as a precedent: if, however, the Court has ruled that no factors indicating invalidity have appeared, then new factors may be suggested in a future case, while of course if the measure has been held invalid the question cannot arise again.

When ruling a measure to be invalid, the Court has treated it as being void *erga omnes*: the ruling under Article 177 EEC is therefore different from a decision under Article 184 EEC which merely declares the measure to be inapplicable in the instant case (for Article 184 and the plea of illegality, see p. 125, above).

Ratione temporis, however, the Court may decide to limit the retrospective effect of its ruling in order to leave previous transactions unaffected. We have already seen in *Defrenne* above how it did this when ruling upon interpretation, but the same concern for legal certainty may operate *a fortiori* when it rules a Community measure to be void.

Thus, in Case 41/84 *Pinna* [1986] ECR 1 the Court declared invalid a provision in a Council regulation which granted to France a special exemption from the obligation to pay family allowances in respect of an immigrant worker's family resident in another Member State. The Court went on to limit the retrospective effect of the ruling: only the claimant and those who had already commenced proceedings prior to the date of its judgment could claim allowances for periods prior to that date. (Subsequently, the Commission, alleging failure to comply with the ruling in *Pinna*, introduced Article 169 proceedings against France in Case 371/88).

Again, in Cases 4, 109 and 145/79, *Providence Agricole de la Champagne and others* (the *Maize and Starch* cases) [1980] ECR 2823, the Court held a Council regulation to be void which had caused the applicants (and other processors of the same products) to receive lower payments for their products than they would otherwise have done. Nevertheless, the Court went on to hold that the applicants should not be entitled to claim against their national authorities the extra sums which would be due to them if transactions concluded prior to the date of the ruling were to be re-opened. The Court claimed jurisdiction to do this in proceedings under Article 177, by analogy with the power conferred upon it by Article 174(2) whereby the Court may state which of the effects of the regulation it has declared void in proceedings under Article 173 shall be considered as definitive: (for the complex consequences of these rulings in the French courts, and the divergent attitudes of the French *Cour de Cassation* and *Conseil d'Etat*, see Hartley, *The Foundations of European Community Law* (2nd ed., 1988), pp. 232–235).

In the result, the Court evolved a doctrine of great flexibility akin to that of prospective overruling in the United States. Whereas, in *Defrenne* and *Pinna*, the applicant—but not *future* applicants—was able to benefit from the ruling, in the *Maize and Starch* cases not even the applicants could benefit from the ruling. In reality, of course, the applicants (and all fellow processors) would be better off in the future by reason of the offending regulation being held void.

Conclusions

Earlier chapters have shown the narrow limits within which the individual can bring a case directly before the Court: limits which the Court itself has strictly construed. In contrast, the Court's policy, as this chapter has shown, has been to welcome references from national courts; and it has availed itself of the opportunity presented by such references to develop the law in ways which are explored in Part Four.

Characteristically, in cases referred under Article 177, what is at stake between the parties in the action before the national court may be relatively little; but the case often raises wider principles concerning the impact of the Communities on the sovereignty of the Member States; and the ruling of the Court is such as to determine authoritatively, and with binding force, the conflict between Community law and national law. In addition, other principles of a constitutional character have been laid down.

The two classic illustrations are the judgments in *Van Gend en Loos* in 1963 and in *Costa* v. *ENEL* in 1964. In the former case, as we have seen, the question concerned a tariff classification made under Dutch law which the plaintiff challenged in the Dutch court as contrary to Article 12 of the EEC Treaty. The action raised the issue of conflict between national legislation and the provisions of the Treaty. The Court not only resolved this issue in favour of the primacy of Community law, but also formulated the doctrine of direct effect, thus providing for a direct guarantee of rights arising under Community law before the national courts, and ensuring, incidentally, that the future development of the law would be the responsibility of the national courts acting, where appropriate, under the guidance of the Court through the use of Article 177.

In *Costa* v. *ENEL* the sum involved, the amount of the plaintiff's electricity bill, was trivial—little more than £1; but by challenging its legality before the Italian magistrate he put in issue the validity, under the EEC Treaty, of State measures of nationalisation. While leaving the magistrate to apply its ruling as he thought fit (he, in fact, upheld the plaintiff's submission), the Court took the opportunity, in this most famous of its judgments, of elaborating its doctrine that membership of the Community limited the sovereignty of the Member States:

> "By contrast with ordinary international treaties, the EEC Treaty has created its own legal system which, on the entry into force of the Treaty, became an integral part of the legal systems of the Member States and which their courts are bound to apply.
>
> By creating a Community of unlimited duration, having its own institutions, its own personality, its own legal capacity and capacity of representation on the international plane and, more particularly, real powers stemming from a limitation of sovereignty or a transfer of powers from the States to the Community, the Member States have limited their sovereign rights, albeit within limited fields, and have thus created a body of law which binds both their nationals and themselves": [1964] ECR 585 at 593.

In another reference from Italy (Case 106/77 *Simmenthal* [1978] ECR 629) the Court was faced with a conflict between a directly applicable Community rule and a later national law. Developing the doctrine in *Costa* v. *ENEL* of the Community as a new legal order and of the paramountcy of Community law, the Court was careful not to rule that the Community rule had made the subsequent Italian law void; rather, it precluded the valid adoption of new legislative measures to the extent to which they would be incompatible with Community provisions. The Court declared:

> "A national court which is called upon, within the limits of its jurisdiction, to apply provisions of Community law is under a duty to give full effect to those provisions, if necessary refusing of its own motion to apply any conflicting provision of national legislation, even if adopted subsequently, and it is not necessary for the court to request or await a prior setting aside of such provisions by legislative or other constitutional means."

The late Professor Hood Phillips commented on this passage that it would not prevent the British Parliament from repealing the whole or part of the European Communities Act 1972 so as to deprive British courts of the relevant jurisdiction referred to above (see (1979) LQR p. 167); but see *contra*, Usher, *European Community Law and National Law: The Irreversible Transfer?* (1981).

Quite apart from the content of its rulings, this aspect of the jurisdiction of the Court of Justice is of constitutional significance in other respects. In the first place, if a reference is made on the validity of, for example, a Council regulation, the Court may be required to consider the compatibility of the Community enactment with the founding Treaties in the same way as a constitutional court is required to consider the constitutionality of national legislation. Second, the ruling of the Court is final in a sense unknown in systems which have a sovereign legislature. Thus in the United Kingdom a decision of even the highest court can, in the last resort, be reversed by an Act of Parliament. In the Communities, however, a ruling on the interpretation of the Treaties could be reversed only by an amendment of them; and such an amendment, requiring the unanimous approval of the Member States in accordance with their respective constitutional provisions, is almost impossible to attain. Here too therefore the Court is more comparable to a constitutional court than to an ordinary court. Moreover, at least so long as the normal law-making processes in the Community were partially paralysed by the lack of power and influence of the Parliament and by the unanimity rule of practice in the Council, the Court assumed a creative law-making role for which the Article 177 system has been the principal vehicle.

Chapter 11

OPINIONS: EXTERNAL RELATIONS

As well as the judgments which it gives in direct
actions, and the rulings which it delivers on references
from national courts, the Court has an advisory
jurisdiction to give "Opinions" under Article 228 of the
EEC Treaty. Article 228 concerns the negotiation and
conclusion of agreements between the Community and
non-Member States or international organisations. It
provides that, where such an agreement is envisaged,
the Council, the Commission or any Member State may
seek, before the agreement is entered into, the opinion
of the Court as to whether the agreement is compatible
with the provisions of the Treaty. There is a corresponding provision under Article 103 of the Euratom
Treaty. Article 228 further provides that, where the
opinion of the Court is adverse, the agreement may
enter into force only by an amendment to the EEC
Treaty in accordance with the process prescribed by
Article 236, a process which has rarely been used, the
most notable recent example being the Single European
Act. Thus although this aspect of the Court's jurisdiction is advisory, and it gives only an "Opinion," it does
rule definitively under Article 228 on the vital question
of the treaty-making power of the Community.

That power has been widely construed, although the
provisions of the EEC Treaty are rudimentary. Remark-
ably, the Treaty leaves the general question as to the
scope of the Community's treaty-making powers
unanswered; in particular, it fails to specify the dividing
line between the treaty-making powers of the Community and those of the Member States. There are only
three relevant articles. Firstly, Article 113 provides for a

203

"common commercial policy" governing the Community's trade with non-Member States and covering in particular "changes in tariff rates, the conclusion of tariff and trade agreements, the achievement of uniformity of liberalisation, export policy and measures to protect trade such as those to be taken in case of dumping and subsidies." By Article 113(3), where agreements with third countries need to be negotiated, the Commission is to conduct the negotiations under the general supervision of the Council. Second, Article 229 instructs the Commission to ensure the maintenance of "all appropriate relations" with the United Nations, with the GATT, and with international organisations generally. Lastly, Article 238 empowers the Community to conclude association agreements. Here the outstanding achievement has been the conclusion of a succession of agreements with African, Caribbean, and Pacific States, currently under the title of the Third Lomé Convention.

The division of competences between the Community institutions is governed by Article 228. According to that Article, where the Treaty provides for the conclusion of international agreements by the Community, the Commission generally negotiates and the Council concludes the agreements. It might be thought, from a reading of Article 228, that the treaty-making powers of the Community are limited to those enumerated in Article 113 (common commercial policy), Article 229 (relations with international organisations) and Article 238 (association agreements). That view has been roundly rejected by the Court of Justice, which has progressively expanded the Community's external competence beyond those limits. In the ERTA case which, as we have seen (p. 98), came before the Court under Article 173 and not under Article 228, the Court held that the Community had the capacity to establish treaty relations with non-Member States over the whole field of objectives specified in Part One of the Treaty.

In order to determine whether the Community had such capacity in a particular case, the Court looked to the whole scheme of the Treaty, as well as to its specific provisions. The capacity was found to arise not only where it was expressly conferred, as by Articles 113 and 238, but also from other provisions of the Treaty, or from measures taken by the Community institutions within the framework of such provisions. In particular, whenever the Community implemented a common internal policy, Member States were deprived of the right to undertake separately any obligations in their external relations which might affect the Community's common rules. As the Court said in the ERTA judgment (at p. 274): "As and when such common rules come into being, the Community alone is in a position to assume and carry out contractual obligations toward third countries affecting the whole sphere of application of the Community legal system."

The Court has developed this approach in a succession of cases, usually at the instigation of the Commission, and often in the face of opposition from the Member States. In this way, the external competence of the Community has been progressively expanded.

The next step in the development of the Court's case law was taken in 1975 in the *Export Credits* case: Opinion 1/75 [1975] ECR 1355. Here an agreement on export credits was being prepared within the OECD in the form of a draft "Understanding on a Local Cost Standard." The Commission recommended the Council to take a decision under Article 113 of the Treaty according to which the attitude of the Community would be expressed by the Commission. When doubts arose about the Community's competence in the matter, the Commission asked the Court for an Opinion pursuant to Article 228(1). The Court took the view not only that the Community was competent to participate in the agreement but that its competence was exclusive:

Member States had no concurrent power. Elsewhere the Court has recognised the possibility of "mixed agreements" where the competence to negotiate and to conclude a treaty may be shared between the Community and the Member States: Opinion 1/78 [1979] ECR 2871, concerning a commodity agreement, the International Agreement on Natural Rubber.

The division of competences between the Community and the Member States may come before the Court by other routes as well, *e.g.* by a question referred for a preliminary ruling under Article 177. It did so in Joined Cases 3, 4 and 6/76 *Kramer* [1976] ECR 1279. Here the question arose when Dutch fishermen were prosecuted in a Dutch court for infringing Dutch conservation measures designed to conserve stocks of sole and plaice in the North East Atlantic. The connection with Community law was not immediately apparent since the Dutch measures had been adopted pursuant to the North East Atlantic Fisheries Convention, which was not a Community treaty: the parties to the Convention were seven Member States and seven non-member States. But the Dutch court asked, among other questions, whether the Member States were still competent to assume commitments on the international plane, or whether the Community alone had authority to enter into such commitments. The Court of Justice answered that, since there was not yet a fully developed Community policy on conservation, the Member States did have, at the time, the competence to assume the commitments in question, but that their competence was only temporary and would expire at the end of the transitional period laid down by Article 102 of the Act of Accession, *viz.*: at the end of 1978.

The international competence of the Community was further explored, under Article 228, in Opinion 1/76 [1977] ECR 741, which concerned an international agreement on a laying-up fund for barges on the Rhine, and in Ruling 1/78 [1978] ECR 2151, concerning a draft convention on the protection of nuclear materials. The latter ruling, given under Article 103 of the Euratom Treaty, provoked an extraordinarily virulent reaction in France, where two parliamentarians introduced a Bill seeking to have the judgment declared illegal on the ground of "fraud" and seeking to provide, in terms designed to recall the re-establishment of French independence after the end of the German occupation in 1944, that any French authority submitting to the Court's ruling should be guilty of the crime of "forfeiture." The Bill did not become law; but the strength of political reactions to the judgments of the Court raises questions to which we must return in the concluding chapter.

Here it may be appropriate to consider why the Court was given this somewhat unusual advisory jurisdiction. Normally, courts do not have, and do not like exercising, advisory functions, nor jurisdiction to rule on measures which are merely proposals or other hypothetical questions. The purpose of this jurisdiction, according to the *Export Credits* case, is to forestall complications which might arise subsequently if the question of compatibility with the Treaty were raised after the Community had concluded an international agreement. It is noteworthy that, under international law, the relations between the parties to a treaty cannot normally be affected, once the treaty is concluded, by a ruling of a court of one of the parties that the treaty is, in its view, invalid: *cf.* Article 46 of the Vienna Convention on the Law of Treaties. As we have seen, the Court has gone well beyond the original purpose of its jurisdiction under Article 228 in order to prevent the Member States from encroaching on the international competence of the Community.

Procedure

Requests for an opinion under Article 228 have usually come from the Commission. The Commission's request is served on the Council and the Member States, and the President of the Court fixes a period within which the institutions and the Member States may submit their written observations. There are no public proceedings; all the advocates general (and sometimes also Member States) are heard in private, and the Court then delivers a reasoned opinion. The Court's Rules of Procedure appear, somewhat unusually, to enlarge the Court's jurisdiction, by providing that the opinion may deal, not only with the question whether the envisaged agreement is compatible with the provisions of the Treaty, but also with the question whether the Community or any Community institution has the power to enter into that agreement.

APPENDIX

JUDICIAL STATISTICS

1. *Cases brought*

	1982	1983	1984	1985	1986	1987	1988	1953-1988
Preliminary rulings	129	98	129	139	91	144	179	1858
Direct actions	131	131	140	229	181	174	136	2063
Staff cases	85	68	43	65	57	77	58	2347
Interim measures	21	12	17	22	23	20	17	274
Total:	366	309	329	455	352	415	390	6542

2. *Direct actions brought by*
3. *Direct actions brought against*

	Direct actions brought by	*Direct actions brought against*
Belgium	7	104
Denmark	5	15
Germany	24	56
Greece	14	53
Spain	7	2
France	29	102
Ireland	8	35
Italy	35	194
Luxembourg	6	28
Netherlands	20	27
Portugal	1	—
United Kingdom	17	24
Total Member States:	173	640
Commission	662	1167
Council	3	125
Commission and Council	—	105
European Parliament	4	19
EIB	—	1
Natural or legal persons	1220	5
Total:	2062	2062

4. *Judgments and interim orders*

	1982	1983	1984	1985	1986	1987	1988	1953–1988
Cases completed	234	210	218	255	197	316	306	3657
Judgments given in cases completed	176	148	163	202	170	208	235	2657
Interlocutory judgments	9	2	1	9	2	—	3	53
Total judgments	185	150	164	211	172	208	238	2710
Interim orders	15	14	16	17	22	19	18	240

5. *Subject matter of direct actions*

	1953–1988
a. EEC	
Discrimination (Tr. Art. 7)	3
Free movement of goods (Tr. Arts. 9–11)	29
Customs duties (Tr. Arts. 12–17)	28
Common customs tariff (Tr. Arts. 18–29)	8
Quantitative restrictions (Tr. Arts. 30–35)	102
Industrial property (Tr. Art. 36)	9
National monopolies (Tr. Art. 37)	4
Agriculture (Tr. Arts. 38–47)	342
Agricultural guidance fund (Tr. Art. 40)	55
Freedom of movement for workers (Tr. Art. 48)	11
Social security (Tr. Art. 51)	11
Right of establishment (Tr. Arts. 52–58)	36
Freedom to provide services (Tr. Arts. 59–66)	25
Capital (Tr. Arts. 67–73)	1
Transport (Tr. Arts. 74–84)	21
Cartel agreements — Dominant positions (Tr. Arts. 85–90)	234
Aids granted by States (Tr. Arts. 92–94)	75
Internal taxation (Tr. Arts. 95–99)	77
Approximation of laws (Tr. Arts. 100–102)	219
Conjunctural Policy (Tr. Art. 103)	5
Commercial policy	31
Dumping	63
Social policy	13
European Social Fund (Tr. Arts. 123–128)	5
Arbitration clause (Tr. Art. 181)	9
Financial provisions (Tr. Arts. 200–209)	8
Non-contractual liability (Tr. Art. 215)	185
Protective measures (Tr. Art. 226)	32
Accession of Greece	7
Accession of Spain and Portugal	12
Convention of Lomé	7
Association between EEC and third countries	1
Staff statute	10

5. *Subject matter of direct actions—continued*

	1953–1988
b. EAEC	
Health and safety (Tr. Arts. 30–39)	1
Joint undertakings (Staff)	8
Supply (Tr. Arts. 52–76)	1
Arbitration clause	5
c. ECSC	
Coal market	15
Control by the High Authority	2
Supply (Tr. Art. 3a)	2
Quantitative restrictions (Tr. Art 4a)	1
Aids granted by States (Tr. Art. 4c)	13
Consultative Committee (Tr. Art. 18)	1
Non-contractual liability (Tr. Art. 40)	65
Checks (Tr. Art. 47)	8
Levies (Tr. Arts. 49–50)	8
Equalisation of scrap metal (Tr. Art. 53)	167
Investments (Tr. Art. 54)	3
Quotas (Tr. Art. 58)	195
Prices (Tr. Arts. 60–64)	43
Cartels and concentrations (Tr. Arts. 65–66)	28
Transport (Tr. Art. 70)	35
d. Privileges and Immunities	9
e. Staff Cases	2347
f. Functioning of the Communities	41

6. *Subject matter of preliminary rulings*

	1961– 1988
a. EEC	
Discrimination (Tr. Art. 7)	13
Common customs tariff	131
Free movement of goods (Tr. Arts. 9–11)	43
Customs duties (Tr. Arts. 12–17)	115
Quantitative restrictions (Tr. Arts. 30–35)	150
Industrial property (Tr. Art. 36)	31
National monopolies (Tr. Art. 37)	16
Agriculture (Tr. Arts. 38–47)	618
Agricultural Guidance (& Guarantee) Fund (Tr. Art. 40)	4
Free movement of workers (Tr. Art. 48)	67
Social security for migrant workers (Tr. Art. 51)	248
Right of establishment (Tr. Arts. 52–58)	29
Services (Tr. Arts. 59–66)	24
Capital (Tr. Arts. 67–73)	4
Transport (Tr. Arts. 74–84)	32
Cartel agreements — Dominant positions (Tr. Arts. 85–90)	89
Aids granted by States (Tr. Arts. 92–94)	21
Internal taxation (Tr. Arts. 95–99)	73
V.A.T.	86
Approximation of laws (Tr. Arts. 100–102)	69
Conjunctural Policy (Tr. Art. 103)	4
Balance of payments (Tr. Arts. 104–109)	6
Commercial policy	23
Dumping	4
Social policy (Tr. Arts. 119–122)	47
Procedural questions (Tr. Art. 177)	20
Non-contractual liability (Tr. Art. 215)	2
Protective measures (Tr. Art. 226)	10
Staff statute	7
Functioning of the Communities	9
Associations between EEC & third countries	20
Convention of Lomé	2
Privileges and Immunities	11
Convention on jurisdiction (27.9.1968)	68
Accession of Greece	3

6. *Subject matter of preliminary rulings—continued*

	1961–1988
a. EEC—*continued*	
Accession of Spain and Portugal	2
b. EAEC	
Privileges and immunities	1
Procedural questions (Tr. Art. 152)	1
Non-contractual liability	1
Health and safety	1
c. ECSC	
Coal market	1
Levies (Tr. Art. 49)	2
Prices (Tr. Art. 60–64)	1
Dumping	1

7. *Courts which have requested a preliminary ruling*

	1961-1988		1961-1988
BELGIUM		**IRELAND**	
Cour de Cassation	27	An Chúirt Uachtarach	—
Conseil d'Etat	10	An Ard-Chúirt (High Court)	13
Others	179	An Chúirt Chúarda	2
		An Chúirt Dúiche	1
Total:	216	Others	4
DENMARK		Total:	20
Højesteret	9		
Others	20	**ITALY**	
Total:	29	Corte Costituzionale	—
		Corte Suprema di	
FRANCE		Cassazione	35
Cour de Cassation	37	Consiglio di Stato	—
Conseil d'Etat	8	Others	167
Others	305	Total:	202
Total:	350		
		LUXEMBOURG	
GERMANY		Cour Supérieure de Justice	8
Bundesverfassungsgericht	—	Conseil d'Etat	7
Bundesgerichtshof	31	Others	8
Bundesarbeitsgericht	4		
Bundesverwaltungsgericht	22	Total:	23
Bundesfinanzhof	89		
Bundessozialgericht	30	**NETHERLANDS**	
Others	427	Raad van State	10
		Hoge Raad	46
Total:	603	Centrale Raad van Beroep	29
		College van Beroep voor het	
GREECE		Bedrijfsleven	74
Cour de Cassation	—	Tariefcommissie	17
Conseil d'Etat	1	Others	125
Others	18		
Total:	19	Total:	301

7. *Courts which have requested a preliminary ruling—continued*

	1961-1988
PORTUGAL	
Tribunal Constitucional	—
Supremo Tribunal de Justiça	—
Supremo Tribunal Administrativo	—
Others	—
Total:	—
SPAIN	
Tribunal Constitucional	—
Tribunal Supremo de Justiça	—
Tribunales Superiores de Justicia de las Comunidades Autonomas	—
Others	3
Total:	3
UNITED KINGDOM	
House of Lords	6
Privy Council	—
Court of Appeal	8
Inner House of Court of Session	—
Court of Appeal of N. Ireland	—
Others	78
Total:	92

PART THREE: PROCEDURE AND PRACTICE

Introductory

It is a lawyer's commonplace that procedure often counts for more than substantive law. But the role of procedure in the Court of Justice is in some ways more limited than in national legal systems. The procedure has no long tradition behind it. It was devised for lawyers from the differing legal backgrounds of the six original Member States and therefore was not tied to any particular national system. When first devised and published in 1953, the Rules of Procedure were based on those of the International Court of Justice at The Hague. There is also a family resemblance to the procedure of the French *Conseil d'Etat*, a resemblance developed, whether consciously or unconsciously, by the presence in Luxembourg over the years of a series of judges and advocates general drawn from the *Conseil*.

Modifications in the procedure have hitherto been few. Minor amendments were introduced after the enlargement of the Communities in 1973 and again in 1979 and 1981. A consolidated version of the Rules was published in the Official Journal in 1982. From 1989, of course, regard must be had to the procedural rules adopted for the Court of First Instance, for the division of competences between that court and the Court of Justice and for the machinery of appeals from the one to the other.

A lawyer from the British Isles is likely to find the procedure very strange. The oral and adversary character of English civil procedure (and its Scottish and Irish counterparts) is in marked contrast with the written and inquisitorial features of the Luxembourg procedure, features which cause the continental lawyer little or no surprise.

219

The emphasis on written procedure is explicable on two grounds, historical and practical. In continental civil procedure there is a very long tradition of a written or documentary process, derived from Roman and canon law models; the absence of the English-type institution of the lay jury meant there was little pressure to evolve towards a more oral process. With this shared background, it was natural for the original framers of the procedure at Luxembourg to devise a process with more emphasis on written argument to persuade the legal mind than on forensic flourishes to impress a jury.

In practical terms, a mainly written procedure makes good sense. For the administration of Community justice is ultimately controlled by its single supreme court at Luxembourg which has to serve a territory stretching from the Shetlands to Sicily, from the Atlantic Ocean to the Aegean Sea. The geographical isolation of Luxembourg from the other capitals (and principal legal centres) of the Member States means that lawyers will not wish to prolong their visits to the Court and burden their clients with additional costs. By the time the oral stage is reached the main work has been done on paper by the lawyers working in the convenience of their own offices or chambers.

The Rules of Procedure binding upon the Court are drawn up by the Court itself but submitted for approval to the Council; as Article 188 EEC states: "The Court of Justice shall adopt its rules of procedure. These shall require the unanimous approval of the Council." The Rules themselves fill out and amplify the organisational and procedural framework set out in the Protocols on the Statute of the Court of Justice which are annexed to the three founding Treaties.

However, the rules themselves are relatively brief and give only schematic guidance: there is much less detail than, for example, in the English Rules of the Supreme Court and although there is a handy compendium of texts, "Selected Instruments Relating to the Organisation, Jurisdiction and Procedure of the Court," published by the Court itself, there is no semi-official practitioner's manual equivalent to the English Supreme Court Practice. In recent years, however, two practice books have been published which provide valuable guidance for English-speaking lawyers: these are Usher's *European Court Practice* (1983) and Lasok's *The European Court of Justice: Practice and Procedure* (1984). Within the framework of the Rules, decisions on procedural questions are taken by the Court, on the advice of the judge-rapporteur and advocate general, but often without the parties being consulted. Such decisions are taken at regular "Administrative Meetings" of the Court, held in private in the Deliberation Room. The decisions are communicated to the parties but are not normally reported, so that a lawyer who needs to know the practice of the Court on a particular point can only inquire of the Registry. There is a need in this respect for some system equivalent to the Practice Notes or Directions issued by English superior courts: a precedent already exists in the Notes for Guidance of Counsel (reproduced in the Appendix to the next chapter, p. 247, below).

Chapter 12

PROCEDURE AND PRACTICE

Introduction

Within the categories of cases coming before the Court a broad distinction is drawn between direct actions and references for preliminary rulings. The latter involves a reference by a national court to Luxembourg for a preliminary ruling on a point of Community law; the procedure is distinctive and forms the subject of a separate section (below, p. 242). The account which follows is confined to direct actions, that is, those where a private individual, a company, a Member State or a Community institution is bringing proceedings directly before the Court—usually with a Member State or a Community institution as the defendant. As we have seen (above, p. 64), cases brought by individuals and companies will now normally go to the Court of First Instance, with an appeal on points of law to the Court of Justice. The Court of First Instance is to adopt its own rules of procedure, but since these rules will require the agreement of the Court of Justice and the unanimous approval of the Council, the Council Decision establishing the Court of First Instance provided that the Rules of Procedure of the Court of Justice should apply *mutatis mutandis* in the interim.

The Court of Justice has also adopted its own rules for dealing with appeals from the Court of First Instance. The procedure in such appeals is modelled, with some modifications, on the procedure governing direct actions which is considered here.

A. *The Usual Stages in Procedure*

The procedure has four stages, of which the second stage is sometimes omitted. These stages are: (1) the written proceedings; (2) the investigation or preparatory inquiry; (3) the oral proceedings; (4) judgment. The first and second stages are essentially private, in contrast to the third which takes place publicly in open court.

Despite the number of stages, and the heavy case-load, the procedure moves along with relative despatch; indeed, by the standards of many national courts it was, until recently, quite swift. Thus, a straightforward direct action takes currently about 18 months from commencement of proceedings to judgment; a preliminary reference may take rather less, as the Court always gives priority to such cases, taking the view that time is here of the essence in order to enable the national court to resume its own adjourned proceedings as soon as possible. Recently, the average time taken has increased by several months for each type of case, but the establishment of the Court of First Instance should enable the earlier standards to be maintained.

1. *Written proceedings*

Proceedings are begun by the filing of an application (*requête*) with the Registrar. No set form is required for the application but under the Rules it must contain certain information. Thus, the plaintiff (in the Rules, "the applicant") must set out the subject matter of the dispute and the grounds upon which the application is based. He must also state the form of order that is being sought (*e.g.* an order to quash or for damages) and the nature of the evidence being relied upon. Any claim for costs must be included in the application.

These are the minimum requirements, but the successful drafting of an application requires considerable skill: see the helpful guidance offered by Advocate General Sir Gordon Slynn in the English Bar's journal

Counsel, September/October 1988. The document is the equivalent neither of an English writ nor of a statement of claim, although it performs the function of both. It is much more, for it contains, in effect, the whole of the applicant's case. It should include a full statement of the facts, of the nature of the complaint, and of the arguments of law upon which the applicant relies; any documentary evidence should be annexed (or its exact whereabouts indicated so as to permit a subsequent court order for production). Moreover, since the form of order sought cannot normally be amended, and since the Court cannot adjudicate *ultra petita*, the contents of the application circumscribe the scope of the action. The case can be expanded in the reply to the defence or at the oral hearing, but no substantial modification is permitted at these later stages.

Other, more technical information required in the application includes an address for service in Luxembourg: usually, this is the office of a Luxembourg *avocat* but the address may be "of any person enjoying the confidence" of the applicant. In addition, the lawyer acting for the applicant must file a certificate of his entitlement to practise before the courts of a Member State. The question of the right of audience is considered in the next chapter. It should be noted that legal representation is obligatory in direct actions, (below, p. 255), but a preliminary application for legal aid may be made without the services of a lawyer (below, p. 261).

The language in which an application is drafted will normally be taken to be the language of the case. Where the applicant is a Member State or an individual (or company) who is proceeding against a Community institution, the general rule is that the applicant has the choice among the 10 languages allowed by the Court: Danish, Dutch, English, French, German, Greek, Irish, Italian, Portuguese or Spanish. But where the action is against a Member State (or, as may exceptionally arise, an individual or company in a Member State), the choice of language belongs to the defendant. As a matter of practical convenience, however, the Court has settled (at least for the present) upon French as its working language. Accordingly, whatever language is chosen for the particular case, the documents will always be translated at least into French for internal use.

The application, if in satisfactory form, is then served upon the defendant. Service of this, as of all other documents, is effected by the Registrar by registered post.

The defendant has one month in which to file his defence. The defence is of similar scope to the application, and should set out the considerations of fact and law on which the defendant relies, an indication of the supporting evidence—again annexed to the pleading—and also any counterclaim or other relief sought. The time for filing a defence can be extended for good reason by the President of the Court.

The Court has adopted the practice, common to many legal systems, of distinguishing generally between the admissibility of the action and its merits or substance. Questions of admissibility include all questions which go to the jurisdiction of the Court: they may include, for example, the question whether the applicant has the necessary standing to challenge the measure in issue, whether the action has not been brought out of time, or whether the "conclusion" or form of relief sought by the applicant is one which the Court can grant.

Accordingly the defendant often sets out his submissions under two heads, admissibility and substance; or he may make a "preliminary objection" to the admissibility of the action, and ask the Court to take a decision on that alone, which may obviate the need for a decision on the substance. The Court may also consider, of its own motion and at any time, whether there is an "absolute bar" to proceeding with a case, what the French term *un moyen d'ordre public*, that is, a bar which does not require to be pleaded by the parties and cannot be waived by them.

In the absence of a defence, judgment can be given in default. Usually, however, a defence is lodged. This allows the applicant to put in a reply, to which the defendant in turn can respond by a rejoinder. Although not obligatory, both reply and rejoinder are common steps in the pleading of a case at Luxembourg. The time limits for each are usually one month. With the rejoinder the pleadings are closed.

2. *Investigation or preparatory inquiry*

Meanwhile, upon the lodging of the application, the case will have been assigned by the President to one of the six Chambers, and he will nominate one of the judges from that Chamber to act as rapporteur while the First Advocate General will designate the advocate general for the case.

All the papers relating to the case will have been distributed to all members of the Court, but at this stage, they will only have been studied closely by the judge-rapporteur and the advocate general to whom the case is assigned—and their legal secretaries.

The pleadings being closed, the Court now takes over the direction of the proceedings. Up to this point the procedure has been adversary; it now becomes inquisitorial, if the Court decides an *instruction* of the case is needed. (This term of French procedure has become "preparatory inquiry" in the English version of the Rules).

This and other procedural decisions are based upon the preliminary report (*rapport préalable*) of the judge-rapporteur. Guided by this report and any views expressed by the advocate general, the Court decides what (if any) issues of fact need to be proved and what evidence is to be adduced for the purpose, including whether witnesses (and if so, which) are to be summoned to testify. This decision is made at an

Administrative Meeting (see p. 221, above) held in private in the Deliberation Room. An order setting out any measures of inquiry is served upon the parties.

The Court may also decide at this stage whether the case will be heard by the Chamber to which it was assigned, or whether it should be heard by a full Court consisting, in the jargon of the Court, of a "Petit Plenum" of nine judges or a "Grand Plenum" consisting of all thirteen judges, a decision depending on the difficulty or importance of the case. Cases are never listed to be heard by only seven judges (the legal quorum for a full Court) because of the risk that one judge may for some reason (*e.g.* ill health) become unavailable later in the proceedings and thus necessitate the reopening of the proceedings before a reconstituted Court. When the Court sits with 11 (or 10 or 12) judges it usually means that the case has been listed for a Grand Plenum but that one or more of the judges is unavailable (or ineligible) to sit on the day of the hearing: a judge who does not sit during the oral hearing or during the advocate-general's opinion may not then take part in the vote on the case.

The Court may also decide that there should be a joinder of the case with other closely related cases (see p. 240, below).

The investigation may include all or any of the following: the personal appearance of the parties; the production of documents or the supply of information by the parties; the summoning of witnesses to appear and give evidence; the commissioning of a report by an expert; or the arranging of a visit or inspection. The Rules permit these measures, where appropriate, to be assigned by the Court either to the Chamber for the case or to the judge-rapporteur individually.

It should be noted that the hearing of witnesses is part of the investigation, not part of the oral proceedings; moreover, the witnesses or the expert are witnesses of the *Court*, not of the parties. It is possible for the parties to request the Court to hear a witness in order to prove certain specified facts; if there is good reason for this request, the Court will accede to it, and the witness then becomes the Court's witness.

The taking of evidence from a witness conforms, for the most part, with the normal practice of continental courts—practice which common lawyers generally regard as much inferior to their own for the establishment of facts where this depends on the credibility of a witness. The order sets out what facts are to be established: see the example in Case 18/63 *Wollast* v. *EEC* [1964] ECR 85, at 95. The witness is heard by the Chamber in the presence of the parties or their representatives. After the witness has given his evidence, questions may be put to the witness by the presiding judge, the other judges or the advocate general. Until the revision of the Rules of Procedure in 1974, the parties' lawyers could only put questions through the medium of the presiding judge, but now they may be permitted to put their questions directly, as in cross-examination—although the different context of the Luxembourg questioning makes it no more than a pale shadow of the English original. The statement of the witness, attested on oath, is recorded and later transcribed.

Letters rogatory are an alternative method for taking evidence. These are in the form of an order for a witness to be examined, on specified facts, by a judicial authority in the Member State where he permanently resides. Their use is extremely rare: indeed, the only instance to date is that in Case 160/84 *Oryzomyli Kavallas* v. *Commission* [1985] ECR 675; [1986] ECR 1633 where it appears that the replies requested took nine months to reach the Court.

A formal investigation or preparatory inquiry is relatively rare. Thus, up to January 1, 1989 (some 36 years after the Court came into existence) the Court had heard witnesses in only 44 cases and had appointed only 16 experts; there had been only one reported instance of an inspection: this was under the ECSC Treaty, where it was necessary to ascertain conditions of production in the iron and steel industry: see Case 14/59 *Société de Fonderies de Pont-à-Mousson* [1959] ECR 215 at 224 and 237 for a visit by the Court to the applicant's foundry at Pont-à-Mousson. If witnesses are to be heard, the inquiry may be fixed on the day preceding, or the same day as, the oral proceedings in order to save the lawyers a double journey to Luxembourg.

More commonly, the Court at its Administrative Meeting may decide, at the prompting of the judge-rapporteur, to ask the parties, or the Commission, to reply, either in writing or at the oral hearing, to questions put by the Court in advance of the hearing, or to produce documents or objects for the Court's inspection: see, *e.g.* the "laughing device" produced in Case 22/76 *Import Gadgets* [1976] ECR 1371.

Whatever material is added to the court file of the case as a result of a preparatory inquiry or the informal requests just mentioned, it must be made freely available to the parties, who have then the right to make written submissions upon its content. In this respect, the procedure conforms with the requirement that it be (as the French would say) *une procédure contradictoire*, that is one in which the arguments and evidence of each party are made available to, and can be commented upon by, the other.

3. *Oral proceedings*

Once the pleadings have been exchanged and the preparatory inquiry (if any) has been conducted, the President of the Court fixes the earliest convenient date for the public hearing. The parties and their lawyers are given at least three weeks' notice to attend. With the current congestion of the Court's time-table, hearings are now often fixed months in advance. Once fixed, the date cannot readily be changed. In England it has been

accepted that a barrister's obligation to attend a
hearing before the Court of Justice takes precedence
over obligations before all courts save the House
of Lords.

Some time before the hearing the judge-rapporteur
issues his report for the hearing (*rapport d'audience*).
This sets out the facts of the case and summarises the
respective arguments of the parties. The original
purpose of the report was that it should be read aloud
at the start of the oral hearing to inform the public and
preserve the public character of the proceedings. But it
is now always taken as read. It now serves different
purposes, including the instruction of members of the
Court who may be less familiar with the full contents of
the file than the judge-rapporteur and advocate general.
It is distributed before the hearing to the parties'
lawyers so that they can make any comments either
formally at the hearing or otherwise. Immediately
before the hearing, copies of the report are placed on a
table outside the Courtroom for interested members of
the public. Subsequently, as we have seen (above,
p. 45) the report will be published in the Court's
reports and may make it easier to understand the
judgment, which will often contain a reference back to
the report for fuller detail of the facts and argument.

Immediately before the case is called, counsel for the
parties and the agents for any Community institution
involved are invited into the judges' retiring room
where there is often informal discussion, for example, as
to the order and length of speeches in the forthcoming
proceedings.

The members of the Court take up their seats on the
bench after the usher has called out "The Court"
(spoken in the language of the case) as a signal to those
present to stand.

The oral proceedings are reduced in practice to the
addresses by the opposing lawyers and the opinion
submitted by the advocate general. This opinion, as we

shall see, is almost always delivered at a subsequent sitting of the Court.

So far as the lawyers' addresses are concerned, strict time limits are now imposed: normally each party is allowed 30 minutes, and only 15 minutes in cases before a Chamber of three judges: see the Court's Notes for the Guidance of Counsel, appended to this chapter. Counsel cannot therefore waste the Court's time by going over again the facts and arguments already fully set out in the written proceedings and so known to the Court. Instead, they show their skill in marshalling the salient points of their case and the weaknesses of the other side. High-flown rhetoric is eschewed. Unless the language of the case is English or French, some members of the Court will be dependent upon their earphones for simultaneous translation, a barrier which not even the oratory of a Demosthenes could surmount.

It is not customary, at least before the full Court, to interrupt the main speeches. Each side is allowed a brief right of reply to the other. In recent years the judges and the advocate general have increasingly exercised their right to put questions: usually, these questions are reserved until after the two main speeches, but before a Chamber, especially a Chamber of three judges, counsel may find himself interrupted with questions—an ordeal with which counsel from the British Isles at least are familiar.

At the end of the hearing, the advocate general will usually announce the date on which he will deliver his opinion, and the case is then adjourned. Only very rarely might the opinion be delivered forthwith, for example, where the case is already exactly covered by a previous decision of the Court to which the advocate general might then simply refer. Usually, the opinion is delivered in open court at a hearing some weeks later; recently, where possible, it may be one week after the hearing. The advocate general stands to address the Court as an indication that he is in no sense a member of the tribunal of judgment but rather their impartial adviser. His opinion closes the oral proceedings, so that it is he, and not the parties, who has the last word. Exceptionally, the Court may order further investigative steps to be taken, which may mean the advocate general has to deliver a second opinion. The same situation may arise if the advocate general delivers a first opinion which urges the Court to decide the case upon a preliminary point without entering into the merits: if the Court decides against him on the preliminary point, it will ask him to deliver a second opinion on the substance.

An illustration of the re-opening of oral proceedings is provided by Case 155/79 *AM & S Europe Limited* v. *Commission* [1982] ECR 1575, which raised the question of the scope of legal professional privilege in Community law. In the course of an investigation by the Commission under the competition rules, AM & S claimed privilege for certain documents which they refused to make available to the Commission. The Commission did not accept the claim and AM & S took the matter to court. After the oral procedure had been completed, with a very full opinion by Advocate General Warner, the Court decided that the oral procedure should be re-opened: it decided itself to look at the documents for which privilege had been claimed, and for this purpose ordered the applicant to produce them under seal, and decided also to hold a further hearing, after which Advocate General Sir Gordon Slynn gave a further opinion.

4. Judgment

The Court always reserves its judgment. Following continental traditions, the Court preserves strictly the principle of the secrecy of its deliberations. Thus, only the judges are admitted to the Deliberation Room, a large room, elegant in the modern style and with a panoramic view of the City of Luxembourg; neither the advocate general for the case nor the Registrar is present. The principle also entails the exclusion of interpreters, so that the judges have had to settle upon a language which they all understand. In the result, the deliberations of the Court are normally conducted in French.

The principle of secrecy of deliberations has an additional consequence. Dissenting judgments cannot be permitted. Where the Court finds itself divided, a majority view must be determined by vote and this will then emerge as the judgment of the Court. The outside world has no way of knowing whether the judgment was unanimous or by a majority. The interesting implications of the single collegiate judgment are discussed in Part Four (below, p. 266).

Where a vote has to be taken the Rules of Procedure require votes be cast in the reverse order to the order of precedence of the judges; as Professor Schermers explains "Voting in the reverse order to the order of seniority is an old judicial custom in European courts and is designed to prevent the votes of the older and more experienced judges from influencing their younger colleagues" (*Judicial Protection in the European Communities* (4th ed., 1987), p. 449). Whether the Rules are always observed on this point, in practice, only the judges will know.

The Statute requires that judgments should state the reasons on which they are based and give the names of the judges who took part in the deliberations. When subsequently drawn up in the language of the case, the judgment is signed by all the judges who took part in the deliberations and authenticated by the signatures of the President (who may not necessarily have sat on the case) and the Registrar. The authentic version is that in the language of the case. Consequently, except where this language is French, the authentic version will be a translation of the text as agreed in the Deliberation Room; but, to ensure conformity, the translation will be checked by the judge whose native tongue is that of the language of the case. Despite this safeguard, slips may occur; *e.g.* in Case 131/79 *Santillo* [1980] ECR 1585, where a ruling was sought on whether lapse of time may deprive a recommendation to deport of its validity under Directive 64/221, the Court, according to the authentic English text, provided a criterion in terms of whether the lapse of time "is liable to deprive" the recommendation of its validity, whereas the more precise French text employs the words *"est de nature à priver"*: the ambiguity of the English may have misled the Divisional Court and the Court of Appeal in their application of the ruling—see Barav (1981) 6 E.L. Rev. 139.

The operative part of the judgment (what the French term *le dispositif*) is read out at the next available public hearing of the Court, either by the President (or President of Chamber) or the judge-rapporteur or as linguistic convenience may dictate; thus, if the language of the case is Danish or Greek, the Danish or Greek judge, as the case may be, may read out the judgment. The *dispositif* must then be published in the Official Journal, in all the different language series. The judgment in its entirety is also published in the special series of the Court's reports, accompanied by the advocate-general's opinion. The official version in English is that in the European Court Reports. The citation before the Court of other series of reports became improper as soon as the English version of the cases prior to 1973 was published. In the event of some discrepancy having legal significance between the different language versions, the version in the language of the case, being regarded as authentic, must prevail.

B. Execution and Enforcement

The Court has no powers to enforce its judgment. It has no criminal jurisdiction whatsoever, nor does it have the power to commit for contempt which is the peculiar weapon at the disposal of the English judge. This has led to certain problems, theoretical rather than practical, for dealing with perjury by witnesses at Luxembourg.

It will be appreciated from what has been said in previous chapters about the effects of judgments of the Court that questions of execution or enforcement rarely arise. The implementation of preliminary rulings is a matter for the national courts. In actions against Community institutions, the consequences of a judgment given against them are either automatic, as in the case of annulment, or at any rate unlikely to raise problems of non-compliance. A judgment against a Member State is declaratory. There is no provision for enforcement of judgments against Member States or Community institutions, although as we have seen (p. 79) the ECSC Treaty contains provisions for sanctions against Member States. The EEC Treaty merely places the State or institution under an obligation to take the necessary measures to comply with the Court's judgment.

So far as the execution of a judgment is concerned, a problem only arises where the judgment imposes a pecuniary obligation on a private individual or company (as distinct from a Member State). By Article 192 EEC it is only such a judgment which has enforceable effect. The same Article then provides that enforcement shall be governed by the rules of civil procedure in the Member State where enforcement is being sought. In other words, the successful party, armed with an authenticated copy of the judgment, is left to pursue his judgment debtor in the national forum.

C. Costs

This is a subject of great practical importance. It is linked with the subject of legal aid, to be dealt with in the next chapter.

One preliminary difference between the Luxembourg Court (and now the Court of First Instance) and most national courts is that there are no court fees, because of the principle that procedure before the former is free of charge. A further saving follows from the principle that the service of pleadings is effected by the Registry of the Court. A minor qualification to the gratuitous principle is that the Court may order a party to pay court costs which could have been avoided or where the proceedings are deemed vexatious.

Regarding party and party costs, the Court is bound by rule to include in its judgment a decision as to costs. The general principle is that the unsuccessful party is ordered to pay the costs if they have been asked for by the successful party in his application (or defence). There are however a number of exceptions, real or apparent, to this principle.

Thus, in staff cases, the Community institution, as "the employer" concerned, has normally to bear its own costs, even if the employee loses his action.

Again, one party may be only partly successful; for example, the Court may grant his application to annul a Community decision but refuse his claim for damages. Or there may be several parties suing jointly, some of whom succeed while others fail. In such cases the Court may apportion the costs as it thinks fit or simply leave each party to bear his own costs.

If a party withdraws or discontinues proceedings, he may be ordered to pay all the costs, unless the withdrawal or discontinuance is justified by the conduct of the other party.

The question of costs on references for preliminary rulings is dealt with below.

What items are included under costs may give rise to dispute. They appear to cover the travelling and subsistence expenses of parties and their lawyers, the fees of lawyers or other specialist advisers, and the costs involved in providing an address for service in Luxembourg. If the parties cannot agree the items, the Rules provide that one of the parties may apply for costs to be taxed by the Court. This is done by one of the Chambers, whose order is not subject to appeal. In the history of the Court there have only been 30 or so applications for taxation.

Taxation in Luxembourg is quite different from taxation in London: the Court will make a rough assessment of the appropriate level of fees, based on what it considers reasonable in the circumstances.

Decisions on taxation are not normally reported, but Case 126/76 *Dietz* v. *Commission* [1979] ECR 2131 established a point of principle. The Commission claimed from the unsuccessful plaintiff the sum of 75,000 Belgian Francs (rather less than £1,000) for the conduct of the case by its agent, a member of its Legal Service. The Court upheld the applicant's challenge to this claim and ruled that, although the Community institutions could recover fees paid to outside counsel, the position was different where they chose to be represented by one of their own officials acting as agent: they could then recover only the travel and subsistence expenses incurred in attending the hearing in Luxembourg.

D. Some Special Matters of Procedure

1. Interim measures

A party involved in litigation before the Court may apply to the President for interim relief (a procedure known in French as *le référé*). For example, the party may wish to obtain a stay of execution of the decision which is being challenged in the principal suit. The circumstances must justify such a stay, and this condition has been strictly construed so as to limit it to cases where there is a risk of irreparable damage or serious prejudice to the applicant. This reluctance to grant stays of execution is in accordance with French practice where *le référé* is seldom successful before the administrative courts.

As we saw in Chapter 6, the Court has even been prepared to order interim measures in proceedings brought by the Commission against Member States under Article 169 EEC. An example occurred in the continuing "Wine war" between France and Italy (above, p. 79), where the President made an order against France: Case 42/82R [1982] ECR 841 (the letter R after the case number denotes *référé*). Interim relief may also be granted to a company appealing against a Commission decision in competition proceedings. Thus in Case 27/76R *United Brands Co.* v. *EC Commission* [1976] ECR 425, the President suspended two provisions of a Commission decision (requiring United Brands to cease to charge dissimilar and unfair prices and to cease prohibiting the resale of green bananas) until the Court had given judgment on the appeal from that decision; United Brands had pleaded that there was a threat to it of irreversible damage and financial disaster.

The application for interim relief is dealt with separately from the principal suit to which it is, in a sense, ancillary. It is made in writing, and the document must set out the grounds of fact and law so as to establish a prima facie case for the relief being sought. A copy of the application is served on the other side, which may then submit written observations within a short time limit. In the not infrequent event of an oral hearing, the President may be assisted by the judge-rapporteur and the advocate general, but the decision is the President's alone whether to grant or refuse the relief sought. Exceptionally, he may refer an application to the full Court: see, *e.g.* Case 792R/79 *Camera Care* v. *Commission* [1980] ECR 119.

The orders granting or refusing interim relief are not always easy to reconcile, one with another: the decisions are by a single judge (the President) and delivered in situations of urgency which may curtail the full articulation of reasons; rather, there has to be a quick assessment of the facts as presented. The approach is on a case by case basis, rather than to construct a consistent body of jurisprudence.

Applications for interim relief have been on the increase and now average some 20 a year, of which only about a quarter have been successful.

2. Preliminary objections to admissibility

In a direct action the defendant, usually a Community institution, may wish to contest the admissibility of the action, without entering into the substance of the case (see p. 225, above). For example in an action for annulment brought by a natural or legal person against the Council or Commission under Article 173(2) EEC, the Council or Commission may contend that the measure at issue is a regulation which the applicant has no *locus standi* to attack (see above, p. 105 *et seq.*). The defendant may then, without entering a full defence, make a preliminary objection to admissibility. The applicant will then reply and the hearing will be limited to the question of admissibility. Only if the Court finds the action admissible, or decides to reserve the issue of admissibility, will the action continue on the substance in the usual way.

3. Interventions by third parties

The Protocols on the Statute of the Court of Justice under both the ECSC and the EEC Treaties permit the intervention in proceedings of third parties provided they have a sufficient interest in the suit between the principal parties. Notice to potential third parties (and to the world at large) of all proceedings before the Court is given by publication in the Official Journal, as required by the Rules, of every application to originate proceedings. An application to intervene must be made within three months of such publication.

Under the ECSC Statute, a Community institution, a Member State, or a private individual or a company may intervene upon proof of sufficient interest, in order to argue for or against the cases put forward by the principal parties. In the EEC Statute it is presumed that a Community institution or Member State has a sufficient interest to intervene: only a private individual or company is put to proof of their interest, but their intervention is never permitted in suits between Member States or between Member States and Community institutions. Where permitted, the intervention may only support the submissions of one of the principal parties.

As we have seen, the intervention of the European Parliament was accepted by the Court in proceedings against the Council in the *Roquette* and *Maizena* cases (above, p. 119), despite the Council's objection that the Parliament was seeking to use the intervention procedure to circumvent its lack of a direct right of action under Article 173. The Court has sometimes been liberal in admitting interventions: for example, by a national consumers' association in the Sugar Cartel case (Joined Cases 40, etc., /73 *Suiker Unie and Others* v. *Commission* [1975] ECR 1663); and by the CCBE, a body representing the Bars and Law Societies of the Member States, in the *AM & S* case concerning the scope of legal professional privilege in Community law (above, p. 232).

4. *Joinder of actions*

Where two (or more) actions are concerned with similar or closely related matters, they may be joined at any stage of the proceedings, This is done by an order of the Court, either on the initiative of the Court itself or at the request of one of the parties.

Joinder of actions is quite a frequent occurrence, as will be apparent from the number of cases cited in this book which bear more than one serial number. But even without a formal joinder, the Court may arrange administratively for suits which are proceeding concurrently and have a common subject matter to come for oral hearing on the same day, or again the advocate general may deliver a single opinion—a sensible economy in time and effort.

5. Can judgments be appealed against?

A judgment of the Court is final and not subject to any appeal. There are, however, five special procedures which may be invoked with reference to a judgment that has already been delivered.

The first is an application for an interpretation by the Court of its judgment. Thus, a party or a Community institution with a sufficient interest may so apply if difficulty arises in understanding the meaning or scope of a judgment of the Court. An early example was Case 5/55 *ASSIDER* [1954–1956] ECR 135. But the Court has been severe in restricting such applications to cases where there is a real ambiguity in the judgment.

Secondly, there is a procedure for rectification of a judgment: the Court may, of its own motion or on application by a party made within two weeks after the delivery of a judgment, rectify clerical mistakes, errors in calculation and obvious slips: see, *e.g.* Case 27/76 *United Brands* v. *Commission* [1976] ECR 446 and 450, and Case 158/80 *Rewe* [1981] ECR 1805 (the "butter boats" case (1982) 7 E.L. Rev. 316 at 322).

Thirdly, there is the application for a judgment to be reconsidered: the French term is *révision*. A party may apply for this reconsideration if the judgment was given in ignorance of facts which subsequently came to light and which would have had a decisive influence. The new facts may even be subsequent to the judgment of the Court: see Case 56/75-rev. *Elz* v. *Commission* [1977] ECR 1617; but the procedure must not be abused as an attempt to appeal: see Case 116/78 *Bellintani* v. *Commission* [1980] ECR 23. Three months are allowed for the lodging of the application from the date when the party learns of the new facts; no application can be brought after the expiration of 10 years from the date of the judgment.

Fourthly, there is the procedure known in French as *tierce opposition* and in the English version of the Rules of Procedure as "third party proceedings." This is an application for reconsideration of a judgment brought by a third party not involved in the original proceedings. The third party may be a private individual or company, a Member State or a Community institution. It must be shown that the judgment adversely affects their interests and that the proceedings had not been brought to their notice. The Rules of Procedure reduce the scope of this procedure by requiring the applicant to show that the judgment would occasion actual damage to the applicant. The application has to be notified to all the original parties and may include a request for a stay of execution. Two months are allowed for such applications from the date of the publication of the judgment in the Official Journal. An example of this procedure is Cases 42 and 49/59 *Breedband* [1962] ECR 145.

Finally, if a judgment by default has been given against a defendant who was properly served with the application but who did not duly enter an appearance, the defendant is allowed one month from the service of the judgment in which to lodge an application for it to be set aside for cause shown.

E. Preliminary Rulings

The procedure that we have considered so far is the procedure in direct actions, which are brought directly before the Court, and which originate and terminate there. The procedure in preliminary rulings is different: here the Court is ruling, at the request of a national court, on a question of Community law in issue before the national court. The procedure is incidental to, or, in the Court's words (above, p. 171), a step in, the action before the national court. Before the Court of Justice the proceedings on such a reference are not, strictly speaking, contentious, and there are formally no parties to such proceedings. As we saw in Chapter 10, it is regarded as more in the nature of a dialogue between the national court and the Court of Justice conducted in a spirit of "judicial cooperation." This has important consequences for the character of the procedure.

When the order for reference has reached the Court from the national court, a copy is sent by the Registry to the parties to the action before the national court, to the Member States, to the Commission and, where a measure of the Council is in issue, to the Council. These may all submit written observations within a single period of two months; they have no obligation to do so. They may also submit oral observations at the hearing of the case; in practice, the Commission always attends such hearings, the parties usually do so, and sometimes also one or more Governments. After the hearing, the advocate-general's opinion and the ruling of the Court follow in the usual way, as in direct actions.

The Court deals with references as expeditiously as possible. Sometimes there is a delay in the transmission of the reference to the Court but, once received, the questions were, until recent years, answered within about six months, which includes the two month period for the submission of written observations. Thus the judgment in the *Import Gadgets* case (see p. 43, above) records that the order for reference was made on January 22 and received on March 5, 1976; the ruling was given on September 22, 1976. In the 1980s the great increase in the Court's case-load has led to considerable delays, the average period rising to about 18 months; but efforts are being made to reduce these delays, notably by the transfer of whole categories of cases to the new Court of First Instance.

Although in principle the same Rules of Procedure apply to both direct actions and preliminary rulings, the various special features of procedure in direct actions which have been described under head D above are inapplicable to preliminary rulings. Thus in one case where the plaintiff before the German court asked the Court of Justice to supplement its ruling, the Court said that "Article 177 of the EEC Treaty establishes a direct form of cooperation between the Court of Justice and the national courts or tribunals by means of a non-contentious procedure, in which the parties to the main action cannot take any initiative and during the course of which they are only invited to submit their observations within the legal context outlined by the court making the reference": Case 13/67 *Becker* v. *Hauptzollamt München* [1968] ECR 187 at 197. Accordingly a further ruling could be given only if a further reference were made by the national court.

Similarly an application by the Edison electricity company to intervene in Case 6/64 *Costa* v. *ENEL* was rejected by the Court which stated that

"Article 177 of the EEC Treaty does not envisage contentious proceedings designed to settle a dispute but prescribes a special procedure whose aim is to ensure a uniform interpretation of Community law by cooperation between the Court of Justice and the national courts and which enables the latter to seek the interpretation of Community provisions which they have to apply in disputes brought before them": [1964] ECR 585 at 614.

The character of the proceedings also determines many other aspects of the procedure which differ from direct actions. No address for service in Luxembourg is necessary. The language of the case is that of the national court or tribunal which made the reference, although a Member State retains the right to submit observations in its own language, and the advocate general will normally deliver his opinion in his own language. Again, in contrast to direct actions, the ruling will *ex hypothesi* be concerned only with an abstract question of law; normally therefore there will be no occasion for any preparatory inquiries.

Objections to the admissibility of a reference, or to the jurisdiction of the Court, also have a more limited scope than in a direct action. As we saw in Chapter 10, the Court will not normally allow such objections as that a decision on the question referred is not necessary to enable the national court to give judgment. Apart from special circumstances such as those of *Foglia* v. *Novello* (above, p. 180), the Court has consistently held that its jurisdiction is dependent on the mere existence of a reference. Thus a question of admissibility is likely to arise only if the very existence of the reference is itself in doubt, as when for example the order for reference has been set aside on appeal in the national courts. But the practice of the Court is to discontinue its proceedings only if the order for reference is withdrawn by the court making it or quashed by a higher court; otherwise the Court proceeds to judgment: Case 127/73 *B.R.T.* v. *S.A.B.A.M* [1974] ECR 51.

The position on costs is also different. The costs of the parties are always reserved to the national court, the Court's decision on costs invariably stating, as the reason for this, that the proceedings are, insofar as the parties to the main action are concerned, in the nature of a step in the action pending before the national court. The costs incurred by the Member States and by the Community institutions in submitting observations, whether written or oral, are not recoverable. When the national court comes to rule on the costs incurred by the parties in connection with the reference, it must do so, as the law now stands, in the context of its own national law: Case 62/72 *Paul G. Bollmann* v. *Hauptzollamt Hamburg-Waltershof* [1973] ECR 269. However the Court of Justice can itself grant legal aid for the purposes of the preliminary ruling procedure. This is laid down in one of the very few provisions in the Rules of Procedure specifically concerned with preliminary rulings. Another provision in the same Article, Article 104, deals with legal representation. We revert to this and to legal aid in the next chapter.

APPENDIX

NOTES FOR THE GUIDANCE OF COUNSEL[1] AT ORAL HEARINGS

These notes are issued by the Court of Justice so that counsel for the parties may better appreciate the purpose of the oral procedure before the Court and so that they may be informed of the Court's new working methods. The notes are inspired by the desire to reconcile in the best possible manner the need to maintain the quality of judicial protection within the Community legal order and the need to ensure that cases before the Court, which are constantly growing in number, are dealt with expeditiously.

I. The purpose of the oral procedure

It should be borne in mind that by the time the hearing takes place the judges and advocate general will already have read the documents on the case and studied attentively the conclusions, submissions and arguments summarised in the Report for the Hearing. It is therefore unnecessary to repeat orally arguments which have already been set forth in writing or to present a commentary on the pleadings or observations.

In all types of case (both direct actions and references for a preliminary ruling) the purpose of the oral procedure is to enable counsel:

---

[1] The word "counsel" is used in a non-technical sense so as to include all those appearing before the Court and acting as advocate, whatever their capacity or professional status.

   (i) to remind the Court, where appropriate, in summary fashion, of the position adopted, emphasising the essential submissions put forward in writing;

  (ii) to present new arguments based on any matters which arise after the closure of the written procedure and which could not therefore be dealt with in the written pleadings;

 (iii) to reply to questions put by the Court.

In addition, in references for a preliminary ruling, the oral procedure gives counsel an opportunity to refute, very briefly, the essential legal arguments put forward in the observations of the opposing party and thus compensates, to some extent, for the absence of any such opportunity in the written procedure.

II. The course of the oral procedure

1. The usefulness of addressing the Court

Counsel should in each case ask himself, having regard to the purpose of the oral procedure as defined above, whether it is necessary for him to address the Court or whether a simple reference to the observations or written pleadings would not suffice.

The Court wishes to emphasise that, if counsel refrains from addressing the Court, his silence will never be construed as acquiescence in the address delivered by opposing counsel, if the arguments in question have already been refuted in the written pleadings.

Finally, the Court considers, in certain circumstances, that it is preferable to open the hearing with questions put by the Court to counsel. In that event, counsel are requested to take that into account if they then wish to deliver a short address.

2. Presentation and structure of the address

Counsel are reminded that, for the sake of clarity and in order to improve the understanding of their addresses on the part of the members of the Court, *it is always preferable to speak freely on the basis of notes rather than to read out a prepared text.* They are also asked to simplify, so far as possible, their presentation of the case. A series of short sentences is always preferable to one long and complicated sentence. In addition, it would be helpful to the Court if counsel were to structure their address and explain at the outset the order in which they intend to present their arguments.

3. Taking into account the constraints of simultaneous interpretation

Counsel are reminded that not all the members of the Court will be able to follow the address in the language in which it is delivered. Some members of the Court will be listening to an interpreter. The interpreters are highly skilled but their task is a difficult one and counsel should bear in mind that the hearing is likely to take a much smoother course if they speak slowly and into the microphone.

4. Length of the address to the court

The Court is fully aware that the length of counsel's address may vary according to the complexity of the case and the existence or absence of new issues of fact or law. It is also aware that counsel generally wish to be allowed to address the Court at some length. However, counsel are asked to bear in mind that, in view of the ever increasing number of cases brought before the Court, the quality of judicial protection within the Community can only be maintained if the average duration of proceedings before the Court is substantially reduced.

Consequently, counsel will henceforth be asked, *as a general rule*, to *restrict the length of their address to 30 minutes. For cases referred to Chambers consisting of three judges, the length of counsel's address will be limited to 15 minutes.* These are of course merely maximum limits and it goes without saying that they apply only to the address itself and do not include the time used to reply to questions asked by members of the Court or to points raised by other counsel.

Exceptions to this rule may be granted by the Court, subject to a request addressed to the Registrar. Such a request must state in detail the reasons on which it is based and stipulate the amount of time considered necessary. It can only be considered if it reaches the Court 14 days before the date of the hearing. The decision on whether to grant it will be taken by the president of the Court or Chamber before which the case is being heard, after seeking the views of the judge-rapporteur and the advocate general. The decision will be notified to the originator of the request at least seven days before the hearing.

When one party is represented by several counsel, no more than two of them will be allowed to address the Court and the total length of their addresses should not exceed the limits stipulated above. However, replies to questions asked by the Court and observations on points raised by opposing counsel do not have to be delivered by the same counsel who addressed the Court.

When several parties wish to argue in favour of the same proposition (as may happen, in particular, in the case of interventions and joined cases), their counsel are urged to concert their efforts before the hearing, in order to avoid needless repetition.

The president of the Court or Chamber hearing the case will seek to ensure observance of the principles set out above, as regards both the purpose of the oral procedure, that is to say, the content of addresses to the Court, and the length of such addresses.

III. Miscellaneous

1. The report for the hearing

The Court will henceforth endeavour to send the Report for the Hearing to counsel three weeks before the hearing. Counsel are reminded that if the report does not faithfully reflect the views of the parties they should inform the Registrar before the hearing and suggest appropriate amendments.

2. Citations

Counsel are requested, when citing in argument a previous judgment of the Court, to indicate the reference in full, including the number of the case. In addition, when citing a passage from a judgment of the Court or from the opinion of the Advocate General, counsel should specify the number of the page on which the passage in question appears.

3. Documents

The Court wishes to point out that under Article 37 of the Rules of Procedure all documents relied on by the parties must be annexed to a pleading. Save in exceptional circumstances and with the agreement of the parties, the Court will not admit any documents produced after the close of pleadings, except those produced at its own request; this also applies to any documents submitted at the hearing.

Since all the oral arguments are recorded, the Court also does not allow notes of oral arguments to be lodged.

Chapter 13

LAWYERS IN THE COURT

Introduction

In this chapter we consider the role of the lawyer representing his client before the Court of Justice. For the English or Scottish lawyer, this role may seem different, in some respects, from that which he plays before the national courts.

In the first place, the nature of the procedure, as described in the previous chapter, is such as to give a different emphasis to the lawyer's task. In the written proceedings, as we have seen, the drafting of the pleadings requires considerable skill; the lawyer will also have to set out in writing the substance of his arguments. In the oral procedure, which has a more limited scope, the opportunity for forensic talents is correspondingly reduced.

Second, the advocate general plays a crucial role which supplements that of the parties' representatives. Indeed, the parties may feel that the judges will be more influenced by the advocate-general's opinion than by anything their own representatives may say. But the advocate general will himself have had a full opportunity to consider the submissions of the parties, both written and oral, since the proceedings are normally adjourned before he delivers his opinion. By contrast, in the French *Conseil d'Etat*, the advocate-general's counterpart, the *commissaire du gouvernement*, gives his view of the case immediately after the oral submissions, if any.

Third, in the Court of Justice, the judges themselves see their role as an active rather than a passive one.

Their function is not only to adjudicate on the basis of the respective strength of the parties' submissions, but (as we shall see in Part Four) to develop the law and to give due weight to the interest of the Communities. Here the lawyer can both serve his client and assist the Court by relating his submissions to those wider interests.

Perhaps the most important limitation for the lawyer arises from the novelty of the Community legal system. In principle, as we shall see, any lawyer qualified to practise before the courts of a Member State is entitled to appear before the Court of Justice. Inevitably, the lawyer trained in his own legal system faces new problems. He will often be unfamiliar with Community law and the procedure of the Court, since even in the original Member States those subjects are still not widely known or taught. He may have to acquaint himself, not merely with a new branch of law, but with a fundamentally new approach to law, with what is in effect a new legal system having, for example, its own principles of interpretation which differ to a greater or lesser extent from those of his own national law, and which derive in part from the plurilingual character of Community law. Indeed, the lawyer must always appreciate that this plurilingual character adds a dimension to Community law not present in his own law: thus, the British lawyer must shed the blinkers interposed by the English language when reading a Community text, or at least be aware of their presence.

Considerable efforts have been and are being made to overcome these problems. The Court for its part regularly invites, and receives visits from, groups of lawyers from the Member States, but out of the enormous total of perhaps a quarter of a million lawyers in the Communities, only a very small proportion can be reached in this way.

Within the Member States, lawyers have set up their own organisations to encourage interest in and knowledge of Community law. A leading part has been played by the International Federation for European Law (*Fédération Internationale pour le Droit Européen*—FIDE), with its national groups such as the United Kingdom Association for European Law, which include both practising and academic lawyers. Practitioners have formed their own associations, such as the Scottish Lawyers European Group, and the Solicitors' European Group and the Bar European Group in England. A Community forum for problems of mutual interest to practitioners is provided by the Consultative Committee of the Bar and Law Societies of the Member States (usually referred to by its French initials CCBE).

In some respects, indeed, more progress has probably been made in the United Kingdom than in other Member States, apart perhaps from the Netherlands. Since the early 1960s the British Institute of International and Comparative Law and the Europa Institute of Leiden University have organised joint annual meetings on Community law attended by academics, practitioners and judiciary. Again, long before British accession the British Institute had provided extensive programmes of lectures and conferences to acquaint British lawyers with developments in Community law. Community law is now widely taught in the universities and in other law schools, and has also featured for many years in the English Bar examinations, although not, regrettably, in solicitors' examinations. Degree courses combining the study of law with another European language have been introduced. Many British lawyers of the future will therefore be better equipped to meet the demands of Community law, but much remains to be done if the lawyer is to play the fullest part and to have a truly European perspective, especially in the light of the prospective demands of the Single Internal Market after 1992.

The role of the lawyer in the Court of Justice is only one aspect of this wider perspective. Articles 52 to 58 EEC envisage, as part of the right of establishment, the

right of nationals of Member States to practise a
profession throughout the EEC, while Articles 59 to 66
envisage the right to provide services, including professional services, across national boundaries. (See on the
right of establishment of lawyers Case 2/74 *Reyners*
[1974] ECR 631, Case 7/76 *Thieffry* [1977] ECR 765,
Case 107/83 *Klopp* [1984] ECR 2971 and Case 292/86
Gullung [1988] 2 C.M.L.R. 57; and on the provision of
legal services Case 33/74 *van Binsbergen* [1974] ECR
1299, *Gullung*, above, and Case 427/85 *Commission* v.
Germany The Times April 5, 1988). This last case
concerned the Directive on Lawyers' Services which was
issued by the Council to facilitate cross-frontier services
by lawyers: in the preparation of this Directive an active
role was played by CCBE (for a critique of the
Directive, see Walters (1978) 3 E.L. Rev. 256 and
Edward in *In Memoriam J. D. B. Mitchell*, (1983),
p. 231, who calls it "a conceptual dog's breakfast since
it is based on the false premise that equivalence of title
implies equivalence of status, function and activity."

Perhaps because of such criticism, the Council has
adopted a broader brush approach in the recently
approved Directive on Mutual Recognition of Higher
Education Diplomas which is intended to facilitate the
right of establishment for all the liberal professions
throughout the Community: special provisions have
(reluctantly) been included in the Directive in regard to
lawyers. In this chapter, however, we are not concerned
with the right of establishment or cross-frontier legal
services but only with the practice of the lawyer before
the Court of Justice. Much of what follows will also now
apply to lawyers practising before the Court of First
Instance.

Legal representation

Parties before the Court must normally be represented
by a lawyer. This rule is laid down in the Statute of the

Court. So in general a litigant cannot plead his own case. The only exception is that, possibly in order to widen the rights of audience on a reference from a national court, the Rules of Procedure (Article 104) require account to be taken of the rules of procedure of the national court concerning the representation of the parties. So where there was a litigant in person before the national court, he may appear in person before the Court of Justice; this happened, for example, on a reference from a Dutch court in Case 39/75 *Coenen* [1975] ECR 1547. It has also been suggested that this Article imposes an obligation, on a reference from an English court where barristers have an exclusive right of audience, that a barrister (as opposed to a solicitor) be instructed before the Court of Justice; but the Court has, as we shall see (p. 258), been prepared to accept that the proceedings in Luxembourg be conducted even by a lawyer from a different jurisdiction.

A Member State or a Community institution is represented by an agent appointed for the case, assisted, as necessary, by an adviser or lawyer. Member States appear quite frequently; apart from their role as parties in direct actions, usually as defendants in proceedings by the Commission under Article 169 EEC, Member States frequently make use of their right to submit observations in references from national courts. The British, German and Italian Governments have been particularly active in exercising this right. The practice on representation varies in the different Member States. The Italian Government has frequently been represented by a member of the diplomatic service, the German Government by an official from a Government department who is also a lawyer. In the United Kingdom the practice in some cases has been to instruct counsel in practice at the Bar, and in this way a number of barristers have gained experience of the workings of the Court. In other cases, the Government has been represented by lawyers employed in the

Treasury Solicitor's Department or in the Government department directly concerned.

The Council and the Commission are usually represented by a member of their Legal Services, although they occasionally instruct private practitioners. The role of the Legal Service of the Commission is particularly important. The Commission, apart from appearing as applicant or defendant in most contentious cases, always submits observations in references from national courts, and can assist the Court by explaining the background to the particular Community instrument in question, which it will often have been responsible for drafting. It can also supply information on the economic context of a provision, or on the way in which it has been implemented in the Member States. Because of the Commission's special expertise it quite often happens that the Court adopts the interpretation proposed by the Commission, although at other times, of course, the Court adopts a more restrictive, or a more adventurous response. An illustration of a more restrictive approach can be found by comparing the observations of the Commission, the opinion of Advocate General Trabucchi, and the judgment of the Court in Case 118/75 *Watson and Belmann* [1976] ECR 1185; and an illustration of a more adventurous approach can be found by means of a similar comparison in Case 43/75 *Defrenne* [1976] ECR 455. For an interesting analysis, see Eric Stein (1981) *Am. Journal of International Law* 1.

Right of audience

No special qualifications are required of a lawyer to appear before the Court. The only requirement is that he is a "lawyer entitled to practise before a court of a Member State" (Article 17 of the Statute of the Court); he must lodge with the Registrar a certificate to this effect when submitting an application or defence

(Article 38(3) of the Rules of Procedure): for this purpose, the Registrar accepts a CCBE identity card issued or validated within the previous year. On a reference for a preliminary ruling, the parties will normally be represented by the lawyers who acted in the national court and who may have had no previous encounter with Community law. In a direct action, the parties are more likely to instruct a lawyer with some experience of the Court, but, perhaps because of the diversity of the Court's jurisdiction, there is little sign at present, with the exception of a few lawyers who appear regularly, of the development of a specialist Bar. As a result, there cannot be the same kind of relationship between Bench and Bar as exists in the English High Court or the Scottish Court of Session. The relations, and also the style of the proceedings, are necessarily less personal.

Moreover, the Court has apparently accepted that a lawyer entitled to practise before a court of *any* Member State has the right of audience in both direct actions and references for preliminary rulings; thus, a French lawyer could, it seems, appear in Luxembourg on a reference from an English court. In Case 234/81 *du Pont* [1982] ECR 3515, a reference from the English High Court, the proceedings in Luxembourg were conducted by an advocate of the Scots Bar practising in Brussels. However, in some cases a broadening of the right of audience could give rise to difficulties. For example, in a case referred by a German court in which questions of German law as well as Community law arose, a lawyer from outside Germany might be at a disadvantage, and might also place the Court of Justice at a disadvantage when it sought to put questions for guidance on German law. Moreover, the national court, when the case returned to it with the ruling of the Court of Justice, might be surprised to discover that proceedings which are, as we have seen (p. 243, above), a step in the proceedings before the national court, had been conducted by a lawyer who had not appeared, and might not be entitled to appear, before it. There might even be difficulties about which rules of professional conduct were applicable in respect of the Luxembourg proceedings, or how they were to be enforced. And where legal aid has been granted by the national authorities for the purpose of those proceedings, it might be doubtful whether public funds could be used to pay the fees of a lawyer from a different jurisdiction who might not be subject to the local code of discipline or whose fees were customarily fixed on a much more generous scale. The Court's liberal approach to the right of audience accords with the literal wording of the Statute which, as we have seen, refers to a lawyer entitled to practise before a court of a Member State; but it may be questioned whether it accords with the requirement of Article 104 of the Rules of Procedure, mentioned above, that, on a reference from a national court, account must be taken of the rules of procedure of that court concerning the representation of the parties.

Special problems of a divided profession

Problems may arise in countries with a divided profession. Within the Communities those countries include England, Wales, Scotland, Northern Ireland, and the Republic of Ireland. Although the United Kingdom is a single entity as a Member State of the European Communities, for many domestic purposes England and Wales, Scotland, and Northern Ireland constitute three separate jurisdictions, and the legal profession is separately regulated in each jurisdiction.

The right of audience at Luxembourg is expressed so widely as to appear to include solicitors as well as barristers and advocates. Has then a solicitor a right of audience before the Court?

In Scotland and Northern Ireland there has been no formal arrangement between the two branches of the profession regarding audience at Luxembourg, and to date very few cases, surprisingly, have come to the Court from these jurisdictions: examples are Case 83/78 *Pig Marketing Board* (*Northern Ireland*) v. *Redmond* [1978] ECR 2347, in which members of the English and Irish Bars represented the parties, Case 24/83 *Gewiese* v. *Mackenzie* [1984] ECR 817, a reference from the Court of Session which brought Edinburgh counsel to Luxembourg, in the person of the Solicitor General for Scotland, and Case 370/88 *Procurator Fiscal* v. *Marshall.*

In England and Wales a working agreement was reached by representatives of the Bar and of the Law Society in 1971 in anticipation of the United Kingdom's entry into the Communities. The general purport of the agreement was to give solicitors almost complete equality of opportunity with barristers to play a full part in the legal professional life of the enlarged Communities. To this end, solicitors as well as barristers were to be placed on equal terms with the French *avocat* and the equivalent categories of lawyers in the other countries of the original Six, wherever reference was made to *avocats* (or their equivalents) in the Treaties or other Community instruments.

The one important exception to such equality was to reserve to barristers the right of audience before the Court of Justice in preliminary references from the English High Court, the Court of Appeal or the House of Lords (these being courts, of course, in which the Bar to date still enjoys an exclusive right of audience).

The 1971 agreement was never embodied into the English Practice Rules. Serious doubts were subsequently expressed as to its validity, at least under Community law, and in 1981 the whole agreement was quietly abandoned by the Law Society, the Bar *non obstante*. And since, as we have seen, the Court of Justice may be willing to extend the right of audience to lawyers from a *different* jurisdiction, it cannot be supposed that the Court would be concerned to uphold purely domestic demarcations. However, from an English perspective, it might still seem curious if a solicitor were to act alone on a reference from, say, the House of Lords.

The first appearance by a solicitor as advocate before the Court was in a staff case, Case 175/80 *Tither* v. *Commission* [1981] ECR 2345, and this precedent has occasionally been followed. *Tither* was, of course, a direct action. It seems unlikely that solicitors will seek to specialise in advocacy at Luxembourg since (as we have seen) very real problems might arise in references for preliminary rulings from English (or Scottish) courts in which they have no right of audience.

It is accepted that an English barrister may appear on behalf of a client without being instructed by a solicitor: as the requirement for such instructions is only a rule of etiquette of the Bar, the Court will accept both his written pleadings and oral argument: see Case 167/80 *Curtis* v. *Parliament and Commission* [1981] ECR 1499; cf. *Prais* v. *Commission* [1976] ECR 1589, where the applicant was herself a solicitor.

Legal aid

Ligitation is an expensive pursuit, although in the Court of Justice it is probably less expensive than, for example, in the High Court in England, because hearings are generally much shorter and the preliminary proceedings generally simpler.

The Court may grant legal aid; the decision is made by a Chamber, after considering the application and the written observations of the other party. The application for legal aid need not be made through a lawyer. Consequently anyone contemplating bringing an action may himself apply for legal aid, stating the subject of the proceedings which he intends to introduce. In practice, applications are a handful each year: in 1985 there were only four. In all, up to March 1988, only 30 grants of legal aid have been accorded.

In granting legal aid the Court acts on the principle of *ex aequo et bono*: it considers the justice and equity of the matter. Acting on this basis it may, therefore, grant legal aid even where the applicant would not be eligible for legal aid in his own country (*e.g.* because he falls outside the financial conditions or because his own country in fact has no system of legal aid: see *Lee* v. *Minister for Agriculture*, below). The Court, in practice, requires a certificate of the applicant's means from the competent authority in his own country.

Legal aid takes the form of a cash grant in aid rather than the payment of a taxed bill of costs. Indeed the Court has no such English device as a taxing master. However, the rules appear to go so far as to provide that if a person is granted legal aid he may, if he loses the case, be ordered to repay the whole or part of the funds advanced to meet his costs, as in Case 25/68 *Schirtzer* v. *European Parliament* [1977] ECR 1729, or if he succeeds, his opponent may be ordered to repay the Court, as in Case 175/80 *Tither* v. *Commission* [1981] ECR 2345.

This provision does not seem to apply to legal aid on a reference for a preliminary ruling. Here there is a separate provision merely empowering the Court to provide funds, in special circumstances, to assist the representation and attendance of a party. Since the reference is to be regarded as a step in the proceedings before the national court, a party may also be able to obtain legal aid for this purpose under national law.

This question arose in England when a stipendiary magistrate's court made a reference in the case of Pierre Bouchereau. Bouchereau was a French national working in England who was convicted by the magistrate of unlawful possession of drugs. For these proceedings he had been granted legal aid. Before deciding whether to recommend deportation, the magistrate referred certain questions to the Court of Justice, but declined to extend the legal aid order to cover proceedings in the Court of Justice on the ground that he had no jurisdiction to do so. The Divisional Court, however, held that the existing legal aid certificate covered the proceedings before the Court of Justice, since these were a step in the proceedings before the national court: *R.* v. *Marlborough Street Stipendiary Magistrate, ex p. Bouchereau* [1977] 1 W.L.R. 414. But in civil proceedings the authority of the Area Committee (after 1988, the Legal Aid Board) is required before a legal aid certificate may extend to proceedings in the Court of Justice.

In other cases, the parties may be unable to obtain legal aid in the particular national proceedings. In the United Kingdom, for example, this may arise in claims before social security tribunals, where legal aid is not available. A person claiming pension rights under Community law would then not be eligible for legal aid before the national tribunals, but, if a reference were made, could apply to the Court of Justice for legal aid to meet the costs of the reference. Again, difficulty may arise where the reference is from a country which has no scheme of legal aid. Thus in Case 152/79 *Lee* v. *Minister for Agriculture* [1980] ECR 1495, a reference was brought from a court in the Irish Republic (where no general provision exists for civil legal aid). The plaintiff in the Irish proceedings then sought, and was granted, legal aid from the Court of Justice in respect of the reference. Although the eventual ruling was unfavourable to the plaintiff and the Irish court subsequently gave judgment against him, the Court of Justice did not seek to recover the funds advanced to him to meet his costs at Luxembourg. The Court may also grant legal aid where the national authority competent in the matter refuses to extend legal aid to cover a reference: Case 320/82 *D'Amario* [1983] ECR 3811 (the report does not refer to this aspect of the case, but see Lasok, *The European Court of Justice: Practice and Procedure* (1984) p. 93).

PART FOUR: THE COURT AS LAW-MAKER

Introductory

In this Part we examine what may be termed judicial legislation by the Court. For the Court's decisions constitute a source of Community law in a number of ways. First, in relation to the Treaties and legislation made thereunder, decisions of the Court provide authoritative interpretations, explaining and developing the texts by reference to concrete cases: as such they supply an essential gloss upon the *corpus* of Community *lex scripta*, which must always be read in the light of the Court's rulings, much as the English statute book (or the French Civil Code) is incomplete unless annotated with references to the relevant case-law. The Court of Justice has evolved its own style of interpretation, and this forms the subject of Chapter 14.

Secondly, the Treaties refer to the general principles of law common to the Member States as a source of Community law. The elucidation of these principles is an important function of the Court and amounts (as we see in Chapter 15) to a creative act of judicial legislation. For whatever the fiction, the legal reality is that the Court largely creates, and does not merely declare, these general principles. Inevitably, a common lawyer will be reminded of the Blackstonian theory of the King's judges ("repositories of the law, the living oracles") declaring the immemorial customs of the realm as the common law of England. That a court established by, and consisting predominantly of, civil lawyers should have this creative function illustrates the increasing convergence in Europe of the common law and civil law traditions; thus, in *Kloppenburg* [1988] 3 C.M.L.R. 1, at 19, the German Federal Constitutional Court, in support of the case-law method of developing Community law, stated that there could be no doubt:

> "that it was the intention of the Member States to provide the Community with a Court which would ascertain and apply the law by methods developed over centuries of common European legal tradition and refinement of law. In Europe the judge was never merely '*la bouche qui prononce les paroles de la loi*.' Roman law, the English common law and the German *Gemeines Recht* were to a large extent the creation of the judges in the same way as in more recent times in France, for instance, the development of general legal principles of administrative law by the *Conseil d'Etat* or, in Germany, general administrative law, a large part of the law of employment or security rights in private-law business transactions."

Thirdly, in fulfilling these interpretative and creative functions, the Court has had to come to terms with the principle of *stare decisis*. Like any court, the Court of Justice seeks to be consistent, and to the extent that consistency prevails over the competing pressure to adjust Community law to ever-changing circumstances, the Court's decisions are "precedents" in the English sense—or (better) in the American sense, being at most persuasive and never binding upon the Court for the future. This topic forms the subject of Chapter 16.

We have seen in previous Parts the style in which the Court's judgments are drafted and the process by which they emerge. Here we consider how far their collegiate character is appropriate for the Court's law-making functions.

Undoubtedly, the great advantage of the single judgment is to enchance its authority. Whatever the hidden reservations or concealed dissents, the judgment moves, syllogistically, to its logical conclusion, to which the appearance of single-mindedness then attaches

greater legal certainty. In 1952 it was practical wisdom
to adopt the rule of unanimity for the new-born Court
of the Coal and Steel Community. Now that the Court
has come of age its authority seems assured, but the
single judgment has special value for reinforcing the
unity of Community law. For the need to prolong
deliberation to secure, if at all possible, a collegiate
judgment without recourse to a vote helps to produce
an agreement (or compromise) which is truly *communautaire*, that is, one in which all the judges, with
their differing viewpoints, bring forward and blend
together in the eventual judgment various elements
from all the national legal systems. In this way, as
Professor Schermers points out, the inability openly to
dissent "aids the amalgamation of rules from all the
national legal orders and their assimilation into Community law" (*Judicial Protection in the European
Communities* (4th ed., 1987), p. 451).

The absence of individual judgments has also the
advantage of not identifying a particular judge with a
particular decision. To this extent it is made easier for
the Court as a whole to adopt a new departure in its
case-law, without fear of the charge of inconsistency
being laid at the door of one judge rather than another.

In addition, the single judgment is seen as a means of
strengthening judicial independence. The twin
principles—of secrecy of deliberation and singleness of
judgment—provide together an effective shield for the
individual judge against pressure from his government
or from public opinion in his own country.

Chapter 14

METHODS OF INTERPRETATION

Introduction

The judicial process is characteristically the two-fold one of the interpretation of the law and then its application to the case in hand. As we have seen, however, the Court of Justice may find its role limited to that of interpretation only; where a preliminary ruling is sought from it, the application of the law is reserved to the national court. Under its other heads of jurisdiction the Court has both to interpret and apply the law. This chapter will survey the methods adopted by the Court in interpreting Community law. Community law includes, of course, both the Treaties and the legislation made thereunder, but the methods of interpretation do not substantially differ as between the two categories of Community law.

The methods of interpretation employed by the Court have added importance for British lawyers since they constitute the "European way" which Lord Denning recognised the courts of England (and Scotland) should follow when called upon themselves to interpret Community law. In *Bulmer* v. *Bollinger* [1974] Ch. 401 at 425 Lord Denning declared:

> "The (EEC) treaty is quite unlike any of the enactments to which we have become accustomed ... It lays down general principles. It expresses its aim and purposes. All in sentences of moderate length and commendable style. But it lacks precision. It uses words and phrases without defining what they mean. An English lawyer would look for

an interpretation clause, but he would look in vain. There is none. All the way through the treaty there are gaps and lacunae. These have to be filled in by the judges, or by regulations or directives. It is the European way... Seeing these differences, what are the English courts to do when they are faced with a problem of interpretation? They must follow the European pattern. No longer must they argue about the precise grammatical sense. They must look to the purpose and intent... They must divine the spirit of the treaty and gain inspiration from it. If they find a gap, they must fill it as best they can... These are the principles, as I understand it, on which the European Court acts."

This view of Lord Denning is reinforced by the terms of section 3(1) of the European Communities Act 1972, which provides:

"For the purposes of all legal proceedings any question as to the meaning or effect of any of the Treaties, or as to the validity, meaning or effect of any Community instrument, shall be treated as a question of law (and, if not referred to the European Court, be for determination as such in accordance with the principles laid down by and any relevant decision of the European Court)."

The reference here to "the principles laid down by the European Court" is wide enough to include its methods of interpretation.

Plurilingual Dimension of Community Law

A problem peculiar to interpreting Community law, as distinct from English law, which we must add to those mentioned by Lord Denning in the passage cited above, is the Community's "linguistic regime." This term describes the principle of linguistic equality which has been accepted in the Communities since the EEC Treaty. With each enlargement of the Communities the principle that the languages of all the Member States should rank equally has been steadfastly upheld, no matter at what cost or inconvenience. In the result, Community law has a plurilingual dimension not encountered in English law nor, indeed, in most national legal systems. In particular, all the texts of Community law rank equally in the different official languages (since Portuguese and Spanish entry, nine in number), so that the Court of Justice has had to evolve methods of interpretation appropriate to plurilingual texts.

The Court's Own Style of Interpretation

Generally, the Court does not discuss in its judgments the methods of interpretation being employed, although its choice of phrase may sometimes serve as a signpost of the road it has followed to reach its conclusions. Fortunately, individual members of the Court have been less laconic in their extra-judicial speeches and writings, and a considerable literature now exists on the subject of interpretation, some of which must be considered authoritative having regard to its source.

Interpretation of law is in no way an exact science but rather a judicial art. In the end, it is a matter of judicial instinct, and because the judge proceeds instinctively, the process cannot be reduced to a series of mechanical rules. Writers sometimes refer to "canons of interpretation," but it is better to think in terms of varying *approaches*: sometimes one approach is preferred, sometimes another, sometimes a combination of several; or one approach may be followed by another as a check upon the result achieved by the first.

The Court of Justice has no special methods of its own but uses those with which national courts are familiar. But the Court's use of traditional methods should not deceive us: the distinctive nature of Community law, when compared with national laws on the one hand and international law on the other, as well as the manner in which the Treaties are drafted, have led the Court to evolve its own style of interpretation. Moreover, as we have emphasised above, the plurilingual character of Community law introduces an extra dimension not normally encountered in the courts of the Member States. In addition, resort to comparative law is more common in the sense that the Court may look to the national laws of the Member States for guidance. This is especially so when the Court is venturing beyond mere interpretation into creative law-making: of this a notable example is the Court's development of the doctrine of the general principles of law, to be discussed in the next chapter.

In the exposition which follows, four methods of interpretation are discussed *seriatim*. These are the literal, historical, contextual and teleological. Although this order has a certain logic and accords broadly with the way in which the approaches to interpretation by national courts are traditionally presented, it would be quite wrong to assume that the methods are placed in descending order of importance. As will become apparent, the dominant approaches of the Court of Justice are the contextual and teleological.

Literal Interpretation

Every court must begin from the words of the text before it. If their meaning is plain, either in their ordinary connotation or in some special sense appropriate to the particular context, then for the national judge the task of interpretation is a light one and ends there. Usually, the same can be said for the Court of Justice, but exceptionally the Court may be led to disregard the plainest of wording in order to give effect to what it deems the overriding aims and objects of the Treaties.

In other words the literal interpretation is displaced by the contextual or teleological approach, although the Court may speak rather in terms of looking to "the spirit" of the text in question.

Case 22/70 *ERTA* [1971] ECR 263 provides a good example. The Commission sought the annulment of a Council discussion to co-ordinate the attitude to be adopted by the six Member States in certain international negotiations to revise the European Road Transport Agreement. The Council's defence included the plea that the discussion did not constitute an "act" subject to annulment within the meaning of that term in Article 173 EEC: any such act was limited to the categories of regulation, directive or decision as enumerated in Article 189. Despite the apparently exhaustive wording of Article 189, the Court found against the Council on this plea, holding that the aim of Article 173 was to subject to judicial review all measures taken by the institutions designed to have legal effect and declaring that "It would be inconsistent with this objective to interpret the conditions under which the action is admissible so restrictively as to limit the availability of this procedure merely to the categories of measures referred to by Article 189."

As Lord Denning has indicated, literal interpretation is made more difficult for the Court by the general absence in the Treaties of definitions of the terms used. An English or Scottish Court may often be able to resolve a question of interpretation by the help of the glossary or dictionary which the legislator has thoughtfully provided in the definition or interpretation section of the particular statute. Such definitions are rare in Community law. Rather, the Treaties adopt the opposing continental approach of preferring to leave to judicial interpretation (assisted by doctrinal opinion) the meaning of terms which have been deliberately left undefined in the texts. Examples from the EEC Treaty include:

"charges having equivalent effect" (Articles 9, 12, 13 and 16) (see the *Gingerbread* case below, p. 281);

"public policy" (Article 48) (see *Van Duyn* v. *Home Office* below);

"abuse of a dominant position" (Article 86) (see *Continental Can* case below, p. 287);

"general principles common to the laws of the Member States" (Article 215(2)) (see Chapter 15).

By contrast, although definitions do not normally feature in the Treaties, the different technique is used of providing either an exhaustive list or a number of examples which is deliberately left open-ended: for the former, see the list of products subject to the Common Agricultural Policy set out in Annex II to the EEC Treaty, and for the latter, see the five examples in Article 85(1) EEC of prohibited agreements under that Article.

By its very nature and purpose, secondary legislation under the Treaties is much more tightly drafted. Thus, the Common Customs Tariff (pursuant to Articles 19–29 EEC) is a detailed catalogue of nearly 3,000 items; it may still however give rise to problems of interpretation: see Case 22/76 *Import Gadgets* above, p. 43. But Community legislation also often makes use of vague terms: see, for example, Council Directive No. 64/221 which failed to clarify sufficiently the reference in Article 48 EEC to "grounds of public policy, public security or public health," a clarification which the Court had to supply in Case 41/74 *Van Duyn* v. *Home Office* [1974] ECR 1337.

Faced as it often is with texts which are vague, ambiguous or incomplete, the Court has recognised the limitations for itself of the literal method of interpretation. Particularly after 1958, when the Court was confronted with the more programmatic EEC Treaty, its interpretation shifted perceptibly towards the contextual and teleological, with emphasis on the *ratio legis* and the objectives of the Treaty. Thus, in Case 6/60 *Humblet* [1960] ECR 559 it declared at 575: "it is not sufficient for the Court to adopt the literal interpretation and the Court considers it necessary to examine the question whether this interpretation is confirmed by other criteria concerning in particular the common intention of the High Contracting Parties and the *ratio legis*." Again in Case 26/62 *Van Gend en Loos* [1963] ECR at 12, the Court stated:

> "To ascertain whether the provisions of an international treaty [*viz.*: Article 12 EEC] extend so far in their effects it is necessary to consider the spirit, the general scheme and the wording of those provisions."

Significantly, the Court ranked the wording in third place, as it did in similar language in Case 6/72 *Continental Can* [1973] ECR at 243: "In order to answer this question, one has to go back to the spirit, general scheme and wording of Article 86 EEC, as well as to the system and objectives of the Treaty." But in its earlier decisions the Court gave greater emphasis to wording: thus in Case 9/56 *Meroni* v. *High Authority* [1958] ECR 133 at 140, it re-affirmed the view it had expressed in Case 8/55 *Fédéchar* [1954–1956] ECR 245, that an argument *a contrario* is only admissible if no other interpretation appears to be appropriate and compatible with the express wording, with the context and with the purpose of the provisions.

In comparison with a national court, the task of the Court of Justice is inevitably more difficult because, as we have seen, there will seldom be a single text before it. In the event of ambiguity it may have to consider the versions in the various Community languages, all equally authentic. Very real difficulties may arise from subtle differences between the alternative texts. Thus, Article 48(3) EEC uses, in the English text, the

expression "public policy," to translate the French term
"ordre public," a false equation with which Advocate
General Warner wrestled valiantly to find the *mot juste*
in Case 30/77 *Bouchereau* [1977] ECR 1999. Likewise,
the French term "détournement de pouvoir" as used in
Article 173 EEC has a more precise meaning than the
vague English term "misuse of powers" employed in the
English texts: the same expression in Article 33 ECSC
has presented problems of interpretation for the Court
because of its various shades of meaning in the original
six Members States: *e.g.* Case 3/54 ASSIDER [1954–
1956] ECR 63. Again, in Case 29/69 *Stauder* [1969]
ECR 419, the Court had to consider the different
versions of a Commission decision addressed to the
Member States permitting the sale of butter at reduced
prices to persons in receipt of welfare benefits. The
Dutch and German texts required the beneficiaries to
receive their butter in exchange for a "coupon
indicating their names." A German citizen challenged
this in his national courts as an infringement of
fundamental rights. The Court referred to the French
and Italian versions which only stipulated the production of a "coupon referring to the person concerned." It
adopted this more liberal version of the decision which
would enable its objective to be achieved by other and
unexceptionable methods of identifying the
beneficiaries.

Faced thus by a disparity of texts the Court looks,
where the context so permits, for that text which offers
the most liberal solution in relation to the rights of the
individual, being guided by the spirit and intention of
the texts rather than by the verbal symbols in which
they are expressed: this is an approach consistent with
its own doctrine of proportionality whereby the Court
requires a Community act to use the minimum of means
to achieve the desired end (see p. 295, below). Other
cases posing problems of textual disparity include: Case
9/79 *Koschniske* [1979] ECR 2717; Case 814/79 *Rüffer*

[1980] ECR 3807; Case 131/79 *Santillo* [1980] ECR 1585: see generally Brown (1981) 15 *Valparaiso Univ. Law Rev.* 319. Only rarely will a national court embark on so elaborate an analysis of the different language versions of the provisions of a regulation as was attempted in the Northern Irish High Court in *Cunningham* v. *Milk Marketing Board for Northern Ireland* [1988] 3 C.M.L.R. 815 at 877–887.

Historical Interpretation

By historical interpretation is usually meant the quest for the subjective intention of the author of the text. It may also mean the discovery of the objective intention of the measure in question, to be deduced from its purpose at the date of enactment. The English so-called "Mischief Rule" as laid down in *Heydon's Case* (1584) 3 Co. Rep. 7a confines the English judge to the objective legislative intent, whereas in most Continental countries the judge may examine the *travaux préparatoires* ("preparatory work") in pursuit of the subjective intention of the legislature. This is only a generalisation, for on both sides of the Channel there is movement towards a more intermediate position, limited access to certain *travaux préparatoires* becoming acceptable in England, while such materials are treated with increasing caution in some continental jurisdictions. (For a valuable survey, see Norman S. Marsh, *Interpretation in the National and International Context*, 1973).

Historical interpretation in either sense is little used by the Court of Justice. In regard to the Treaties, the negotiations have remained shrouded in secrecy by common agreement of the contracting States. Professor Pescatore, later a distinguished judge of the Court, was himself the head of the Luxembourg team which negotiated the EEC Treaty, and he has explained in a public lecture in 1963 the wisdom of excluding recourse to the records of the negotiations:

"Treaties are not established unilaterally, they are negotiated. In order to interpret an international treaty correctly, account must therefore be taken of the actual conditions in which it was negotiated. However, it is precisely one of the rules of negotiation that one does not always reveal one's intentions. It is not, in actual fact, on the intentions of the contracting parties that agreement is reached, but on the written formulas of the treaties and only on that. It is by no means certain that agreement on a text in any way implies agreement as to intentions. On the contrary, divergent, even conflicting intentions may perfectly well underlie a given text and I would even go so far as to say...that the art of treaty-making is in part the art of disguising irresolvable differences between the contracting States."

A former President of the Court, Robert Lecourt, in his Geneva Lectures *Le juge devant le Marché commun* (1970), confirms the view of Judge Pescatore that it is not the function of the Luxembourg Court to rediscover the intention of the parties in the manner which is traditional for interpreting treaties in international law. He explains (at p. 64) that:

"In the Community the judge is the repository of the will of the authors of the Treaties, who moved into the background on the day of signature, to re-appear only at rare moments when they sign new agreements. They have made the judge the guardian of their common achievement, that is to say, of its objectives, institutions and law. They have carried so far the trust which they have placed in the judge as the custodian of their common will that they have even destroyed every official trace of their *travaux préparatoires.*"

Somewhat greater freedom in resorting to *travaux préparatoires* is manifested by the advocates general of the Court in their opinions. In particular, they have occasionally referred to the record of proceedings in the national parliaments when the Treaties were being submitted for ratification. Thus, in Case 6/54 *Netherlands* v. *High Authority* [1954–1956] ECR 103 concerning the interpretation of Article 33 ECSC Advocate General Roemer suggested, after citing the explanations given to their national legislatures by the German and French Governments, that "the Court should examine the statement of reasons laid before the parliaments of the other countries." And the Court itself in Case 6/60 *Humblet* [1960] ECR 559 referred in its judgment to the fact that "the opinions of the governments put forward during the parliamentary debates on the ECSC Treaty do not touch on this question. The same is true of the parliamentary votes on the EEC and EAEC Treaties which contain a provision in substantially the same terms." In *Humblet* the Court had to determine the scope of the provision in the Protocol on the Privileges and Immunities which exempted the salaries of Community officials from national charges; having found the parliamentary debates silent on the point, the Court then resorted to a comparison of different national laws as an aid to interpretation of the Protocol.

Because of the dynamic character of the Treaties as laying down programmes for the future, such reference to *travaux préparatoires*, whether by the Court or its advocates general, tends to diminish as the dates of concluding the Treaties (or Protocols) recede into the past. Former President Kutscher has declared indeed that "It is useless to look at such pointers in the more recent judgments . . . interpretations based on the original situation would in no way be in keeping with a Community law orientated towards the future." (H. Kutscher, *Methods of Interpretation as seen by a judge of the Court of Justice* (1976), pp. 21–22).

So far as Community legislation is concerned, both the Council and the Commission deliberate in secret, and especially in the Council hard bargaining is common. Accordingly, even if available, the records of deliberations in these bodies would be open to the same objections as those attached by MM. Pescatore and Lecourt to the negotiations of the Treaties. On the other hand, certain official *travaux préparatoires* are available for Community legislation. Thus, the Official Journal publishes all legislative proposals by the Commission as well as formal opinions of the European Parliament, which may relate to proposed legislation.

In addition, the regulations, directives and decisions of the Council and Commission are required by Article 190 EEC to state the reasons on which they are based and to refer to any proposals or opinions which were required to be obtained pursuant to the Treaty. These obligatory recitals in the preamble to such legislation throw light on the intention of the Council or Commission and are frequently referred to by the Court as a guide to the interpretation of their provisions. Thus, in Case 14/69 *Markus* v. *Hauptzollamt Hamburg-Jonas* [1969] ECR 349 the Court held that:

> "according to the seventh recital of the preamble to the regulation in question ... the eighth recital of the same preamble states ... It must therefore be assumed that the authors of the first paragraph of Article 16 intended ... This solution is confirmed by the penultimate recital of the preamble to the said regulation according to which ... "

Again, in Case 9/72 *Brunner* [1972] ECR 961 the Court held that: "It is clear from the recitals of the preamble to that regulation that ... " And in the *Import Gadgets* case (Case 22/76 [1976] ECR 1371, discussed pp. 43–44 above) the Court followed its normal practice of interpreting the Common Customs Tariff by reference to the Explanatory Notes to the Brussels Nomenclature, that is, notes relating to the Convention of December 15, 1950 on nomenclature for the classification of goods in customs tariffs, this Nomenclature, which provides the historical basis for the Common Customs Tariff, being legally binding as an international obligation on all the Member States and, in the view of the Court, on the Community itself.

Contextual Interpretation

This method is extensively used by the Court in interpreting both the Treaties and Community legislation. It involves placing the provision in issue within its context and interpreting it in relation to other provisions of Community law. The Treaties, in particular the EEC Treaty, set out a grand design or programme, and it is natural to stress the interrelationship of the individual provisions as component parts of the total scheme. Not seeing the wood for the trees is, for the Court, a cardinal sin. Hence, its judgments abound with references such as:

> "the context of all the provisions establishing a common organisation of the market": Case 190/73 *Van Haaster* [1974] ECR 1123;
> "the general scheme of the Treaty as a whole": Cases 2 and 3/62 *Gingerbread* case [1962] ECR 425;
> "taking account of the fundamental nature, in the scheme of the Treaty, of the principles of freedom of movement and equality of treatment of workers": Case 152/73 *Sotgiu* [1974] ECR 153;
> "one must have regard to the whole scheme of the Treaty no less than to its specific provisions": Case 22/70 *ERTA* case [1971] ECR 263;
> "the context of the Treaty": Case 23/75 *Rey Soda* [1975] ECR 1279;
> "the framework of Community law": Cases 90 and 91/63 *Dairy Products* case [1964] ECR 625; Case 6/64 *Costa* v. *ENEL* [1964] ECR 585.
> "Article 37(1) EEC must be interpreted in its context in relation to the other provisions of the

article and taking account of its place in the general scheme of the Treaty": Case 59/75 *Manghera* [1976] ECR 91.

A striking example of the effect of this systematic interpretation of the Treaty can be found in the Court's treatment of customs duties and charges having equivalent effect in Article 12 of the EEC Treaty. Article 12 provides that

"Member States shall refrain from introducing between themselves any new customs duties on imports or exports or any charges having equivalent effect, and from increasing those which they already apply in their trade with each other."

In the *Gingerbread* case, Cases 2 and 3/62 *Commission* v. *Luxembourg and Belgium* [1962] ECR 425 the Court held that

"The position of those Articles (Articles 9 and 12) towards the beginning of that Part of the Treaty dealing with the 'Foundations of the Community'— Article 9 being placed at the beginning of the Title relating to 'Free Movement of Goods,' and Article 12 at the beginning of the section dealing with the 'Elimination of Custom Duties'—is sufficient to emphasise the essential nature of the prohibitions which they impose."

Relying on, among other things, the "general scheme" of these provisions and of the Treaty as a whole, the Court went on to argue that there was evidence of "a general intention to prohibit not only measures which obviously take the form of the classic customs duty but also all those which, presented under other names or introduced by the indirect means of other procedures, would lead to the same discriminatory or protective results as customs duties."

It is interesting to compare the approach which an English court might adopt to the expression "customs

duties and charges having equivalent effect." An
English court would be likely to apply the more
restrictive approach, according to which, when general
words are used, they are to be confined to those kinds
of things with which the context deals explicitly or
implicitly: the *eiusdem generis* rule is a specific instance
of this approach where two examples of a category are
given, followed by a general expression. An English
court, therefore, would refer to the context of the
provision "customs duties and charges having equivalent
effect," but rather with a view to *limiting* the general
expression in the light of that context. In the
Gingerbread case, on the contrary, the Court uses the
general expression "any charges having equivalent
effect" as a "catch all" concept to cover not only
charges of the *same* kind but charges of *all* kinds having
the same effect. Hence it takes Chapter 1 of this part of
the Treaty as prohibiting all pecuniary obstacles to trade
between Member States. In other cases, the same result
is achieved in relation to Chapter 2, on the elimination
of quantitative restrictions. All measures having equivalent effect to quotas, prohibited by Article 30, are taken
to exclude, in effect, all non-pecuniary trade barriers,
subject only to the exceptions expressly provided (and
narrowly construed) in Article 36. Thus, by looking at
this Title of the Treaty as a whole, and construing its
very general provisions in the light of its supposed aims,
the Court takes it as abolishing at a stroke, with very
limited exceptions, all barriers, pecuniary or otherwise,
to trade between Member States.

In a characteristic passage in case 24/68 *Commission*
v. *Italian Republic* [1969] ECR 193, the Court held (at
200–201):

> "Thus, in order to ascribe to a charge an effect
> equivalent to a customs duty, it is important to
> consider this effect in the light of the objectives of
> the Treaty, in the Parts, Titles and Chapters in

which Articles 9, 12, 13 and 16 are to be found, particularly in relation to the free movement of goods. Consequently, any pecuniary charge, however small and whatever its designation and mode of application, which is imposed unilaterally on domestic or foreign goods by reason of the fact that they cross a frontier, and which is not a customs duty in the strict sense, constitutes a charge having equivalent effect within the meaning of Articles 9, 12, 13 and 16 of the Treaty, even if it is not imposed for the benefit of the State, is not discriminatory or protective in effect and if the product on which the charge is imposed is not in competition with any domestic product."

Contextual interpretation is no less important in relation to Community legislation. Typically, the Court may have to interpret a regulation of the Commission which implements a regulation of the Council which itself is issued pursuant to a provision in the Treaties: Case 64/69 *Compagnie Française Commerciale et Financière* v. *Commission* [1970] ECR 221 was such a case. The Court will necessarily examine the subordinate regulation immediately in issue for its compatibility both with the enabling regulation and with the superior law of the treaty provision. Having examined the vertical context it will also consider the horizontal relationship of the regulation with other Commission regulations *in pari materia*. Again, the language of the Court's judgments is indicative of this approach, for example:

"the Regulation (No. 3 on social security for migrant workers made pursuant to Article 51 EEC) must be interpreted in the context and within the bounds of this article and having regard to the fundamental principles which it lays down": Case 28/68 *Torrekens* [1969] ECR 125. And in Case

17/76 *Brack* v. *The Insurance Officer* [1976] ECR 1429 "The Regulation [No. 1408/71 which superseded No. 3 above] must be interpreted above all in the light of the spirit and of the objectives of the Treaty."

Comparative Law as Aid to Interpretation

Part of the context in which Community law operates is its interrelationship with the national laws of the Member States. The judges themselves of the Court bring to their task the conceptual background and instinctive reactions derived from previous careers in their own legal systems. Almost subconsciously, therefore, comparative law must be influencing their interpretative function.

In addition, Community law may use terms or concepts which are well known in the national laws, without itself defining them. In this case, the Community sense of the term may involve a comparison of the relevant national laws: see, for example, the opinion of Advocate General Lagrange in Case 3/54 *ASSIDER* v. *High Authority* [1954–1956] ECR 63 concerning the term *détournement de pouvoir* in the authentic French text and its Dutch, German and Italian equivalents in Article 33 ECSC. The Brusselss Convention (p. 176, above) offers particular scope for the comparative method in its interpretation. To secure its uniform application in all the Member States, the Court has been persuaded to adopt autonomous Community meanings for legal terms and concepts employed in the Convention: the advocates general have demonstrated in several cases that such terms lack any consistent meaning in the various national laws (see, *e.g.* Case 29/76 *LTU* v. *Eurocontrol* [1976] ECR 1541 Opinion of Advocate General Reischl; Case 814/79 *Rüffer* [1980] ECR 3807 Opinion of Advocate General Warner).

Likewise, Community law may simply be silent on questions of principle which have received solutions in the laws of the Member States. Thus, the question whether Community law admitted the revocation of measures creating subjective rights was answered by the Court in Cases 7/56 and 3–7/57 *Algera* [1957–1958] ECR 39 "by reference to the rules acknowledged by the legislation, the learned writing and the case-law of the member countries," and there followed in the judgment "a comparative study of this problem of law" (for the facts of this case, see p. 162, above).

So extensive a comparative examination in an actual judgment is rare, indeed unique; but the opinions of the advocates general contain much comparative analysis. The judgment of the Court may then briefly adopt the result of such analysis, as, for example, in Case 32/62 *Alvis* [1963] ECR 49, which upheld in Community law the generally accepted principle of administrative law in the Member States whereby a civil servant must be allowed the opportunity to reply to allegations against him before being disciplined (see further p. 164 above). Again in Case 155/79 *AM & S* [1982] ECR 1575 both Advocate General Warner and (in the re-opened oral proceedings) Advocate General Slynn included in their opinions extensive comparative analysis of the scope of legal professional privilege in all the Member States with a view to guiding the Court how far that privilege should extend as a general principle of Community law.

More specifically, as we have seen in Chapter 8, Article 215(2) EEC bases the non-contractual liability of the Community for damage caused by its institutions or by its servants in the performance of their duties upon "the general principles common to the laws of the Member States." In the earlier chapter we saw how the Court had drawn, by an eclectic process, upon the national legal systems to create a uniform Community law governing tortious liability or reparation.

Resort to *ius commune Europaeum*, which is explicitly required by Article 215(2) EEC (Article 188 Euratom), is also an underlying feature of the wider doctrine of "general principles of law" which the Court has developed as an additional source of Community law. This important topic is returned to more fully in Chapter 15, but it is relevant here as a further example of the Court's use of comparative law as an aid to interpretation. Of necessity, much comparative research is constantly undertaken on behalf of the members of the Court, and we have seen in Chapter 2 what internal arrangements exist to facilitate this. In addition, the Commission's Legal Service often includes comparative material in presenting its observations to the Court, or the Commission may be expressly requested by the Court to include such material in its observations (Pescatore (1980) *Revue Internationale de Droit Comparé* 337).

Teleological Interpretation

The term teleological is applied to an interpretation which is based upon the purpose or object of the text facing the judge. This approach, which is increasingly favoured by the Court, is peculiarly appropriate in Community law where, as we have seen, the Treaties provide mainly a broad programme or design rather than a detailed blue-print. In setting forth the grand design the Treaties, both in their preambles and in certain Articles, express the objectives of the Communities in very general terms; in turn, these objectives are knit together by the underlying assumption that they will lead eventually to an economic and political union. Article 2 EEC is a striking example with its declaration of intent that:

> "The Community shall have as its task, by
> establishing a common market and progressively

approximating the economic policies of Member States, to promote throughout the Community a harmonious development of economic activities, a continuous and balanced expansion, an increase in stability, an accelerated raising of the standard of living and closer relations between the States belonging to it."

Faced with a body of law whose core is couched in such terms the Court of Justice has naturally adopted the teleological method in interpreting both the Treaties and the legislation derived from them. For Judge Pescatore, as for President Kutscher, the teleological and contextual methods assume greater importance than the historical or literal methods; see above, p. 276 and p. 278.

From the case law of the Court we have already discussed one notable example, Case 22/70 *ERTA* [1971] ECR 263 (see p. 272, above). A further illustration is a leading case on Article 86 EEC, Case 6/72 *Europemballage Corporation and Continental Can Co. Inc.* v. *Commission* [1973] ECR 215. Article 86 prohibits any "abuse of a dominant position within the common market or in a substantial part of it . . . in so far as it may affect trade between Member States." The *Continental Can* case raised the question whether Article 86 could apply to take-overs or mergers.

According to a decision taken by the Commission, Continental Can Company Inc. of New York, which held, through the medium of its German subsidiary, a dominant position over a substantial part of the common market in certain packaging products, had abused that dominant position by acquiring, through a Belgian subsidiary Europemballage Corporation, a Dutch company which was the only significant competitor in those products.

The Commission's decision required Continental Can to put an end to its alleged infringement of Article 86 and to submit proposals to the Commission for that purpose by a specified date. The decision was challenged before the Court by Continental Can and by Europemballage, who argued that the Commission had wrongly interpreted Article 86 and was trying to introduce merger control in the EEC Treaty. The ECSC Treaty made express provision for merger control but there was no such express provision in the EEC Treaty. The Court rejected comparison with the ECSC Treaty as a method of interpretation and referred instead to "the spirit, general scheme and wording of Article 86, as well as to the system and objectives of the Treaty." It went on to examine the Article in the context of the other treaty provisions on competition and in the light of the principles and objectives set out in Articles 2 and 3. Ultimately it annulled the decision on other grounds, but it upheld the Commission's extensive interpretation of Article 86.

The use of the teleological method of filling gaps in codes or statutes is a familiar one in continental legal systems. It is expressly enjoined upon the Swiss courts by the Swiss Civil Code of 1922. In Community law the original Treaties were designed to have their details filled out by legislation of the Council and Commission. The political near-paralysis which has often crippled the legislative institutions of the Communities in the past has left yawning gaps in the enacted Community law. The Court of Justice sees itself as charged by the Treaties with upholding Community law, and accordingly it must fill the gaps left in that law by the default of the other institutions or the inactivity of the Member States.

Thus, the adjustment of State monopolies of a commercial character was required of Member States under Article 37 EEC during the transitional period; in default of the adjustment by the Italian Government of its tobacco monopoly (albeit this default was with the tacit acquiescence of the Council), the Court, in Case

59/75 *Manghera* [1976] ECR 91, took upon itself to declare the incompatibility of that monopoly with the Treaty and to draw the necessary consequences.

Again, in the second *Defrenne* case (Case 43/75 [1976] ECR 455), the Court had to consider the application of the principle of equal pay for equal work imposed by Article 119 EEC, and whether that principle had become directly enforceable in the national courts at the end of the first stage of the transitional period (December 31, 1961), or whether the further period of grace granted by the Council to Member States for implementing Article 119 was valid. The Court held the Article to have come into operation on January 1, 1962 and to have direct effect. It supported this conclusion by reference to the nature of the equal pay principle and the objective of this principle and its place in the EEC Treaty. It combined the teleological with the contextual approach in emphasising not only the dual purpose (economic and social) of Article 119 but also its relationship to other provisions, particularly Article 117 concerning the need to promote improved working conditions and an improved standard of living for workers.

That the Court has consciously assumed a legislative role in this case is confirmed by the further (and controversial) component of its judgment in which, in the interest of legal certainty, it declined to give a general retrospective effect to its ruling on Article 119: only those who had already commenced legal proceedings could claim pay for periods prior to the date of judgment. For a similar limitation on the retrospectivity of a ruling on validity, see Case 41/84 *Pinna* [1986] ECR 1 (discussed p. 198, above). But the Court has emphasised that such a limitation should only be introduced where there were overriding considerations of legal certainty: Case 24/86 *Blaizot* v. *University of Liège*, *The Times*, April 4, 1988.

This teleological approach is also extensively used in interpreting Community legislation. Thus, in Case 9/67 *Colditz* [1967] ECR 229, concerning certain social security regulations, the Court declared that

> "the solution to this question . . . can only emerge from the interpretation of those regulations in the light of the objectives of the provisions of the Treaty (Articles 48 to 51)."

Also, as we have seen in considering contextual interpretation, regulations and directives recite in their preambles the reasons on which they are based. This enables the Court to invoke the objectives of the measure by reference to such recitals and to interpret it accordingly.

As part of its teleological approach the Court not infrequently refers to the principle of effectiveness (*l'effet utile*), a concept borrowed from international law which is sometimes rendered inelegantly into English as "useful effect." In Community law this has come to mean that "preference should be given to the construction which gives the rule its fullest effect and maximum practical value" (Kutscher, *op. cit.* 41). Cases in which the Court has invoked this principle of what we would term "Community efficacy" (compare the principle of "business efficacy" as laid down for English law in *The Moorcock* (1889) 14 P.D. 64) include Case 8/55 *Fédéchar* [1954–1956] ECR 245 and 292; Case 20/59 *Italy* v. *High Authority* and Case 25/59 *Netherlands* v. *High Authority* [1960] ECR 325 and 355; *and Case 34/62 Germany* v. *Commission* [1963] ECR 131.

The European Way

The separating out in this chapter of the various methods or approaches which the Court brings to its task of interpreting Community law should not mislead the reader into concluding that the Court operates in some mechanical way. As we have said, interpretation is an art in which the judicial instinct looms large. Frequently the Court uses a combination of methods, much as the artist blends the primary colours of his palette. A characteristic example is provided (as we have seen) by Case 6/72 *Continental Can* [1973] ECR 215 at 243 where the judgment states:

> "In order to answer this question (whether Art. 86 EEC applies to changes in the structure of an undertaking) one has to go back to the spirit, general scheme and wording of Article 86, as well as to the system and objectives of the Treaty."

Literal, contextual and teleological approaches are here all mixed together to enable the Court to reach its landmark decision on the full scope of Article 86.

Finally, over the 36 years of its existence the Court has changed the emphasis of its methods, especially in interpreting the founding Treaties. The earlier reliance on literal interpretation has given place increasingly to the contextual and teleological approaches, approaches which befit a jurisdiction charged with a quasi-constitutional function as the guardian of the grand objectives laid down in the Treaties.

Pitfalls for the Common Lawyer

The non-civilian lawyer, be he English, Irish or Scottish, should beware of approaching Community law as if it were no different from his national law: he must heed the injunction of Lord Denning with which we began this chapter. In particular, he should not strain to apply to Community law the canons of interpretation which the common law judges have evolved over the centuries. It would be a salutary exercise for the English-speaking lawyer who has some French to make a practice of looking at the French as well as the English version of the text in issue. As illustrations of where English courts may have gone astray in interpreting Community law, see *Schorsch Meier* v. *Hennin* [1975] Q.B. 416 (Lord Denning M.R.); *R.* v. *Henn and Darby* [1980] 2 All E.R. 166 (Lord Widgery C.J.), see above, p. 170; *R.* v. *Secchi* [1975] 1 C.M.L.R. 383 (Metropolitan Magistrate), see Plender [1976] Crim.L.R. 676; Durand (1979) 4 E.L. Rev. 3 at 9; Case 131/79 *R.* v. *Santillo* [1980] ECR 1585 (Divisional Court and Court of Appeal), see Dashwood (1981) 6 E.L. Rev. 73.

Chapter 15

GENERAL PRINCIPLES OF LAW

Introduction

We have already had occasion to refer to the "general principles of law" used by the Court to supplement the written sources of Community law. But, for several reasons, the subject requires fuller treatment. Firstly, it illustrates both the character of Community law as developed by the Court and the interaction of that law with the national laws of the Member States. Second, the use made by the Court of the general principles of law illustrates, as well as does any other of its techniques, the law-making function of the Court. Third, this technique has enabled the Court to elaborate a doctrine of far-reaching importance, no less than the protection of fundamental rights in Community law.

The use of general principles of law, or something very similar in effect, is found in many legal systems. The Statute of the International Court of Justice requires that Court to apply, *inter alia*, "the general principles of law recognized by civilised nations" (Article 38(1)). In the European Communities there is no such comprehensive direction to the Court to apply the general principles of law; and the criterion is less exacting, since the general principles need be found only in the legal systems of the Member States, and, in the Court's practice, need not be common to all nor even to a majority of them. As Advocate General Lagrange stated:

"In this way the case law of the Court, in so far as it invokes national laws (as it does to a large

293

extent) to define the rules of law relating to the application of the Treaty, is not content to draw on more or less arithmetical 'common denominators' between the different national solutions, but chooses from each of the Member States those solutions which, having regard to the objects of the Treaty, appear to it to be the best or, if one may use the expression, the most progressive. That is the spirit, moreover, which has guided the Court hitherto": Case 14/61 *Hoogovens* v. *High Authority* [1962] ECR 253 at 283–284.

General principles of law are found, not only in international law, but also in many municipal legal systems. The principle of proportionality (below) is especially prominent in German law, where it has a status similar to that of a general principle. Although not expressly mentioned in the German Basic Law, it has been held by the German courts to be the principle underlying two fundamental Articles of the Basic Law, Articles 2 and 12. Indeed German law has made perhaps the greatest contribution to the development of the general principles of law applied by the Court, including the principle of proportionality (*Verhältnis-mässigkeit*) and the principle of protection of legitimate expectations (*Vertrauensschutz*) (below, p. 300).

For the English lawyer the closest analogies are perhaps to be found in the rules of natural justice in administrative law, in the common law notion of reasonableness, and in the maxims of equity; we shall see that these also are now making their mark on Community law.

The French lawyer is familiar with the doctrine of *les principes généraux du droit*. In French administrative law, the general principles of law have restrictive effect in relation to *règlements* or governmental decrees which they do not have on legislation, that is, *lois* enacted by the French parliament. But in the last two decades the

Conseil Constitutionnel has developed its own doctrine of general principles as constitutional norms by reference to which it may veto bills (*projets de loi*), before their enactment, as unconstitutional.

In Community law, general principles may be invoked to interpret the treaty provisions, but they cannot prevail over the express terms of the Treaty. In the *Sgarlata* case, Case 40/64 [1965] ECR 215, the applicants sought to challenge Commission regulations fixing the reference prices for lemons and other citrus fruits. Faced with the objection that the application was inadmissible under Article 173 EEC as being directed against regulations rather than decisions, the applicants argued that if recourse to Article 173 were to be refused by reason of a restrictive interpretation of its terms, individuals would be deprived of all judicial protection under both Community law and national law, which would be contrary to the fundamental principles prevailing in all the Member States. Advocate General Roemer considered that this argument would require the Court not to interpret but to amend the Treaty on this point and the Court agreed that the considerations invoked by the applicants could not be allowed to override the clearly restrictive wording of Article 173. Hence the application was inadmissible. The result would of course have been different if the measures challenged, although in the form of regulations, had been in substance decisions of direct and individual concern to the applicants (above, p. 109). This they also alleged, but were unable to establish.

While general principles of law, or their analogue, can be found in many legal systems, they play a special part in Community law, as will be seen when we look in turn at those principles upon which the Court has most often relied.

1. Proportionality

The earliest decisions of the Court under the Coal and Steel Treaty contain references to general principles of

law such as the principle of proportionality. Mention
has already been made of Case 8/55 *Fédéchar* [1954–
1956] ECR 254 and 292, where the Court held (at 299)
that, by a generally accepted rule of law, the reaction of
the High Authority to an unlawful act must be
proportional to the scale of the act. The principle of
proportionality, expressed in those terms, sounds
unfamiliar to the English lawyer, but he uses a similar
concept when he talks of what is reasonable: see for
example *R.* v. *Barnsley Metropolitan Borough Council,
ex parte Hook* [1976] 1 W.L.R. 1052. The Court too has
used the language of reasonableness. In another early
case, it held that the High Authority must go no further
than is reasonable and must avoid causing harm to the
extent that it is, within reason, possible to do so: Case
15/57 *Chasse* [1958] ECR 211 at 228.

A graphic illustration of proportionality (or, rather,
disproportionality) is afforded by Case 181/84 *R.* v.
*Intervention Board for Agricultural Produce, ex parte
Man (Sugar)* [1986] 2 All E.R. 115: here an export
company had paid to the Board a substantial deposit
(some £1,670,000) in anticipation of its application for
an export licence; when the application reached the
Commission four hours past the deadline, the Board
declared the whole deposit to be forfeit, as it was
required to do by the Commission legislation; the Court
ruled, upon a reference from the English court under
Article 177 EEC, that the forfeiture of the entire
deposit for so trival a breach of the deadline was a
disproportionate act: the company could recover the
entire sum, with interest and costs.

These cases illustrate the characteristic role of general
principles of law as limiting the power of the administration to take measures affecting the citizen, even in the
absence of any written text to this effect. Such
principles were typically applied in actions for annulment under Article 33 ECSC, and subsequently under
Article 173 EEC: an administrative act could be

annulled as contrary to the general principles of law. If a formal justification were required for annulling measures on this ground, it could be found in the references in those Articles to infringement of a rule of law relating to the application of the Treaties. Further, the Court is required to ensure that, in the interpretation and application of the Treaties, "the law is observed" (Article 31 ECSC, Article 164 EEC). The reference here to "the law" is manifestly to a body of law outside the Treaties themselves, and can only be to unwritten rules whose origin it is natural to seek in the legal systems of the Member States.

The general principles of law are thus one, but only one example of the contribution of national law to Community law. Whenever the Court is faced with a question of law which is not resolved by any written Community text, it is likely to be influenced by the laws of the Member States. The advocate general, in his opinion, will very often survey these laws and the Court in its judgment will apply the most appropriate solution. Many concepts undefined in the Treaties, such as "misuse of powers" (above, p. 120), and many other legal problems, have been clarified in this way; we have seen examples of the approach in the previous chapter (p. 284).

The principle of proportionality has also played an important part in the Court's approach to the treaty provisions on the free movement of goods (Articles 30 to 36 EEC), which the Court has treated as imposing far-reaching prohibitions on national measures restricting trade between Member States: see above, p. 281. While such measures may be defended by the State on public policy grounds under Article 36, a defence of this kind is subject to the important proviso that the measures do not constitute, in the words of Article 36, "a means of arbitrary discrimination or a disguised restriction on trade between Member States." In applying this proviso, the Court has used the principle of proportionality so as to declare State measures unlawful if other, less restrictive measures would achieve the same purpose: see, *e.g.* Case 104/75 *de Peijper* [1976] ECR 613. Here the principle is parallel to the doctrine of the "less restrictive alternative" applied by American courts to assess the compatibility of State legislation with the United States Constitution: the question there too is whether the State interest, however legitimate, could be achieved by a measure less damaging to free trade than the one adopted: see T. Sandalow and E. Stein, *Courts and Free Markets* (1982), *Vol. I*, p. 28.

2. Freedom of commercial activity

The principle of proportionality in some situations appears to reflect a broader notion, still to be fully defined, that of freedom of commercial activity—a freedom which accords with the mercantilist philosophy of the EEC Treaty and is found entrenched in the Federal German Constitution. Under this freedom we have grouped, as well as the principle of proportionality: the freedom to pursue a trade or profession, the freedom from unfair competition, and a general freedom to act as one wishes unless the law prohibits the act in question.

All these four principles were invoked together in Cases 133–136/85 *Walter Rau* v. *B.A.L.M.* (1987) 12 E.L.Rev. 451 and Case 249/85 *ALBAKO* v. *B.A.L.M.* [1987] ECR 2354. A scheme of "Free Butter for Free Berlin," a brainwave of the Commission to help increase butter consumption, was introduced in the summer of 1985: for 10 weeks, up to 900 tons of butter held in store were to be offered to West Berliners on the basis of one free 250 gram block of butter for each 250 gram block purchased. This scheme of two blocks of butter for the price of one naturally outraged the manufacturers of margarine, one of whom (Rau) challenged the Commission decision both by a direct action under Article 173 EEC and in proceedings in the German courts against the German Intervention Agency (B.A.L.M.) charged with administering the scheme. The Court of Justice adjudged that none of the four principles above were infringed by the scheme—a not surprising decision in view of the Court's earlier upholding of a cheap "Christmas Butter" scheme in *Walter Rau* v. *EEC*, Cases 279, 280, 285 and 286/84 [1987] ECR 1069.

3. Non-discrimination

Several provisions of the EEC Treaty, and many provisions of EEC legislation, prohibit specific forms of discrimination. Article 7 EEC prohibits discrimination on grounds of nationality across the whole field of the Treaty; Article 40(3) EEC prohibits discrimination in relation to agriculture; Article 119 contains the principle that men and women should receive equal pay for equal work. However the Court of Justice has taken the view that, beyond those specific provisions, the guarantee of equal treatment or the prohibition of discrimination, is a general principle of law which must be observed in the whole field of Community law: see, *e.g.* Case 1/72 *Frilli* [1972] ECR 457 at 466: the rule of equality of treatment "is one of the fundamental principles of Community law."

Similarly in one of the *Isoglucose* cases the Court held that the provisions of Council Regulation 1111/77 establishing the production levy system for isoglucose "offend against the general principle of equality of which the prohibition on discrimination set out in Article 40(3) of the Treaty is a specific expression": Joined Cases 103 and 145/77 [1978] ECR 2037 at 2081.

A different form of discrimination was at issue in a staff case. Signora Sabbatini (née Bertoni) was employed by the European Parliament and benefited, under the Staff Regulations, from an expatriation allowance. On her marriage she lost this allowance since the Staff Regulations provided that an official should forfeit it if, on marriage, he did not become a head of household. Under the Regulations, a married man was classified *ipso facto* as a head of household, but a married female official was so treated only if her husband was unable to work being an invalid or seriously ill. Signora Sabbatini successfully contended that the Regulations were discriminatory on grounds of sex, and therefore contrary both to a general principle of law and to Article 119 EEC. Accepting her plea of illegality under Article 184 (see above, p. 125), the Court held that the Regulations were unlawful and annulled the decision withdrawing the applicant's expatriation allowance: Case 20/71 *Sabbatini* v. *European Parliament* [1972] ECR 345. In accordance, however, with the nature of the plea of illegality, the judgment only declared the offending Regulations to be inapplicable *inter partes*: consequently, other female officials could not rely on this judgment to bring their own claims out of time (see Case 15–33, etc., /73 *Schots–Kortner* [1974] ECR 177, p. 163 above). The offending Regulations were subsequently amended by the Council.

4. Protection of legitimate expectations, etc.

Another rather exceptional case concerned the annual review by the Council of staff salaries: Case 81/72 *Commission* v. *Council* [1973] ECR 575. Here the Court held that the discretion which the Council enjoyed, under Article 65 of the Staff Regulations, in fixing those salaries was subject to the principle of protection of legitimate expectations so that the staff of the Community institutions were entitled to rely on the implementation of a system which the Council had adopted experimentally for a three-year period. When the Council departed from that system, after only nine months, in adopting a new Regulation on salaries, the Commission took the Council to court, and obtained the partial annulment of the Regulation, which was promptly replaced by a Regulation made in conformity with the new system (see above, p. 103).

The judgment illustrates effectively the technique of the Court in handling the general principles of law. Although such principles were considered extensively by the advocate general with full references to national law, the principle of protection of confidence, which had not been considered by the advocate general or relied upon by the Commission, at least in that form, was adopted by the Court without reference to its origins and with only limited explicit justification.

The principle of protection of confidence applied in this case is related to a number of other general principles which have featured in the reports. This family includes the protection of legitimate expectations, the principle of non-retroactivity of legislation, legal certainty, and respect for acquired rights; these principles shade into one another, and the same case may raise one or more of them: see, *e.g.* Case 62/70 *Bock* v. *Commission* [1971] ECR 897; Case 74/74 *CNTA* v. *Commission* [1975] ECR 533, esp. at 556; Case 2/75 *Mackprang* [1975] ECR 607, esp. at 622 *et seq.*; and Case 98/78 *Racke* [1979] ECR 69. All these principles had their origin in the laws of the original Member States, particularly in German administrative law; for although the system of remedies contained in the Treaties was principally based on French administrative law, the German courts have been and remain by far the most active in referring cases to the Court of Justice, with consequent opportunities for the German lawyer to draw the Court's attention to the principles of his legal system.

5. *The right to be heard*

The enlargement of the Communities in 1973 left intact the general principles derived from the legal systems of the founding Member States, but enabled the Court to extend its sources to the laws of the new Member States. English and Scottish decisions were cited by the advocate general as early as March 1973, in the *Staff Salaries* case, and later cases contain frequent references to Danish, English, Irish, and Scots law, especially in the opinions of the first advocate general from the new Member States, Mr. J-P. Warner, and of his successor, Sir Gordon Slynn. Perhaps the best illustration is the *Transocean* case, in which Advocate General Warner invoked a close analogy in English law to the general principles of law, namely the rules of natural justice: Case 17/74 [1974] ECR 1063.

Here the applicant Association had been exempted by the Commission from the provisions of Article 85 of the EEC Treaty, but the exemption was subject to certain conditions, one of which the applicant considered too onerous. The condition in question was a requirement that the members of the Association, who were medium-sized firms manufacturing ship paint, should inform the Commission without delay of any links between them and any other company or firm in the paint sector. The Association, which was a loosely-knit grouping designed to enable its members to compete with the big multinational manufacturers, brought an action before the Court to annul this single condition in the decision, which it considered would be difficult if not impossible to comply with. It contended that the requirement was not mentioned in the notice of objections which the Commission had sent it and that it was never given the opportunity of making its views known on the subject. It relied on Regulation No. 99/63 which governs the procedure before the Commission and maintained that the Commission, by not giving it an opportunity to make its views known, had not followed the proper procedure.

The difficulty with that argument was that Regulation No. 99/63 was not sufficiently detailed to provide for a hearing on the particular matter to which the applicant objected. However the Court is not limited to the arguments which the parties put before it; and the advocate general took the view that the procedure had infringed, not the terms of the Regulation, but one of the rules of natural justice, the principle *audi alteram partem*, which, he said, requires an administrative authority, before wielding statutory power to the detriment of a particular person, to hear what that person has to say about the matter, even if the statute does not expressly require it. Having reviewed the scope of the principle in the laws of the Member States, the advocate general concluded that "the right to be heard forms part of those rights which 'the law' referred to in Article 164 of the Treaty upholds, and of which, accordingly, it is the duty of this Court to ensure the observance."

In its judgment the Court, while following the advocate general, stated the principle in even broader terms, referring to "the general rule that a person whose interests are perceptibly affected by a decision taken by a public authority must be given the opportunity to make his point of view known." It is doubtful, however, whether the principle is to be treated as going as far as this formulation suggests. It is characteristic of the Court's jurisprudential approach to lay down a principle in broad, even absolute terms, but to leave its application to be refined by subsequent developments in the case-law.

6. Fundamental rights

Some of the cases cited in the previous section have what might be called a "human rights flavour." The Court has accepted general principles of law which serve to protect the individual or undertaking from the administration. In some cases, such as the sex equality cases, the same result was secured by the use of general principles as might have been achieved by an express catalogue of fundamental rights written into the Treaties. But the Treaties contain no such bill of rights, despite suggestions that they should be amended to include one. And the Court over a period of years rejected appeals to the fundamental rights protected by national laws such as the German Basic Law.

In a series of cases, notably *Stork* (Case 1/58 [1959] ECR 17), *Geitling* (Joined Cases 36–38, 40/59 [1960] ECR 423) and *Sgarlata* (Case 40/64 [1965] ECR 215), the Court refused to recognise fundamental rights as such. Perhaps its reaction is, with hindsight, explicable; the issue may have been presented to it in the wrong way. When an applicant sought to rely directly on a fundamental right protected by his own law, even by his national constitution, the Court reacted by re-asserting the supremacy of Community law over the laws, even the constitutional laws, of the Member States. The development of Community law has often naturally responded to the way in which a question has been put to it, whether by an applicant in a direct action or by a court of a Member State on a reference.

So it was only when an administrative judge in Stuttgart asked the Court whether a particular requirement was compatible, not with the fundamental rights of national law, but with "the general principles of Community law," that the Court expressly included the protection of fundamental rights within those principles. The case, mentioned above, p. 275, arose out of an attempt by the Commission to reduce the Community "butter mountain." A decision of the Commission authorised Member States to sell butter at a reduced price to persons receiving social assistance. To ensure that the cheap butter reached only those persons for whom it was intended, provision was made in the decision for them to be issued with coupons. The wording of that provision was not precisely the same in all the official language versions, and led to doubts as to whether the beneficiary was required to disclose his name to the shop assistant. As implemented by the German authorities, he was required to do so, and one such beneficiary, Erich Stauder, challenged that requirement.

The Court interpreted the provision on the basis of all the language versions and having regard to its purpose, and held that it did not require—although it did not prohibit—the identification of beneficiaries by name. Then the Court ruled that, so interpreted, that provision contained nothing capable of prejudicing "the fundamental human rights enshrined in the general principles of Community law and protected by the Court": Case 29/69 *Stauder* v. *Ulm* [1969] ECR 419 at 425.

Two linguistic comments must be made on this formula which recognises for the first time the principle of protection of fundamental rights under Community law. Firstly, the expression "general principles of *Community* law"—the term used by the Stuttgart court—must be taken as shorthand for the general principles of law recognised in the Community legal order. The term "general principles of law" is to be preferred and has been used in subsequent decisions. Second, the original French text of the judgment refers to "les principes généraux du droit communautaire *dont la Cour assure le respect.*" These words repeat the formulation of Article 164 EEC requiring the Court to ensure that in the interpretation and application of the Treaty *the law is observed.* They show that the general principles, including fundamental rights, are part of "the law" referred to in Article 164—a point which is lost in the English version of the judgment.

The recognition of fundamental rights was taken a step further in the *Internationale Handelsgesellschaft* case (Case 11/70 [1970] ECR 1125). What was stated elliptically, almost parenthetically, in *Stauder* v. *Ulm* (that the general principles of law include the protection of fundamental rights) is here put into the forefront of the judgment. This was understandable, since the Court was here faced with a direct challenge by the German courts to the supremacy of Community law. The Frankfurt administrative court had already held certain provisions of Community law, relating to the system of agricultural export licences and the deposits attached to them, to be invalid as contrary to fundamental rights protected by the German Basic Law. A German company had forfeited a deposit of about £3,000 for not using export licences for ground maize which it had been granted. On a reference from the Frankfurt court, the Court again refused to look at German constitutional law but asked instead whether there was any analogous guarantee of fundamental rights in Community law. It held that there was. The respect for such rights formed part of the general principles of law. But, having examined the provisions in question, the Court ruled that those rights had not been infringed.

The sequel is well known. The Frankfurt court, not content with this reply, referred the case to the German Federal Constitutional Court and asked whether the Community provisions were compatible with the German Basic Law. The Second Chamber of the Constitutional Court agreed with the Court of Justice on the substance. But the important question was whether the reference was admissible. Could the German courts pronounce, after a ruling of the Court of Justice, on the validity of Community law? The Constitutional Court ruled, by a five to three majority, that the German courts could. So long as Community law contained no catalogue of fundamental rights, passed by a Parliament and equivalent to the catalogue of rights contained in the Basic Law, the German courts remained competent to examine whether the acts of German authorities, although done under Community law, were compatible with the Basic Law.

The judgment of the Federal Constitutional Court was much criticised, not least by the dissenting minority in the Court itself, then was qualified by a later judgment of the same Court (see *Steinike und Weinlig* [1980] 2 C.M.L.R. 531) and was finally overruled, in effect, by the same Court in *Wünsche Handelgesellschaft* [1987] 3 C.M.L.R. 225. But the challenge to the supremacy of Community law at least had the merit of reinforcing concern at the Community level for the protection of fundamental rights. The Court of Justice had already gone somewhat further. After the Council of Europe's European Convention on Human Rights had finally been ratified by all the Member States, it accepted, in the second *Nold* case, that the European Convention, and also more generally "international treaties for the protection of human rights on which the Member States have collaborated or of which they are signatories, can supply guidelines which should be followed within the framework of Community law": Case 4/73 [1974] ECR 491 at 507.

Subsequently, in its judgment in the *Rutili* case, Case 36/75 [1975] ECR 1219, the Court took further the applicability of the European Convention. Rutili was an Italian national resident in France whose trade union and political activities had incurred the disapproval of the French authorities. His residence permit was subjected to a restriction prohibiting him from residing in certain parts of France. On a reference from the administrative court of Paris, before which he had challenged that restriction, the Court of Justice considered the limitations imposed by Community law on the powers of Member States in respect of the control of aliens, in particular under Council Directive No. 64/221 and Regulation No. 1612/68. It held that these limitations were "a specific manifestation of the more general principle," enshrined in the European Convention, to the effect that (in the words of the Convention) "no restrictions in the interests of national security or public safety shall be placed on the rights secured by [Articles 8, 9, 10 and 11 of the Convention] other than such as are necessary for the protection of those interests 'in a democratic society.' "

Here the Court appeared to come close to giving direct effect to the Convention, but in Case 118/75 *Watson and Belmann* [1976] ECR 1185, Advocate General Trabucchi considered that the *Rutili* judgment "did not involve any substantive reference to the [Convention] provisions themselves, but merely a reference to the general principles of law of which, like the Community rules with which the judgment drew an analogy, they are a specific expression."

A further development in the Court's approach can be seen in the *Haur* case, Case 44/79 [1979] ECR 3727. A Council regulation prohibiting the new planting of vines was in issue. The German administrative court, putting questions on the interpretation of the regulation to the Court of Justice, had suggested that the regulation might not be applicable in Germany as being incompatible with fundamental rights protected by the German Basic Law including the right of property. The Court of Justice sought to dispel those doubts by not merely repeating its earlier references to "general principles," but citing specific provisions of the Basic Law and of the Irish and Italian Constitutions, as well as the European Convention on Human Rights, in order to show that the right of property was subject to limitations in the public interest and that the regulation in issue did not go beyond the limitations generally allowed. It has been suggested (by J. A. Usher (1980) 5 E.L. Rev. 209) that the unusual course taken by the Court, in referring expressly to provisions of national law, may be explained as an attempt to reassure those courts "which fear that their fundamental principles are threatened by the primacy of Community law, that in practice these principles *are* taken into account at the Community level."

From the point of view of the general principles of law, the recent judgments of the Court dealing with fundamental rights are of particular interest as showing the sources on which the Court will rely. In the *Internationale Handelsgesellschaft* case the Court refers to "the constitutional traditions common to the Member States"—a very wide term. In the *Nold* and *Rutili* cases it goes further and refers to international treaties as a source of such general principles. In the *Hauer* case it cites specific provisions of national constitutions, a practice hitherto avoided.

Despite the efforts which the Court had made to develop its case-law, debate continued on whether the case-law approach provides sufficient protection on this sensitive issue, or whether, as the Federal Constitutional Court suggested in the *Internationale Handelsgesellschaft* case, an enacted catalogue of fundamental rights was required (see below, p. 310.) The European Parliament, the Council and the Commission appeared to endorse the approach of the Court of Justice when they adopted, on April 5, 1977, a joint declaration in which they underline the paramount importance which they attach to the respect for fundamental rights and especially those derived from the constitutions of the Member States, and from the European Convention on Human Rights, and declare that, in the exercise of their powers and in pursuance of the objectives of the European Communities, they respect and will continue to respect those rights. This commitment was endorsed by the Heads of State and Government at the European Council of April 1978.

As we have seen (above p. 307), by 1986 the German Federal Constitutional Court was sufficiently reassured by the developments just outlined to overrule its previous decision in the *Internationale Handelsgesellschaft* case: the German court accepted that fundamental rights were now sufficiently protected in Community law despite the absence still of any enacted catalogue (see *Wünsche Handelsgesellschaft* [1987] C.M.L.R. 225 p. 307, above).

The Commission, in the past, has advocated the adoption of a Community Bill of Rights (see *The Protection of Fundamental Rights in the European Community*, Bulletin of the EC, Supplement 5/76), but, in recognition of the difficulties inherent in such a proposal, has suggested that, as a first step, the Community should itself accede to the European Convention on Human Rights (Bulletin of the EC, Supplement 2/79). But accession too raises a number of legal, political and institutional problems (see House of Lords Select Committee on the European Communities, Session 1979/80, 71st Report, "Human Rights"; and J. McBride and L. N. Brown, *Yearbook of European Law* (1981), p. 167); and the question of the place of human rights in the Community legal order is far from resolved. A comparable debate continues concerning the entrenchment of human rights in the law of the United Kingdom.

The view, however, of the European Parliament is clear. The Draft Treaty establishing the European Union, adopted by the Parliament in February 1984, made specific provision (Article 4) for the protection of fundamental rights "derived from the common principles of the Constitutions of the Member States and from the European Convention on Human Rights."

And in April 1989 the Parliament adopted its own catalogue of fundamental rights which, while having no legal force, sets out the Parliament's view of those rights deserving of special protection in the European Community.

Chapter 16

PRECEDENT AND THE COURT

It is a fundamental principle of the administration of justice that like cases should be decided alike. Inconsistency in judicial decisions affronts even the most elementary sense of justice. In this sense the principle of *stare decisis*, of abiding by previous decisions, figures prominently in most legal systems, including those of all the Member States of the Communities. In England, whose law, at least in some important areas, is still based largely on case-law, the principle of *stare decisis* has been elaborated and extended into a complex doctrine of precedent, to which whole books have been devoted, *e.g.* Rupert Cross, *Precedent in English Law* (3rd ed., 1977). Strict rules have developed, based on the practice of the courts, as to the circumstances in which one court must follow its own decision, or the decision of another court, in a previous case. Much depends on the respective positions of the courts within the hierarchy of the legal system. According to Professor Cross's "preliminary statement" of the English doctrine of precedent (*op. cit.* p. 7), every court is bound to follow any case decided by a court above it in the hierarchy, and appellate courts (except, since 1966, the House of Lords) are bound by their own previous decisions. But a decision of the High Court, for example, is a persuasive precedent, although not of course binding, even for courts above it in the hierarchy.

In France, at any rate in theory, such a doctrine of precedent has no place; indeed, it is expressly prohibited by Article 5 of the Civil Code. In France, as in other countries sharing the civil law tradition, the predominant view is that judicial decisions are not a formal source of law at all. The reasons for this contrast

311

between England and France throw much light not only on the law and constitution, but also on the politics and history of the two countries: see Kahn-Freund, Lévy and Rudden, *A Source-book on French Law* (2nd ed., 1979), Part I. Here it must suffice to note that the French judge does not regard himself as bound by a single decision of any court; instead, he tries, with the aid of the writings of legal scholars (the *doctrine*), to discern the general trend of decisions on a particular point. Unlike the English (or Scottish) judge, he does not feel compelled to analyse or to reconcile earlier judgments, or to explain his own judgments in those terms.

Judicial decisions are of great importance in Community law, where many fundamental doctrines, as well as much of the elaboration of the texts, are the creation of the Court. However, it is a feature of the Community legal system that Community law is applied by the courts of the Member States, but can be authoritatively interpreted by the Court of Justice alone. Accordingly this chapter is divided into two parts: the first part considers precedent in the Court of Justice, the second considers precedent in the national courts.

A. Precedent in the Court of Justice

The Court's decisions are of course authoritative. But what does this mean? Certainly the English rules for ascertaining the principle upon which the case was decided, the *ratio decidendi*, have no automatic application to the Court's judgments. These judgments, as has already been remarked, have been strongly influenced by the model of the higher French courts. They are abstract and syllogistic, rather than concrete and discursive like the typical English or Scottish judgment: Judge Pescatore speaks of their "lapidary serenity." Although they now sometimes refer to previous decisions which they are following, they rarely allude to any earlier decisions from which they may be departing.

Their character has a decisive impact on the question of precedent. First, it means that the judgments often start from broad propositions of law which may not be intended to be taken at face value, in absolute terms, but rather to be refined by subsequent decisions. If taken literally, these propositions are sometimes strikingly broad: we have seen an example in the general principle stated in the *Transocean* case, above, p. 302. Second, judgments of this kind do not easily lend themselves to the characteristic technique of distinguishing earlier judgments in the way of an English lawyer. But in Case 112/76 *Manzoni* [1977] ECR 1647 at 1662, Advocate General Warner did use the language of *stare decisis* and *ratio decidendi* in his opinion.

Like any other court, the Court prefers to follow its own previous decisions. For example, in Case 35/75 *Matisa* [1975] ECR 1205 at 1210, it cited its previous decision (Case 14/70 *Bakels* [1970] ECR 1001) on the authority of the Brussels Nomenclature in interpreting the Common Customs Tariff and continued: "Since there is nothing in the present case capable of leading to a different conclusion, it is proper to reply to the same effect." And, as we have seen (above, pp. 43–45), in the *Import Gadgets* case the Court followed, but without citing, both the earlier cases on this point. It can be expected, too, that the Court of First Instance (above, Chapter 5) will normally follow previous decisions of the Court of Justice, as any lower court will normally follow the decisions of an appellate court superior to it.

The Court of Justice has not hesitated however to depart from its own previous decisions where it thought it necessary. Such departures may take different forms. Sometimes it is a matter of developing a particular doctrine, such as the doctrine of the direct effect of provisions of Community law. Here the Court started from rather narrow criteria in deciding whether a treaty provision had direct effect, as in Case 26/62 *Van Gend en Loos* (above, p. 183). Subsequently it has taken a progressively broader view of the circumstances in which the Treaty has direct effect in cases such as the second *Defrenne* case (above, p. 289); and the doctrine was extended to directives in cases such as *Van Duyn* (above, p. 273) and *Becker* (above, p. 47) In this way the Court has been able to give direct effect to a far wider range of Community provisions than would have been possible if the narrower criteria had been retained. At other times the Court has appeared to overrule directly, if not explicitly, an earlier decision.

An example of the Court changing its mind was on the question whether an act had to be annulled before a claim for damages for the injury caused by that act could be successful. As we have already seen (p. 144, above), the Court's original view was that prior annulment was a condition precedent to the action for damages. This was so decided in Case 25/62 *Plaumann* [1963] ECR 95, which discouraged for several years the bringing of such actions. Then, in Case 4/69, *Lütticke* [1971] ECR 325, the Court adopted the view that the action for damages was established by the EEC Treaty as an independent form of action and could, in consequence, be brought in respect of an act that had not already been annulled. After a return to the *Plaumann* approach in Case 96/71 *Haegeman* [1972] ECR 1005, the Court finally confirmed the *Lütticke* view in Case 43/72 *Merkur* [1973] ECR 1055.

The Court thus showed that it does not regard itself as bound by its previous decisions. Although the English lawyers may find it strange that the Court should not expressly recognise that it is departing from precedent let alone give no reasons for doing so, the fact that it should have this freedom can be readily understood. A final court can only be bound by its previous decisions if the law established by those decisions can, in the last resort, be amended by legislation. Since the decisions of the Court of Justice could be affected only by an amendment of the Treaties, a practical impossibility, it is inevitable that it should be flexible in its approach to precedent. Like a constitutional court, its freedom can be explained by the finality of its decisions. But such departures from precedent are very much the exception. Difficulties do arise, however, where the Court does not make clear whether it is reversing itself: *e.g.* Cases 115 and 116/81 *Adouai and Cornuaille* [1982] ECR 1665 in relation to Case 41/74 *van Duyn* [1974] ECR 1337; Case 104/79 *Foglia* v. *Novello* (*No. 1*) [1980] ECR 745 in relation to Case 244/80 *Foglia* v. *Novello* (*No. 2*) [1981] ECR 3045 (see p. 181, above); Case 121/85 *Conegate* [1986] ECR 1007 relation to Case 34/79 *R.* v. *Henn & Darby* [1979] ECR 3795: see the subsequent struggle of the Divisional Court in *Noncyp* [1988] 3 C.M.L.R. 84.

The problem arises in a different form in decisions of the Chambers. The Chambers may disagree *inter se* on a question of law, so that, again very exceptionally, there are conflicting precedents. This has occasionally happened in staff cases, but in future the wider use of a Chamber as the normal organ of judgment (see p. 26, above) will increase the danger of conflicting precedents unless care is taken to channel difficult cases to the full Court. Experience in other divided courts shows that it is often difficult to foresee such a potential conflict; fortunately, the Rules (Article 95(4)) permit a Chamber at any time to refer to the Court a case assigned to it.

So far we have considered the authority of judgments of the Court and of the Chambers. A separate question is that of the authority of opinions of the advocates general. These may be, and frequently are, cited in subsequent cases, both by counsel and by advocates general themselves. They may be considered in three separate situations.

First, they may be the only authority available on a particular point: this will be the case if the judgment has

not dealt with a point on which the advocate general
has expressed a view. Since the opinions are more wide-
ranging than the judgments, this situation arises very
frequently; there are many unsettled areas of Community law where only the dicta of the advocates general
can be cited as directly in point. Such dicta might be
compared with the statements of a single judge in the
English Court of Appeal on an issue on which the other
judges have not pronounced.

Secondly, the Court may have dealt with the point
considered by the advocate general, but have differed
from him. Should one then treat the opinion as having
been, in effect, overruled; or should one treat it rather
as a dissenting opinion? The answer would seem to be
that, since the Court is not bound by its own decisions,
it should be treated as a dissenting opinion; and here
too the advocate general is, in practice, cited by
counsel, although they must then of course seek to show
that the judges were wrong and the advocate general
was right.

Thirdly, and perhaps most commonly, where the
Court has followed the advocate general on the point in
question, it may be unnecessary to refer to the opinion
at all, except perhaps to strengthen the authority of the
judgment. But, whether the Court has followed it or
not, the opinion may help to show for precisely what
proposition the case is indeed authority.

So far we have considered the significance for the
Court of its own decisions. What then is the significance
for the Court of national court decisions? These are not,
of course, authoritative for the Court on questions of
Community law; they are most frequently cited as
evidence of the existence of one or more general
principles of law (considered in the previous chapter).
Often, as we have seen, fundamental concepts have
been elucidated with the aid of comparative law. But
decisions of national courts are rarely cited directly on
questions of Community law, unless for purposes of

comparison; and for these purposes even decisions from non-Member States have occasionally been cited, as in the American cases on extra-territorial jurisdiction cited by Advocate General Mayras in the *Dyestuffs* cases, Cases 48, etc., /69 [1972] ECR 619 and by Advocate General Darmon in the *Woodpulp* cases, Cases 89/85, etc., Opinion of May 25, 1988.

Decisions of national courts may also be relevant where questions of national law have to be decided by the Court. Such cases are infrequent but three examples may be given. Firstly, in Case 18/57 *Nold* v. *High Authority* [1957] ECR 121 the Court had to consider questions of German law in order to decide whether Nold himself had the necessary capacity to bring proceedings before the Court in the name of his company, then in liquidation. Second, just as the question may arise, in a direct action, whether the applicant has the capacity to bring proceedings, so on a reference for a preliminary ruling the question may arise whether the body making the reference is competent to do so, that is, whether it is a "court or tribunal of a Member State"; and the answer to this question may, as we have seen (p. 186), depend partly on national law. Finally, national law may be in issue, not as a preliminary question but on the substance of the case, in direct actions against Member States (Chapter 6), if it is alleged that the law of that State is contrary to the Treaty: see, for example, Case 167/73 *Commission* v. *French Republic* (above, p. 84). Here the question whether a provision of national law infringes Community law is a two-part one: first, the Court must determine the rule of Community law which is allegedly infringed, and this is a question of law; secondly, the Court must determine the rule of national law under attack as infringing that Community rule, and this for the Court is a question of fact: see Audretsch, *Supervision in European Community Law* (2nd ed., 1986), p. 73.

It is significant of the relationship between the Court of Justice and the national courts that, in all these cases, the questions of national law are, for the Court of Justice, merely questions of fact, which require to be proved, just as questions of national law are questions of fact for international courts and questions of foreign law are questions of fact for national courts. In contrast, it is a fundamental principle of the Community legal order that questions of Community law are questions of law, not questions of fact, for the courts of the Member States, which must take judicial notice of the provisions of Community law. In the United Kingdom this is expressly recognised by section 3 of the European Communities Act 1972 (below, p. 320), but this is merely declaratory, and the principle is valid for all Member States.

B. *Precedent in the National Courts*

Apart from the role of precedent in the Court itself, the authority of judicial decisions on Community law must also be considered from the point of view of the courts of the Member States, since, as we have seen, they too are Community courts. Three questions arise: Firstly, what is the authority, for them, of decisions of the Court of Justice? Second, what is the authority, within the national hierarchy of the courts, of the decisions on Community law of their supreme courts—for example, the House of Lords in the United Kingdom, the *Cour de Cassation* and *Conseil d'Etat* in France, or the various federal supreme courts in Germany? And finally, what is the authority, within the courts of one Member State, of the decisions of the courts of other Member States?

Two overriding principles may be of guidance in attempting to answer these questions. Firstly, there is no Community hierarchy of courts. The judicial systems of the Member States remain intact. In the absence of any federal structure, the Community system respects the judicial independence of the Member States, subject always of course to the principle that the courts, like all other State organs, are bound by the obligations of the Community Treaties.

Second, while the courts of the Member States remain sovereign, subject to that principle, in the *application* of Community law, only the Court of Justice can pronounce authoritatively on its *interpretation*. So much indeed is apparent from the last paragraph of Article 177 EEC, which obliges the national courts of last instance to refer questions of Community law to the Court.

What then, in the light of these principles, is the status for national courts of decisions of the Court of Justice?

Plainly, in a case where it has given a ruling on a question referred to it, that ruling is binding on the referring court. But is the ruling also binding on other courts in subsequent cases raising the same question? The Court itself has taken the view that, where it has already answered the question in a previous case, there is no need for even a court of last instance, which would otherwise be obliged to refer under the third paragraph of Article 177, to do so, since "the authority of an interpretation under Article 177 already given by the Court may deprive the obligation of its purpose and thus empty it of its substance": Cases 28, 29 and 30/62 *Da Costa en Schaake* [1963] ECR 31 at 38. On the other hand, the Court held in the same cases that a national court may always, if it considers it desirable, refer questions of interpretation to the Court again. Even where the same question has already been answered, it may do so if it considers for some reason that a different answer might be appropriate in the case before it. Since the Court of Justice does not regard itself as strictly bound by its previous decisions, it will be able to modify its previous ruling if necessary. Thus the conclusion would seem to be that, in a case raising a question on which the Court has already ruled, the national court has a choice: it can either apply the ruling, or seek a new ruling. But it is bound by the ruling in the sense that it cannot simply disregard it.

Cases in the Court of Justice have even gone so far as to lay down a principle of construction that national courts should follow in the interpretation and application of national legislation. Where this legislation was passed to implement a directive, the national courts must interpret the national measure (at least where it is ambiguous) so as to give effect to the directive: Case 14/83 *van Colson* [1984] ECR 1891, reaffirmed in Case 80/86 *Kolpinghuis Nijmegen*, judgment of October 8, 1987 [1988] P.L. 317. In *Duke* v. *GEC Reliance* [1988] 1 All E.R. 626, the House of Lords refused "to distort the meaning" of an Act of Parliament in order to give effect to a directive which (in their view) the Act was not passed to implement: see the criticism of this case by Anthony Arnull in (1988) *Public Law* 313.

So far as the courts in the United Kingdom are concerned, the binding force of decisions of the Court is recognised and given effect (albeit parenthetically) by the European Communities Act 1972. Section 3(1) of the Act provides that:

> "For the purposes of all legal proceedings any question as to the meaning or effect of any of the Treaties, or as to the validity, meaning or effect of any Community instrument, shall be treated as a question of law (and, if not referred to the European Court, be for determination as such in accordance with the principles laid down by and any relevant decision of the European Court)."

It would seem to follow also, from what has been said, that, no matter what the national rules of precedent may provide, the lower courts of a Member State cannot be bound by any decision of a higher court in that State on a question of Community law. It could only be so bound if the higher court had obtained a ruling from the Court of Justice on the point in issue; and even then the lower court would be bound by that ruling rather than by the higher court's decision. And it would remain free to refer any new question of Community law.

This point was established by the Court in Cases 146 and 166/73 the *Rheinmühlen* cases [1974] ECR 33 and 139, which were episodes in a long legal battle between a German cereal exporter, Rheinmühlen-Düsseldorf, and the German intervention agency for cereals. The Hessisches Finanzgericht had decided that Rheinmühlen was not entitled, under Community law, to any refunds on the export of certain consignments of barley. On appeal the Federal Finance Court (*Bundesfinanzhof*), having obtained a preliminary ruling on certain questions of Community law (Case 6/71), quashed this judgment and ruled that Rheinmühlen was at least entitled to a refund at a lower rate. The case was accordingly sent back to the Hessian Court to decide certain questions of fact.

Under German law the Hessian court was bound by the Bundesfinanzhof's ruling on the point of law. However, the court considered that that ruling raised a new question of Community law, which it accordingly referred to the Court (Case 146/73). It also asked whether it is permissible for a lower court to make a reference only when the case comes before it for the first time or whether it may do so also when reconsidering the case after the judgment of a lower court has been quashed by a higher court.

This reference by the Hessian court was challenged by Rheinmühlen in the Bundesfinanzhof, which then itself made a further reference (Case 166/73). It asked whether a lower court has a completely unfettered right to make a reference or whether Article 177 leaves unaffected rules of national law under which a lower court is bound on points of law by the judgment of a higher court.

On this question the Court of Justice ruled that the power of a lower court to make a reference cannot be abrogated by such a rule of national law; and it gave the same answer to the Hessian court. Advocate General Warner went further, arguing that the discretion of a lower court to make a reference cannot be fettered by any rule of national law, and he concluded from this that the Treaty does not allow appeals against a decision to refer. The Court held, however, that Article 177 does not preclude an appeal of a type normally available under national law. But the Court's judgments on the two references do establish that, although a lower court may be bound under national law to follow the ruling of a higher national court, it remains free to refer a new question under Article 177, and to follow the ruling given by the Court in reply. To that extent any national rule concerning the binding force of a higher court's decision upon a lower court, whether in the same litigation (as in *Rheinmühlen*) or *a fortiori* under the doctrine of precedent, is displaced by Community law.

Finally, what is the authority of decisions of courts of other Member States on questions of Community law? Again, it seems clear that such decisions can in no sense be regarded as binding, although any rulings given by the Court of Justice on references in such cases will be followed unless a new reference is considered necessary. In the absence of a reference, the authority of the national decision will be at best persuasive.

Chapter 17

FUTURE OF THE COURT: CONCLUSIONS

We have seen, in previous chapters, the ways in which the Court has carried out its task, under Article 164 EEC, of ensuring that, in the interpretation and application of the Treaty, the law is observed. The Communities themselves are creatures of law, and are governed by law in every aspect of their operations. The reader may be left to judge for himself the extent to which the Court has succeeded in preserving the rule of law, and in ensuring that on the judicial level, at least, European integration is being progressively realised.

Here we shall attempt, instead of a retrospective survey of the 35 years or more since the setting up of the Coal and Steel Community in 1952, a brief look forward into the future as well as a critique of the present.

As we said in our first edition, it would of course be rash to venture firm predictions on the future of the Court, which must largely depend upon the unpredictable future of the Communities themselves. The Communities are volatile structures which, if they do not progress, are liable to slip backwards: like a man walking a tight-rope, they need momentum if they are not to fall. Being relatively young and artificial creations, they cannot be left to fend for themselves but need constantly to be nurtured in order to survive. Yet, plagued as they are both by economic difficulties and by political weaknesses, their future development must remain a matter of conjecture. At best we can only base ourselves on a number of hypotheses.

Enlargement of the Communities

Since our first edition, the Communities have been enlarged by the accession of Greece, Portugal and Spain. Turkey has made a formal application to join, and EFTA countries, such as Austria, Norway and Sweden, are re-opening the question of their membership as they face the bleak prospect of exclusion from the Single European Market after 1992.

The successive enlargements of 1981 and 1986 have already had a practical impact on the working of the institutions, and especially of the Court of Justice.

In the first place, the composition of the Court has been increased to include a judge of each of the new Member States. The increased work-load has required an additional (sixth) advocate general to be recruited (like the fifth) from the eight smaller Member States.

In the second place, the enlargement of the Court has reinforced the tendency for the Chambers to become the normal organ of judgment and for the Court to sit in plenary session only exceptionally. The 13-judge Court has permitted the creation of six Chambers, four of three and two of five judges, so that the Court can sit simultaneously in several divisions. When a plenary session is still necessary, the retention of the low quorum of seven judges permits, as we have seen, a Petty Plenum (usually of nine) to sit in cases not warranting a Grand Plenum (above, p. 227).

In the third place, enlargement of the Communities made imperative the creation of the Court of First Instance to help bear the increased case-load. How far this will bring sufficient relief to the senior Court remains to be seen: the probability is that some system of filtering will have to be devised in both the appellate and the original jurisdiction of the Court of Justice.

Perhaps English experience in judicial administration in the wake of the Beeching Commission still has something to teach the Communities about the conservation of that most precious commodity, "judge-power."

Another question of practical importance is the problem of languages, which the enlargement of the Communities has inevitably aggravated. Within the Court it seems an inescapable requirement, at least in preliminary rulings, that any of the national languages of all the Member States should be available, but it may become necessary to restrict the choice of languages for other purposes. The principle of linguistic equality may be in danger of becoming the Community's sacred cow impeding the path of justice and discouraging further enlargement.

Again, the addition of the legal systems of Spain and Portugal will, if past experience is a guide, further encourage the Court to resort extensively to national law in developing the general principles of law, the role of which we have explored in Chapter 15.

Developments in the Court's Jurisdiction

Other developments, apart from the enlargement of the Communities, may affect the Court's work-load. There are likely to be developments in its jurisdiction. Some of these have been mentioned in previous chapters; for example the jurisdiction to give advisory opinions (Chapter 11) and to interpret Conventions concluded between Member States (Chapter 10). The latter jurisdiction might be further extended to include other international agreements in the economic field which have not been entered into pursuant to the Treaties but which may nonetheless require uniform interpretation in the different Member States. Conversely, the work-load in staff cases and competition cases will have been lightened as a result of the creation of the Court of First Instance (see Chapter 5, above). Nevertheless, the principle of "unity of jurisdiction" has been preserved by the right of appeal (on law) from the new Court to the Court of Justice.

To assist it in its formidable task the Court has made frequent pleas, especially to the Council, for more generous staffing, and, as we have seen (Chapter 3, above), the establishment of legal secretaries has been more than doubled since 1980, and the total number of staff has increased from 244 in 1977 to 682 in January 1989. The establishment of the Court of First Instance will necessitate a further increase in the staff of the Court to some 700, including both staff permanently assigned to the Court of First Instance and necessary increase in staffing of the existing departments of the Court.

Such growth in personnel, however, has its dangers. Professor Vining of Michigan has warned that the American federal court system is becoming a "depersonalized bureaucracy" as judges increasingly rely on the growing cadre of law clerks to write a major share of their opinions, which then cease to be authoritative reflections of the workings of a single legal mind or the joint efforts of judges accurately to reflect the dialogue that produced the collegiate decision (26 *Law Quadrangle Notes*, Ann Arbor, 1981, no. 1, 5).

Another, but not dissimilar danger, if the Court becomes overloaded, has been stressed by Professor Cappelletti of Florence. He points out that "constitutional decision-making demands that kind of careful consideration which it is unrealistic to expect from courts which are submerged under thousands of cases they are obliged to decide; it requires a high degree of creativity and of policy-oriented balancing of interests and values which bureaucratic and routine-oriented judges can hardly provide" (*Festschrift für Konrad Zweigert* 1981, p. 391).

The 1980s have brought increasing signs that the Court is indeed becoming over-burdened. To give only one example: if a national court has now to wait some

18 months for a ruling on its preliminary reference (in our first edition, the period was six months), this may well be intolerable: in practice, justice delayed may mean justice denied. How then to lighten the load at Luxembourg and cut down delay? As well as the creation of the Court of First Instance and the subdivision of the Court itself into Chambers, could one envisage purely routine cases proceeding direct to judgment without the benefit of any advocate-general's opinion or with a merely formal opinion deferring to the wisdom of the Court? French administrative courts have adopted or are contemplating such reforms to relieve their backlog of cases; and the Court of First Instance has abandoned the principle of an advocate-general's opinion in every case.

Another common device for easing congestion and one very familiar in common law systems is the filter provided by leave to appeal (or the application for judicial review made subject to leave). But without treaty revision such a filter is incompatible with the terms of Article 177 EEC. Its only use might be in direct actions, so as to stop unmeritorious applications *in limine* where a single judge refused leave.

Comparisons, however, with a fully fledged federal legal system are not entirely apt when describing the court as the Community's supreme constitutional court. For the Community legal system is one in which any national court or tribunal may rule upon constitutionality of its national law in relation to Community law: if the national (*i.e.* State) judge elects to decide such a "federal" question instead of referring it to Luxembourg under Article 177, he is usually free to do so (only a final court *must* refer). To this extent, the burden of adjudicating upon constitutional issues is shared by the Court with the national judiciary.

European Union

At the "summit conference" held in Paris in October 1972 the ambitious but obscure objective was fixed of "transforming, before the end of the present decade and with the fullest respect for the Treaties already signed, the whole complex of the relations of Member States into a European Union." Specific proposals with a view to achieving this "European Union" were made by the Community institutions, and Mr Leo Tindemans, Prime Minister of Belgium, when invited to define what was meant by this term, duly presented a report to the European Council (Bulletin of the European Communities, Supplement 1/76).

The following section of the Tindemans report deals with the Court:

"The Court of Justice stressed in its report on European Union that the Community constitutes a 'state of law' (*Rechtsstaat*) and that this characteristic must be maintained within the Union. This is an essential factor conferring legitimacy upon our undertaking which leads me to formulate the following:

(a) In the new sectors covered by the Union, the Court must have powers identical to those which it has at present, so as to be able to interpret the law of the Union, to annul the acts of the institutions not in accordance with the Treaties and to point out when the Member States fail to comply with their obligations;

(b) Individuals must also be able to appeal directly to the Court of Justice against an act of one of the institutions of the Union infringing their basic rights;

(c) Once European Union has gained its own momentum we should examine whether the Community's current legal system can be improved or extended: the Court has made proposals about this."

A number of specific proposals for strengthening the jurisdiction of the Court were made in the reports of the Commission and of the Court (Bulletin of the European Communities, Supplements 5/75 and 9/75). The Court emphasised, however, and the Commission agreed, that a single court should be preserved: "Because of the need to ensure uniform application of the law in all the Member States, it is of fundamental importance that the judicial system should be subject to a single supreme court." But the reference to a "supreme court" does not imply the creation of a supreme court on the lines of the United States Supreme Court, a model which would be appropriate only in a federal Europe. None of the reports on European Union went as far as this; on the contrary they sought to preserve, with relatively minor modifications, the judicial structure in substantially its present form, in which the Court of Justice and the national courts cooperate in the administration of Community justice. Nor has the creation of the Court of First Instance impaired the supremacy of the Court of Justice as the ultimate arbiter on Community Law.

In retrospect, the hopes of the Paris summit were dashed by the deepening economic depression of the subsequent decade, and the Tindemans report remains only a blueprint of what might have been achieved, given the political will. It was however to be overtaken by the more pragmatic approach leading in 1986 to the Single European Act.

The Protection of Fundamental Rights

Apart from the possible accession of the Community to the European Convention on Human Rights (see p. 310, above), it may also prove necessary to review the mechanisms for the protection of fundamental rights which are divided between the Court on the one hand, and the bodies set up under the Convention (the European Commission and Court of Human Rights) on the other. For at present the acts of Member States are subject to review by the Convention bodies in Strasbourg, and the acts of the Community institutions by the Court of Justice in Luxembourg, while the possibility cannot be excluded that measures taken by Member States in implementation of their Community obligations may be open to challenge in both Strasbourg and Luxembourg, with perhaps conflicting results.

If the field of activity of the Community institutions continues to widen, more matters may fall outside the competence of the Convention bodies. Although the Court of Justice will have the power to ensure that Community action complies with respect for fundamental rights, its paramount concern may be the promotion of integration and the standards it applies may not be the same as those of bodies whose main function is to preserve the rights of the individual.

Again, various proposals have been made to overcome these difficulties. In a different context, the suggestion has been made that the Court of Justice should be empowered, when faced with a question of interpretation of the Convention, to seek a ruling from the European Court of Human Rights (see the opinion of Advocate General Warner in Case 130/75 *Prais* v. *Council* [1976] ECR 1589).

Defiance of the Court and Other Criticisms

The plea made by President Giscard d'Estaing at the Dublin summit in 1975 "to do something about the Court and its illegal decisions" did not fall on deaf ears in his own country. As we have seen (above, p. 194), the *Conseil d'Etat* later went out of its way, in *Cohn-*

Bendit, to confront the Court with an uncompromising rejection of its case-law on the doctrine of direct effect of directives. It is to be expected that governments in the Member States may sometimes, under political pressure, be slow to comply with Community law. But defiance by the national judiciary is a more alarming phenomenon which, if it were to spread, would be the death-knell of that doctrine of judicial co-operation which is the hallmark of the procedure under Article 177. Happily, the German Federal Constitutional Court has moderated its earlier attitude (see p. 306, above), and the bark of the *Conseil d'Etat* may be worse than its bite.

The reaction of the Court has been deliberately restrained and low key. Recent judgments have defined more clearly the limits upon the direct effect doctrine; judicial conferences have continued to bring national judiciary to Luxembourg to become better informed about the Court and to improve mutual understanding under the mellowing influence of wine and good cheer; and the great majority of national judges have loyally accepted the supremacy of Community law and its concomitant, the authority of the Court's rulings and decisions.

Falling far short of defiance of the Court, there has been informed criticism of its procedures and decisions in the Member States, notably by the House of Lords Select Committee on the European Communities, which reviewed the Court's procedures and recommended that there should be formal collaboration between the Court and practitioners on questions of procedure, with consideration being given to the establishment of a Joint Committee (House of Lords, Session 1979–80, 23rd report, p. 18).

Certainly, the Court has shown itself responsive to criticism, some of it, indeed, self-criticism. Thus, in the *Sugar Cartel* cases (Cases 40–48, etc., /73 [1975] ECR 1663), it reformed its procedure for taking evidence of

witnesses so as to expedite consideration of the factual issues before it; in its longest judgment (to date)
the Court demonstrated its ability to deal with
complicated facts, every point of fact and every
argument of the parties being given due consideration in
the decision. Nevertheless, this was only achieved after
prodigious expenditure of effort and time. So too in the
Pioneer case (Cases 100–103/80 [1983] ECR 1825),
where even more voluminous evidence fell to be
examined.

The Court of First Instance, for matters falling within
its jurisdiction, will improve judicial protection by its
careful scrutiny of the factual basis of its decisions.

A criticism of the Court that has not been met is that
it frequently adjudicates on points (usually of law but
sometimes of fact) which have not been argued before
it. This inspires more objection in common lawyers,
accustomed as they are to an adversarial process of trial
in which the court makes up its mind according to the
ebb and flow of argument by counsel: the judge who
engages in his own research is hardly playing the game.
The civil lawyers, by contrast, have been conditioned to
accept that the judge may turn inquisitor—a change of
role not unfamiliar to those dispensing justice in British
administrative tribunals.

A particular aspect of this problem is the lack of
general provision in the Rules of Procedure to permit
counsel to comment upon the advocate-general's opinion, even though this raises new issues upon which no
argument has been presented. Only exceptionally will
the Court order the re-opening of the oral proceedings:
see Case 155/79 *AM & S* [1982] ECR 1575, above,
p. 232; and even then, counsel are in no better position
in relation to the *second* opinion. The House of Lords
Select Committee proposed that the Court should give
parties a right to submit, within a limited period,
written comments on statements of fact in an advocate-
general's opinion, and should be willing to re-open the

oral procedure where it is alleged that the advocate general has introduced a new point of law.

Judicial Activism

The new mood of confidence in the Community, born of the Single European Act, and the improvement in the legislative process through a new readiness to cooperate on the part of the political institutions may argue for a change of attitude on the part of the Court, which for some 20 years past has felt constrained to fill the legislative vacuum by promoting legal integration by judicial decision. But the line between legal and political integration is a fine one and, if crossed, may produce conflicts with the political organs of government both in the Community and the Member States. What Professor Rasmussen has called "uncontrolled pro-Community activism" may now, in his view, have dangers for the Court, not least a perception of it in the Member States as a not fully trustworthy neutral arbiter (H. Rasmussen, *On Law and Policy in the European Court of Justice* (1986)). Professor Cappelletti has cogently refuted this suggestion ("Is the European Court of Justice 'Running Wild'?" in (1987) 12 E.L. Rev. 3); but from the Court itself Judge Koopmans has recently reflected whether it should not go back to a *mininal* role, stripping its case-law of its more daring and activist sidelines (Koopmans, "The Role of Law in the Next Stage of European Integration": (1986) 35 I.C.L.Q. 925).

How far these arguments for judicial restraint will convince the Court is a question made more difficult by the changes in its membership after October 1988 to which we have already referred. Past history, however, suggests that the Court does not easily succumb to faint hearts or cold feet.

Cross-Fertilisation of National and Community Legal Systems

Finally, we turn to what may be, in legal terms, the most significant future development: the cross-fertilisation of Community law and the national legal systems. This is a two-way process.

First, in previous chapters, and especially in Chapter 15, we have seen examples of the impact of national law upon Community law. Until 1973 Community law was largely a product of the relatively homogeneous laws of the Six: only competition law reflected outside influence, that of the United States. But, since the first enlargement, the distinctive legal families of the British Isles and of Scandinavia have added their important contribution, to be joined in the present decade by the laws of Greece, Portugal and Spain. The scope for comparative legal research at Luxembourg is now obviously immense, and we have seen how well equipped are the various services of the Court for this purpose. The fruits of this research emerge in the opinions of the advocates general and more indirectly in the Court's decisions. Moreover, by a kind of process of osmosis, common law concepts and modes of thought now permeate the Court by the mere presence there of British (and Irish) lawyers, whether as judge, advocate general, member of the Commission's Legal Service, or counsel for the parties.

Secondly, Community law, as it becomes more widely known, is having an increasing influence upon national law. So far as the United Kingdom is concerned, two developments in particular may already be remarked in this direction. The first relates to the principles of interpretation (which we have examined in Chapter 14) applied by the Court and applied also now by United Kingdom courts to provisions of Community law. These principles, as they become increasingly familiar, are having some impact in our own courts' approach to domestic legislation: see, *e.g.* the judgment of Lord Denning M.R. in *Macarthys* v. *Smith* [1979] 3 All E.R. 325, C.A.; also the judgments of the Court of Appeal in *James Buchanan & Co.* v. *Babco*, judgments with which the House of Lords pointedly disagreed in favour of the traditional English methods of construction: [1978] A.C. 141, H.L. In the longer term, the Community methods may influence also the style of our own legislative drafting, as may closer acquaintance with our Community neighbours (see Sir Wm. Dale (ed.) *British and French Statutory Drafting*, (1987), reviewed in (1988) 37 I.C.L.Q. 696).

Thirdly, the wider basis of judicial review in the Community legal order (discussed in particular in Chapter 7) throws into relief the more restrictive approach of our own law, although in recent years English administrative law has been revitalised through the twin principles of reasonableness (*alias*, proportionality) and fairness. Judicial review as effected at Luxembourg for constitutionality has also prompted English reformers, such as Lord Scarman, to propose a United Kingdom Bill of Rights by reference to which our judges would invalidate offending legislation.

Parallel developments may occur in the field of procedure, a subject to which we have adverted in Chapter 12. The simplicity, flexibility, and relative speed of the Court's procedures may in the course of time have some effect on the reform of national court procedure, at least in the higher courts and in cases concerned primarily with questions of law. For the determination of questions of law, the Court's methods have proved themselves effective and have made savings in time and in costs which are hard to quantify but must be very great. Conversely, the practitioner accustomed to English methods may find cause for concern in the Court's methods for resolving issues of fact. Here the English lawyer will feel that there is scope for contributions from his own practices to the working of the Court: since 1973 there have already been changes in the hearing of witnesses.

Improvements can obviously be made in both directions; in any event, the greater exposure of judges, practitioners and students (the practitioners of tomorrow) from the Member States to the Luxembourg method can only be salutary.

An increasing convergence of ways of thinking and of practices, both in law and procedure, would thus be of mutual benefit. Beyond the development of Community law itself, this may lead to a wider integration within the Community. For as Mr Roy Jenkins reminded the European Parliament in his inaugural address as President of the Commission on January 11, 1977: "In all our activities, we must remember our underlying political purposes. Our means are largely economic, but our end is and always has been political. It is to make a European Union."

Since those words were spoken, the fulfilment of such Union has been advanced by the Single European Act with its goal of a single internal market by 1992; and Jacques Delors, the current President of the Commission, endorses and even goes beyond the Jenkins' vision. But Prime Minister Margaret Thatcher, in her speech to the College of Europe in September 1988, put a different view: for her, "willing and active co-operation between independent sovereign states is the best way to build a successful European Community. To try to suppress nationhood and concentrate power at the centre of a European conglomerate would be highly damaging and would jeopardise the objectives we seek to achieve." The Community in its history has lived with, and survived, such tensions between the whole and the parts. In the future, as in the past, the Court of Justice has a vital role to play in helping relieve the tensions inherent in the very concept of Community, whilst remaining constant to the ultimate objective, however shadowy its nature, of European Union.

SELECT BIBLIOGRAPHY

Note. This bibliography is confined to a selection of recent English-language publications giving special emphasis to the Court of Justice.

Books

H. Audretsch, *Supervision in European Community Law* (North Holland, 2nd ed., 1986).

St. John Bates & Others, *In Memoriam J. D. B. Mitchell* (Sweet & Maxwell, London, 1983).

Gerhard Bebr, *Development of Judicial Control of the European Communities* (Martinus Nijhoff, 1981).

Lawrence Collins, *European Community Law in the United Kingdom* (Butterworths, London, 3rd ed., 1984)

T. C. Hartley, *The Foundations of European Community Law* (Oxford University Press, 2nd ed., 1988).

K. P. E. Lasok, *The European Court of Justice: Practice and Procedure* (Butterworths, London 1984).

A. J. Mackenzie Stuart, *The European Communities and the Rule of Law* (Hamlyn Lectures, Sweet & Maxwell, London, 1977).

Hjalte Rasmussen, *On Law and Policy in the European Court of Justice* (Nijhoff, 1986).

H. G. Schermers & Denis Waelbroeck, *Judicial Protection in the European Communities* (Kluwer, Deventer, Netherlands, 4th ed., 1987).

H. G. Schermers & Others, *Article 177 EEC: Experience and Problems* (North Holland, 1987).

H. G. Schermers & Others, *Non-Contractual Liability of the European Communities* (Kluwer, 1989).

John A. Usher, *European Court Practice* (Sweet & Maxwell, London, 1983).

Articles

Ami Barav, "Preliminary Censorship? The judgment of the European Court in Foglia v. Novello" (1980) 5 E.L. Rev. 443.

Gerhard Bebr, "Preliminary rulings of the Court of Justice, their authority and temporal effect" (1981) 18 C.M.L.R. Rev. 475.

A. A. Dashwood, "The Advocate General in the Court of Justice of the European Communities" (1982) 2 *Legal Studies* 202.

Alan Dashwood and Anthony Arnull, "English Courts and Article 177 of the EEC Treaty" (1984) 4 *Yearbook of European Law*, 255.

V. L. Everling, "The Member States of the European Community before their Court of Justice" (1984) 9 E.L. Rev. 215.

Christine Gray, "Interim measures of protection in the European Court" (1979) 4 E.L. Rev. 80.

Christopher Harding, "The impact of Article 177 of the EEC Treaty on the review of Community action" (1981) 1 *Yearbook of European Law* 93.

Tom Kennedy, "Paying the Piper" (1988) 25 C.M.L. Rev. 559.

Tom Kennedy, "The essential minimum: the establishment of the Court of First Instance" (1989) 14 E.L. Rev. 7.

T. Koopmans, "*Stare Decisis* in European Law" *Essays in European Law and Integration* (eds. O'Keeffe and Schermers; Kluwer, Deventer, Netherlands, 1982), p. 11.

T. Koopmans, "The Role of Law in the Next Stage of European Integration" (1986) 35 I.C.L.Q. 925.

Jeremy McBride and L. Neville Brown, "The United Kingdom, the European Community and the European Convention on Human Rights" (1981) 1 *Yearbook of European Law* 167.

M. H. Mendelson, "The European Court of Justice and human rights" (1981) 1 *Yearbook of European Law* 125.

T. Millett, "Rules of Interpretation of EEC Legislation" (1989) *Statute Law Review* (forthcoming).

Peter Oliver, "Limitation of actions before the European Court" (1978) 3 E.L. Rev. 3.

Richard Plender, "The Interpretation of Community Acts by Reference to the Intentions of the Authors" (1982) 2 *Yearbook of European Law* 57.

Sir Gordon Slynn, "The Court of Justice of the European Communities" (1984) 33 I.C.L.Q. 409.

Eric Stein, "Lawyers, judges and the making of a transnational Constitution" (1981) 75 Am.J.Int.Law 1.

M. Waelbroeck, "May the Court of Justice limit the retrospective operation of its judgments?" (1981) 1 *Yearbook of European Law* 115.

Reports presented to a Judicial and Academic Conference, Court of Justice of the European Communities, Luxembourg, 1976

House of Lords, Select Committee on the European Communities, Session 1979/80, 23rd Report, "European Court of Justice"; Session 1979/80, 71st Report "Human Rights"; Session 1987/88, 5th Report, "A European Court of First Instance."

INDEX

Actions,
  annulment, for, 96 *et seq.*, 158
  contractual, 132–134
  inactivity, for, 123 *et seq.*
  joinder, 240
  judicial statistics, 210 *et seq.*
  Member State, against, 76 *et seq.*
  non-contractual, 134 *et seq.*
  tortious, 134
Advisory jurisdiction, 203 *et seq.*
Advocates General, 53 *et seq.*
  appointment of, 34, 55, 56
  biographical backgrounds,
    61–63
  contribution of, 58
  independence of, 36, 54, 56
  national origin, 60–63
  number of, 15, 60, 61
  opinions, 55–60, 63, 231, 315 *et
    seq.*, 332
  role of, 53 *et seq.*
Annulment,
  actions for, 96 *et seq.*, 158
  effect of, 122
  grounds for, 116, 120
  interest to bring action, 102 *et
    seq.*
  limitation period, 115
Appeal, 241–242
Audience,
  right of, 257 *et seq.*, 301–303

Barristers,
  right of audience, 258–259

Case reports, 21–22
Cases. *See* Judicial statistics.
Chambers, 15, 26, 324
  assignment of cases to, 26–28,
    226, 324

Chambers—*cont.*
  disagreement between, 315
  presidents of, 35–36
  staff cases, hearing of, 26, 165
Commission,
  actions against Member States,
    77 *et seq.*
  work of, 8, 9
Community acts,
  interpretation of, 98–99
  judicial review of, 95 *et seq.*
  preliminary rulings on, 184–185
Community institutions, 1 *et seq.*
  competence to negotiate
    treaties, 205–206
  positioning of, 11
  relationships between, 3, 4, 8, 9
Community servants,
  acts of, 150–152
  immunity of, 150
Comparative law,
  influence of, 334 *et seq.*
  interpretation influenced by,
    284–286
Costs, 166, 235 *et seq.*, 245
Counsel,
  notes for the guidance of,
    247–251
  See also Lawyers.
Courthouse, 29–31
Court of First Instance, 9, 12, 64 *et
    seq.*, 71, 150, 165–167, 219,
    324
  jurisdiction, 65, 75, 132
  members of, 65
  right of appeal from, 66–67
  procedure, 222 *et seq.*
Court of Justice, 12
  composition of, 42
  creation, 1, 2

Court of Justice—*cont.*
jurisdiction and function, 9, 15, 71 *et seq.*, 201, 203
members of, 15, 324
organisation of, 14 *et seq.*
precedent in, 311 *et seq.*
work-load, increase in, 64, 167, 324
Cross-fertilisation, 334 *et seq.*

Damage,
causation and liability, 137 *et seq.*, 145 *et seq.*, 163
proof, 146
Direct actions,
articles 93, 169 and 170, under, 77 *et seq.*
judicial statistics, 210–214
procedure, 222 *et seq.*
Directorate of Administration, 25
Documentation Service, 22, 23

Enforcement,
judgment, of, 88 *et seq.*, 234–235
Enlargement,
Community, of, 324 *et seq.*
European Council, 7, 11
European Parliament, 5, 6, 11, 12, 104
European Union, 328–329, 336
Evidence,
taking of, 228
Execution,
judgment, of, 234–235

Fault,
concept of, 139–140
Member State, 152–153
Fundamental rights, 329–330

General principles of law, 119, 293 *et seq.*
fundamental rights, 120, 303 *et seq.*, 329–330
national legal systems, in, 294, 301

General principles of law—*cont.*
non-discrimination, prohibition of, 299
proportionality, 275, 295–298
protection of legitimate expectations, 300
right to be heard, 301–303
source of Community Law, 265

Human rights, 308 *et seq.*, 329–330

Illegality,
plea of, 125 *et seq.*, 158
Immunity,
community servants, 150–152
judicial, 40–41
Inactivity,
actions for, 123–125
Information Office, 25
Institutions. *See* Community institutions.
Interim measures, 88, 237 *et seq.*
International court,
role as, 73, 74
International Federation for European Law, 254
Interpretation, 196, 268 *et seq.*
approaches to, 270
common law rules, 291
comparative law influence, 284 *et seq.*
contextual, 271 *et seq.*, 280
historical, 276 *et seq.*
literal, 271 *et seq.*
plurilingual dimension, 269–270
teleological, 271 *et seq.*, 286 *et seq.*
Interpretation Division, 24, 25
Intervention,
third parties by, 239

Joinder of actions, 227, 240
Judge-rapporteur, 54, 226
Judges, 33 *et seq.*, 56
appointment of, 34

Judges—*cont.*
 biographical backgrounds, 47–52
 dismissal, 39
 immunity, 40
 incompatibility with office, 41
 number of, 34
 oath taken by, 38
 qualifications, 36, 37
 resignation, 39
 salaries, 41
 term of appointment, 38
Judgment,
 appeal against, 241–242
 collegiate character, 16, 42, 233, 266–267
 declaratory, 77, 88
 delivery of, 234
 enforcement, 88 *et seq.*, 234
 form of, 42–45
 publication of, 21, 22, 234
 ratio, 312
 style of, 43, 46, 56, 57
Judicial legislation, 265
Judicial personnel, 14
Judicial review, 71, 95 *et seq.*
 actions for inactivity (article 175), 96, 123 *et seq.*
 actions to annul (article 173), 96, 97 *et seq.*, 119
 competence, lack of, 116
 grounds for, 116
 infringement of law, 119
 infringement of procedure, 117–118
 limitation period, 115
 locus standi, 102 *et seq.*, 113–115, 124, 127
 misuse of powers, 120
 plea of illegality (article 184) 125 *et seq.*
Judicial sittings, 31
Judicial statistics, 210–218
Judicial style, 46
Jurisdiction, 10, 15, 71 *et seq.*, 177, 325, 329

Jurisdiction—*cont.*
 advisory opinions, 203
 article 88 (ECSC) procedure, 78–79
 article 93 procedure, 86
 article 169 procedure, 77 *et seq.*
 article 170 procedure, 85
 conflict of, 201
 developments in, 177, 325 *et seq.*
 international court, as, 73, 74
 judicial review, 72, 95 *et seq.*
 non-contractual actions, 134 *et seq.*
 plenary, 132 *et seq.*, 164
 preliminary rulings, 72, 169, 171–172, 180, 182
 remedy, nature of, 144–145
 staff cases, 160 *et seq.*

Language,
 choice, restriction of, 325
 court, before, 16, 244
 decision as to, 224
Language Divisions, 23
Lawyers, 252 *et seq.*
 qualifications required, 253, 257
 representation of parties, 255–256
 right of audience, 257 *et seq.*
 role of, 254–255
 technique, 253
Legal aid, 261–264
Legal secretaries, 17, 18, 57, 326
Liability,
 contractual, 132–133
 damage for, 137, 163
 legislation, arising from, 141–143
 non-contractual, 134 *et seq.*
 vicarious, 150, 151, 152–153
Library, 22
Limitation period,
 article 173 actions, 115–116
 article 215 actions, 143–144
 judicial review, 115–116

Locus standi,
  actions for judicial review, 102 *et seq.*, 113, 126, 127, 129, 239
Luxembourg, 12, 29
Luxembourg Accords, 7

Member States,
  actions against, 76 *et seq.*
  competence to negotiate treaties, 204
  compliance with obligations, 88 *et seq.*
  courts of, what constitutes, 185 *et seq.*
  defiance of Court, 330 *et seq.*
  enforcement of judgments against, 88 *et seq.*
  fault on part of, 152 *et seq.*
  intervention by, 239
  judicial systems of, 318–319
  sovereignty of, 88, 199, 200, 319
  tribunals of, what constitutes, 185 *et seq.*

National courts,
  Community law applied in, 10, 11, 170, 174
  conflict of jurisdiction, 170
  co-operation with, 192 *et seq.*
  decisions of, 316
  exclusive jurisdiction of, 132
  precedent in, 196, 311 *et seq.*, 318 *et seq.*
  question referred, formulation of, 181–182
  referral from, 171, 172, 177–178, 179–180, 189 *et seq.*, 322
  remedy in, 154 *et seq.*
Normative injustice, 141–143, 149, 158

Opinions,
  advocates general, of, 43, 54 *et seq.*, 230–231, 315 *et seq.*, 332
  external relations, on, 203 *et seq.*

Organigramme, 26, 32

Plenary jurisdiction, 131 *et seq.*, 164–165
Power,
  misuse of, 121, 275
Precedent, 196, 312 *et seq.*
  Court of Justice, in, 196, 312 *et seq.*
  departure from, 196, 313
  national courts in, 196, 311 *et seq.*
  opinions of advocates general, 315 *et seq.*
  reversal of decisions, 4, 313–315
Preliminary ruling, 169 *et seq.*, 242 *et seq.*
  Community law, questions of, 183, 184
  decision to refer, 179 *et seq.*
  effects of, 195 *et seq.*
  interpretation of Community law, 176
  legal aid for, 263
  national courts, co-operation with, 192–193
  nature of, 171
  obligation to refer, 172, 180, 189 *et seq.*
  origins of, 178
  procedure, 177, 242 *et seq.*
  validity of Community law, on, 171, 173
President of Chambers, 39
President of the Court, 20, 39, 40
Procedure, 219 *et seq.*
  administrative meeting, 20, 227
  admissibility, 225, 239, 245
  article 88 (ECSC), under, 78–79
  article 93, under, 86–88
  article 169, under, 77 *et seq.*
  article 170, under, 85 *et seq.*
  article 228, opinions, 207–208
  defence, filing of, 225
  developments in, 335
  evidence, taking of, 228

Procedure—*cont.*
  infringements of, 117–119
  interim measures, 88, 237 *et seq.*
  investigation, 226
  judgment, delivery of, 232
  lawyers' addresses, 230–231
  oral proceedings, 229 *et seq.*
  preliminary objection, 239
  preliminary ruling, 177, 242 *et seq.*
  preparatory inquiry, 166, 226, 228
  report for the hearing, 230
  Rules of, 219 *et seq.*
  staff cases, in, 165 *et seq.*
  witnesses, hearing of, 166, 227
  written proceedings, 223 *et seq.*

Rapporteurs,
  assistant, 18
  See Judge-rapporteur.
Referral,
  preliminary ruling for, 177 *et seq.*, 189 *et seq.*
Registrar, 14, 19–21
  appointment, 19
  residence, 19
  responsibility, 20
Registry, 14, 19–21
Relief,
  interim, 237–239
Remedies. *See* Judicial review and Jurisdiction.
Representation,
  legal, 255–257

Salaries, 41
Secretaries,
  legal, 17, 18, 57, 326

Servants. *See* Community servants.
Single European Act, 3, 6, 7, 64, 65, 71, 336
Sittings, 31
Solicitors,
  right of audience, 259
Sources of law, 5, 265, 293, 301, 311
Staff cases, 159 *et seq.*
  costs in, 166, 236
  jurisdiction of Court, 65, 132, 160 *et seq.*
  plenary jurisdiction of Court, 164
  procedure in, 165 *et seq.*
Staff Regulations,
  jurisdiction of Court, 160
  legality of, 162
Stare decisis doctrine, 266, 311
  And see Precedent.
State aids,
  enforcement procedure, 86–88
Summit meetings, 3, 7, 328–329

Third parties,
  intervention by, 239
Translation Directorate, 23, 24
Travaux préparatoires, 276 *et seq.*
Treaty-making powers,
  review of by Court, 203 *et seq.*

Validity,
  preliminary rulings on, 173 *et seq.*, 197

Witnesses, 166, 227